THOMSON
—★—
COURSE TECHNOLOGY

Professional ■ Technical ■ Reference

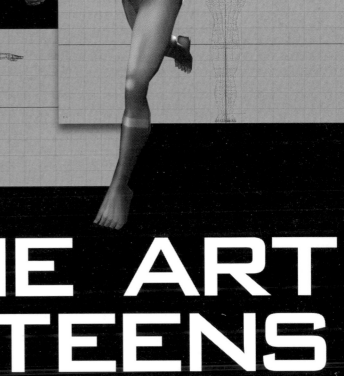

M000251509

GAME ART FOR TEENS

SECOND EDITION

INCLUDES CD-ROM

LES PARDEW

ISBN: 1-59200-959-X

Library of Congress Catalog Card Number: 2005929813

Printed in the United States of America

06 07 08 09 10 BU 10 9 8 7 6 5 4 3 2 1

Publisher and General Manager, Thomson Course Technology PTR:
Stacy L. Hiquet

Associate Director of Marketing:
Sarah O'Donnell

Manager of Editorial Services:
Heather Talbot

Marketing Manager:
Jordan Casey

Senior Acquisitions Editor:
Emi Smith

Senior Editor:
Mark Garvey

Project Editor:
Jenny Davidson

Technical Reviewer:
Dan Whittington

Thomson Course Technology PTR Editorial Services Coordinator:
Elizabeth Furbish

Interior Layout Tech:
Bill Hartman

Cover Designer:
Mike Tanamachi

CD-ROM Producer:
Brandon Penticuff

Indexer:
Katherine Stimson

Proofreader:
Brad Crawford

THOMSON

COURSE TECHNOLOGY ™

Professional ■ Technical ■ Reference

Thomson Course Technology PTR, a division of Thomson Course Technology
25 Thomson Place ■ Boston, MA 02210 ■ http://www.courseptr.com

This book is dedicated to all the young artists.
Keep the dream alive.
Without art, much of beauty would be lost.
You are needed.

ACKNOWLEDGMENTS

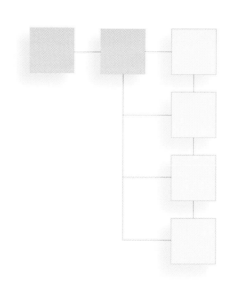

This book is the culmination of the work of many individuals. Some, such as Emi Smith, Jenny Davidson, and Dan Whittington have worked on the book directly. Others, such as Carl Lundgren, Dave Wolverton, and Don Seegmiller, have helped by teaching me their craft. My biggest thanks go to my wife and family, who have put up with my countless hours away from them to write this book, and to my parents, who have always believed in me. To all who had a role in helping me to write this book, I express my deepest appreciation and gratitude.

About the Author

Les Pardew was born and grew up in Idaho. His hometown was a small farming community where he learned the benefits of hard work. His graduating high school class only numbered 33 individuals. From this small beginning, Pardew has grown to become a recognized leader in interactive entertainment.

Pardew is a video game and entertainment industry veteran with over 20 years of industry experience. His artwork includes film and video production, magazine and book illustration, and more than 100 video game titles. He is the author or co-author of six books.

Game Art for Teens

Beginning Illustration and Storyboarding

Game Design for Teens

Mastering Digital Art

The Animator's Reference Book

Basic Drawing for Games

Pardew started his career in video games doing animation for *Magic Johnson Fast Break Basketball* for the Commodore 64. He went on to help create several major games including *Robin Hood Prince of Thieves, Star Wars, Wrestle Mania, NCAA Basketball, Stanley Cup Hockey, Jack Nicklaus Golf, Where in the World/USA Is Carmen Sandiego?, StarCraft Brood Wars, Rainbow Six,* and *Cyber Tiger Woods Golf,* to name a few.

Pardew is an accomplished teacher having taught numerous art and business courses, including teaching as an adjunct faculty member at Brigham Young University's Marriott School of Management.

Pardew is a business leader, founding two separate game development studios. He is also a favorite speaker at video game conferences and events.

Pardew is the father of five wonderful children and the grandfather of one beautiful granddaughter. He loves being with his wife and children, serving in his church, and teaching art.

CONTENTS

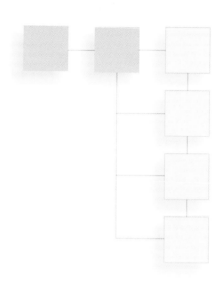

INTRODUCTION

I remember growing up in a small town in southern Idaho. Our high school didn't have an art teacher. The only place that I could gain any instruction in art was from books. I loved reading about artists and I loved the step-by-step instruction books. Now, after years of success in commercial art, I felt it was time to help the young students who are looking for guidance with their dream of becoming a game artist.

This book is designed to give real-world instruction with solid examples of game art creation. The chapters are full of step-by-step projects that show you in detail how game art is created. The examples are taken from projects that could be right out of any game.

To best understand and learn from this book, you should complete each project as shown in the step-by-step instructions. From there, you should practice the concepts on your own to broaden your knowledge of the tools and master the techniques.

The CD contains tools and links to all the resources you will need to complete the projects. The tools are trial versions or learning versions of professional software.

I hope you enjoy reading this book and doing the projects. I wish you success and fulfillment as an artist in this dynamic and exciting field. If you need help or just want to talk, you can e-mail me at les@alpine-studios.com.

Chapter 1

Getting Started in Game Art

Creating art for games is fun and exciting. This book is your gateway to the fascinating world of game art development. In this second edition I have updated many of the methods and processes from the first edition. I have also updated the programs used in the book. In the following chapters, you will learn how art is made and used in games. You will also have a chance to create art yourself by following the many projects in each chapter. As you read each chapter and try out each project, you will gain a good understanding of game art development.

In this book I only want to deal with game art. Completing each project will require some level of artistic talent. Because you are interested in reading this book, I will assume that you have some skill in art. I will not go into the basics of drawing and painting. If you want to learn more about the basics, pick up my book entitled *Basic Drawing for Games*, also by Thomson Course Technology (www.courseptr.com).

This book contains step-by-step instructions on a number of topics. I have worked hard to be as detailed as possible so you can follow along with me; however, no book can provide every single step to every process in something as complex as game art development. The best way to use this book is to become familiar with the tools by reading the instructions that come with the art software. Once you are comfortable with the basic features of the art software, following the step-by-step instructions will be easier.

How Art Is Displayed

The best way to begin any discussion on game art is to clarify how art is displayed in a game. Most people play games on a computer, handheld

1

device, or console game system. The pictures we see in games on the monitors of these systems are made up of small, colored square dots of light called *pixels*. More precisely, a pixel could be defined as the smallest controllable segment of a display. Back when computer games first came out, the resolution of video-game pixels was very low and they appeared as big blocks of color. As technology has advanced, the size of pixels has shrunk to the point that in some game systems it is difficult to see a single pixel.

Figure 1.1 shows a typical character used in early PC games. The character is 32 pixels high. Notice that the pixels are very easy to see. I remember creating hundreds of these kinds of characters, or sprites, as they were called

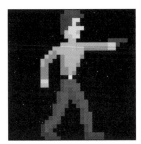

Figure 1.1 This game character for an old PC game is 32 pixels high.

for the early game systems. Even though they were simple, they still needed to follow good artistic principles. Try drawing a few yourself and I am sure you will agree.

Figure 1.2 shows a scene from a more recent game. Notice that the pixels are so small that they are very difficult to distinguish as small blocks of light. As new game platforms continue to become more powerful, screen resolutions will increase and individual pixels will continue to be harder to detect.

Pixels are small dots of colored light that make up pictures on a computer

Figure 1.2 This scene is for a contemporary game system.

screen. This is very important. Each pixel has its own color that is a combination of Red, Green, or Blue light, or RBG for short. So if a game is 800 by 600 pixels in resolution, that is 480,000 pixels that the game has to keep track of. Games usually run at 30 frames a second or higher, so the game has to process at least 14,400,000 every second. So in one minute of playing a game, the game system has to deal with 864,000,000 pixels. Now multiply that number by the number of minutes you typically play a game, and you might begin to see how complex games are to create. Fortunately, most of the hard work has already been done by the pioneers of game development.

In traditional art, artists work mostly with the reflected light of a painted surface. For games, artists work with pure light as it is displayed on a screen. This fundamental difference takes a little getting used to, particularly in the area of color.

A game artist uses colored light to create images. Most other forms of art are reflected light. For example, when a person looks at an oil painting, he sees colors that are reflected from light in the room. On the other hand, when a person looks at the same painting displayed on a color monitor or TV, he is looking at direct light—not reflected light (see Figure 1.3).

Reflected light is not as bright and vibrant as direct light; however, we live in a world of reflected light. When you are creating game art, it is important to remember that the art will look unrealistic or cartoonlike if you don't take care to reduce the intensity of the color to match how things look in real life.

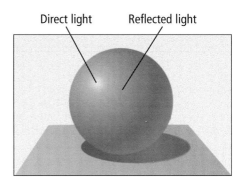

Figure 1.3 Reflected light and direct light.

Working with Pixels

Artists use a variety of computer programs to work with pixels on the screen. These programs fit into two basic categories—two-dimensional (or 2D) programs and three-dimensional (or 3D) programs. 2D programs are the easiest to understand because computer screens and video-game screens are basically flat. A 2D art program directly manipulates pixels on screen. Many of these programs are very sophisticated, and some even simulate natural media such as airbrush, oil paint, or even watercolor. 3D programs create virtual 3D objects used in the creation of 3D characters and worlds in games. 3D programs simulate how we see things in the real world.

Included on the CD for this book are several 2D programs and one 3D program:

- Corel Painter
- CorelDRAW Suite
- Alias SketchBook Pro
- Maya

Hint

Take some time to explore and become familiar with the art programs on the accompanying CD-ROM. Each program is a professional tool. The better you understand these programs, the more you will gain from the projects in this book.

In later chapters I will get into several specific exercises that deal directly with these programs. They are all programs that I use regularly in my own work, and each one is a true professional program. In this chapter, I will give you a brief overview of these programs.

Using Painting Programs

Game artists use painting programs to create 2D art for games. 2D art is often created by the artist from scratch instead of through manipulation of other art or photographs. The CD for this book will give you access to two painting programs—Corel Painter 9 and Alias SketchBook Pro 2. Both of these programs are great programs for creating art. They both have very powerful features that allow you to use tools that simulate natural drawing and painting tools.

Drawing on a computer is much like drawing on paper, if you have the right hardware. I like to use a Wacom Intuos tablet. Figure 1.4 shows the Intuos tablet in use.

The tablet uses a stylus pen whose weight and feel is a lot like a pencil's.

It is pressure-sensitive, so it reacts very similarly to a real pencil. The tablet is nice because it can be held in any position, like a sketchbook.

New touch-screen technology is also available for those who want to work directly on the screen. Figure 1.5 shows the Wacom Cintiq tablet/monitor in use.

When you move the pen over the tablet, the cursor on the computer screen moves. Like clicking with a

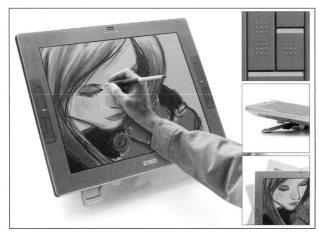

mouse button, you can select or execute commands on the screen by touching the tip of the stylus to the tablet. Unlike the mouse, however, the stylus has a pressure-sensitive tip, which paint programs use to simulate the pressure the artist uses in drawing.

If you are serious about making art for games, I highly recommend getting a digitizing tablet, because it helps make the drawing and painting process on the computer more natural. Don't worry if you don't have one, though. You can still complete the projects in the book, because all of the

art programs used in the projects work with a mouse.

Using Brushes

Painting programs simulate natural drawing and painting with a set of tools called *brushes*. Imagine a fully equipped artist studio with all the latest tools and media. In the studio you might see things like watercolor brushes, oil paint brushes, pastel chalks, airbrushes, and any number of other artist tools. Now imagine all those tools and media in a painting program. That is exactly what a painting program is meant to simulate.

In a painting program, the brush defines not only the type of instrument the painting program is trying to simulate, but also the media. Painting programs allow for a wide range of flexibility in the brushes. For example, an artist might start a picture by sketching in a rough outline with a pencil brush.

Hint

The purpose of this initial chapter is not to train you in all aspects of the tools that will be used in this book; rather, I want to give you a quick example of how the program will be used. Greater detail on each art program will be provided later in the book.

The following example will use Corel Painter. Painter is a great program with a very powerful set of drawing and painting tools.

Figure 1.6 shows the base drawing for a female ranger for a fantasy game. The drawing should be detailed but not shaded. The shading will be applied in the painting.

The media for this painting will be the airbrush brush. You can select the airbrush by clicking on the small arrow on the Brush Selector. A drop-down menu with several brush icons will appear. Select the one that looks like the airbrush shown in Figure 1.6. Now select the paintbrush tool. It is located in the top-left-hand corner of the toolbox. Notice that the property bar shows several brush attributes. Change the brush attributes to match those shown in Figure 1.6

The airbrush is used to lay in a simple background for the illustration. The background colors are applied to the entire surface of the drawing. As the painting progresses, the background colors in the character will help to unify the colors of the painting. Figure 1.7 shows the first pass of color on the painting.

Brush Tool   Brush Attributes   Brush Selector

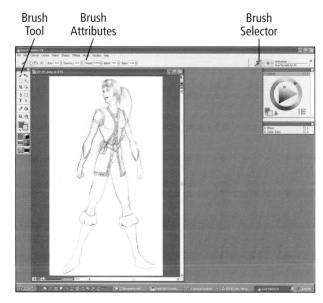

Figure 1.6 Start with a drawing of the character.

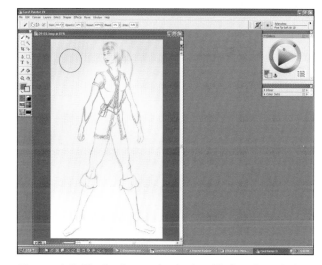

Figure 1.7 The background color is added to the painting.

In Figure 1.8 the background is enhanced with darker colors around the edges of the painting and a lighter color directly behind the character. The design principle here is to focus the attention toward the center of the painting. The lighter background color will be contrasted with the darker colors used in the character.

Figure 1.8 also shows the beginning of the flesh tone colors added to the painting. Notice that the background colors are used in the flesh tones.

In Figure 1.9 the lighter pinks of the flesh are added filling out the face and arms.

The next area is the character's hair. The character will have blond hair so the basic shades of light to dark are applied with the airbrush. See Figure 1.10.

Individual strands of hair are painted in with a very fine airbrush. Reduce the brush size to 1 using the properties bar. To get a good feeling of hair, a small brush is used to apply the darker and lighter areas one at a time. The most important area is the transition from light to dark color. This is where the detail is most important. Figure 1.11 shows the progress of the hair.

The character has a large ponytail, which is also painted in using the same technique as the hair on the top of her head.

From the hair, the next area to paint is the character tunic. This area is masked off and the airbrush is used to paint in the darker, then lighter, areas, as shown in Figure 1.12.

When using an airbrush the artist will move from one area of the painting to the next. The areas that are not being painted are masked off so the artist can apply paint only to those areas that the color applies to. In Figure 1.12 the tunic was left open while the rest of the painting was masked. The dotted lines show the mask. There are several ways to mask an area. For more information on masks in Painter refer to the Help Topics in the Help menu. The best way is to use the lasso selection tool and draw around the selection area. The lasso tool is located directly below the brush icon in the toolbox.

The borders of the tunic have some golden embroidery. Like the hair, the airbrush does not do a very good job for creating the embroidery. The base darker color is painted in with the airbrush and the finer detail is then painted last. Figure 1.13 shows the results.

Several other detail items need to be painted around the upper torso area. Figure 1.14 shows the addition of these parts of the color sketch. The facial features are painted in as well as some of the arm jewelry. The pouch strap and collar broach are also painted.

The only remaining elements to finish the upper body of the character are to paint in the pouch belt and gloves of the character. These are painted in the same way as the other elements with the airbrush laying in the base darker colors and the finer detail over the top. See Figure 1.15.

Next the legs are masked off and painted using the airbrush. See Figure 1.16.

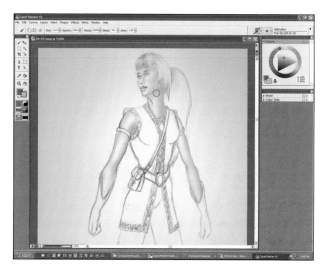

Figure 1.8 The background is used to highlight the character.

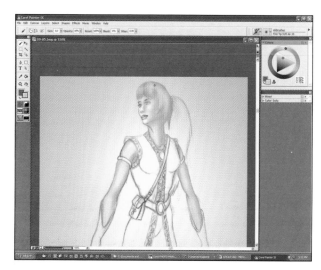

Figure 1.10 Block in the basic shape of the hair.

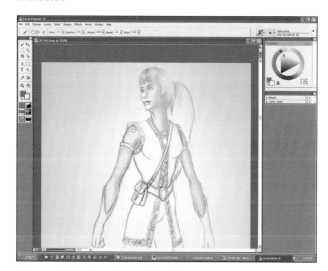

Figure 1.9 The colors of the skin are painted in.

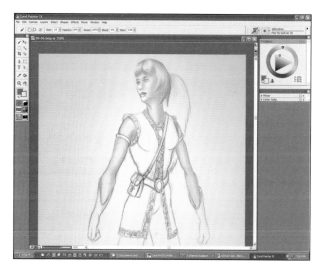

Figure 1.11 Individual strands of hair are indicated one at a time.

Figure 1.12 The tunic is painted.

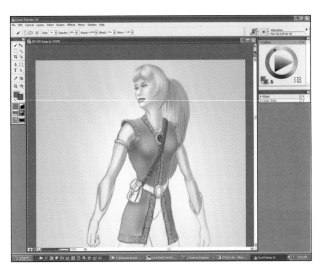

Figure 1.14 Some of the smaller items are painted by hand.

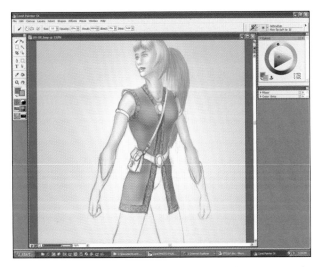

Figure 1.13 The finer detail of the embroidery is painted in by hand.

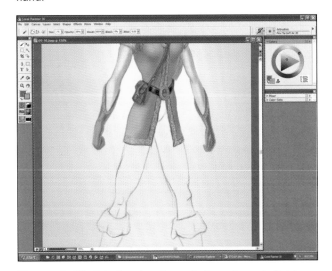

Figure 1.15 Painting the gloves, belt, and pouch finishes the upper portion of the character.

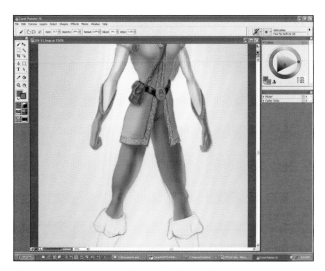

Figure 1.16 Next, airbrush the legs of the character.

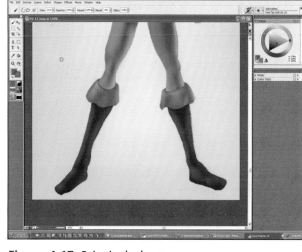

Figure 1.17 Paint in the boots.

The last step is to airbrush in her boots and clean up some of the pencil lines that are still showing. See Figure 1.17.

The pencil lines can be removed by using an opaque paint that is the same color as the background around the character. Figure 1.18 shows the finished character illustration.

Notice that the contrast of the background with the character brings out the character as the focal point of the picture. There is greater detail in the upper part of the body so the focus is on that area. The subtle touch is that the character's lips are red. They are the only real red part of the picture. The illustration is made up of mostly a blue-yellow scheme so the use of red on the character's mouth draws the eye to that area.

Hint

Often when I am working on a project, I will have a paint program, a photo paint program, and a 3D program all running on my computer at the same time. I often switch between programs because photo paint programs are good for some things and Paint programs are good for others.

Figure 1.18 Finish the illustration by cleaning up the remaining pencil lines.

Photo Paint Programs

A photo paint program is designed for photo manipulation and retouching. Some artists use them for creating art, but I find painting programs work better for the former purposes. The CD for this book includes the CorelDRAW Suite; one of the programs in the suite is Corel Photo Paint. This is an excellent program for working with photographs or drawings.

Creating a Door Texture

When it comes to the textures you create from photographs, the quality will depend heavily on the quality of the photograph. The best way to get good photographs is to learn to take them yourself, but sometimes that is impractical, or maybe a subject isn't readily available for you to take a picture of it. Sometimes it is easier to access a library of photographs. A great library for photographic textures can be found at www.environment-textures.com. A picture of the website is shown in Figure 1.19. The site charges a subscription fee but is well worth the price for the quality and quantity of photographs available. Remember that if you don't have permission to use a photograph, you can get in trouble because using photographs without permission is illegal.

This section will provide an example of how you might use a photo paint program to create a door texture for a game. First you load the digital photograph into the program. The picture of the doorway is supplied from the website. Figure 1.20 shows a nice picture of a doorway.

Figure 1.19 www.environment-textures.com is a great site for photographs for building textures.

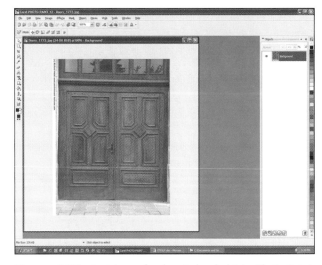

Figure 1.20 A picture of a door is loaded into Photo Paint.

The first step to converting the photo of the door into a usable texture is to isolate the door from the rest of the picture. Drag a mask around the door to select it (see Figure 1.21). A *mask* is a selected area of a picture. You cannot manipulate areas outside the selected area; you *can* manipulate areas inside the mask.

Notice that the door is not square with the camera. A photo is seldom perfectly flat with the viewer. Textures need to be flat, as if they were seen in an isometric view. Go to the Edit menu and select Copy to copy the selected area into the clipboard, as shown in Figure 1.22.

Now you need to paste the selection as a new object into the picture, as shown in Figure 1.23.

Click on the new object twice to change the manipulators to Distort. The Distort manipulators allow you to stretch the corners of the object in any direction. (See Figure 1.24.)

Pull the corners of the object until the door is square with the mask, as shown in Figure 1.25.

Now combine the object with the background by using the menu command under Objects or pressing Ctrl+down arrow on the keyboard. (See Figure 1.26.)

Now the door is flat to the viewer and lined up with the mask. Copy the selected area back into the clipboard. Now instead of pasting it back into the picture, select New From Clipboard from the File menu, as shown in Figure 1.27.

Figure 1.21 Mask around the door in the picture.

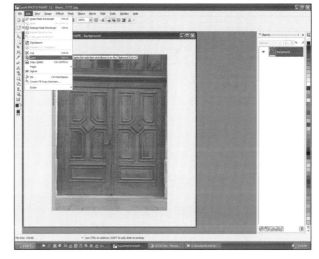

Figure 1.22 Copy the selected area into the clipboard.

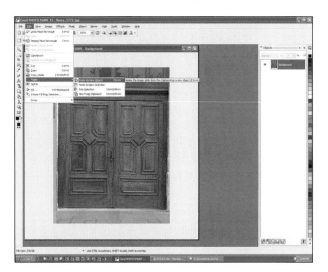

Figure 1.23 Paste the selection back over the picture.

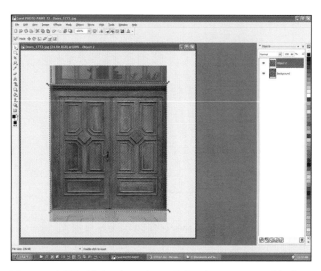

Figure 1.25 Make the edges of the door square with the mask.

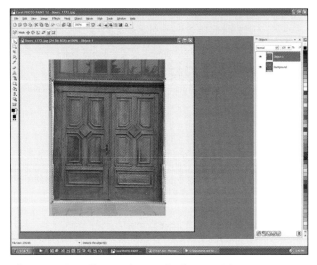

Figure 1.24 Change the manipulator to Distort.

Figure 1.26 Combine the object with the background.

Figure 1.27 Select New From Clipboard.

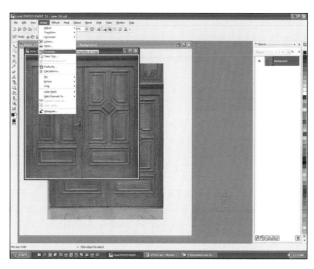

Figure 1.28 Select Resample from the Edit menu.

The result will be a new image that is the door isolated without the surrounding area and square with the image. The image is now ready to resample into the correct dimensions for a texture map. Choose Edit > Resample from the menu, as shown in Figure 1.28.

A Resample dialog box will appear on screen. Change the measurement increments to pixel, as shown in Figure 1.29.

Now click to uncheck the Maintain Aspect Ratio check box so you can freely change the image dimensions.

Textures for games are usually a *power of two*; this means that the height and width of the image must be one of the following number of pixels:

- 8
- 16
- 32
- 64
- 128
- 256
- 512
- 1024
- 2048
- 4096

Keeping the texture dimensions to a power of two helps the game

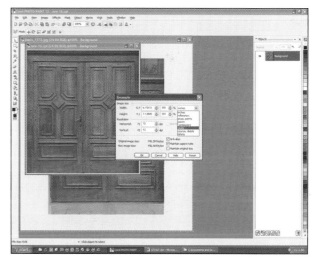

Figure 1.29 Bring up the Resample dialog box.

graphics engine to run faster. Set the height and width of the image to 256, as shown in Figure 1.30.

The finished texture should now look like Figure 1.31.

Working with Vector-Drawing Programs

Vector-drawing programs are art tools in which you create images using vector graphics. Unlike painting on pixels, every line or shape in a vector program is defined by a line or curve between two points. Vector-drawing programs are primarily used in print production, but occasionally they come in handy for creating art for games. The CD for this book includes a trial version of the CorelDRAW Suite. CorelDRAW 12 is one of the programs in the CorelDRAW Suite. It is one of the most powerful vector-drawing programs on the market.

Vector-drawing programs are great for anything that deals with typography, such as signs or interface art for menus. This section shows you a simple example of how you could use a vector-drawing program to create a graphic for a game. The graphic is a layout chart for the menu system in a game called *Flame*. The chart is part of a *game design document*.

Bring up CorelDRAW and select New from the start-up dialog box. The first element of the chart will be a background graphic. The graphic is imported into the scene by selecting Import from the File menu, as shown in Figure 1.32.

Because the game is called *Flame*, I select a picture of a fire, as shown in Figure 1.33. I size the picture to roughly fit within the page size of the workspace.

The first element to add to the chart is the game title. The word *flame* is printed across the top of the chart in bold letters, as shown in Figure 1.34.

The background motif for the chart is now set. Each page will share this motif to give the chart a consistent look. Most games are too complex to adequately fit on a single page. Tying the chart together with a single motif helps to define each page as part of the chart. In this example we will only be showing the first page. If you want

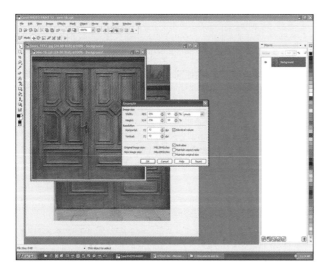

Figure 1.31 The finished texture is now ready for use in a game.

Figure 1.30 Make the texture 256 pixels square.

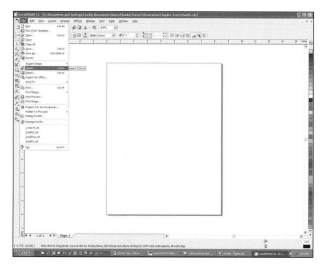

Figure 1.32 Use the Import feature to load a background graphic into the workspace.

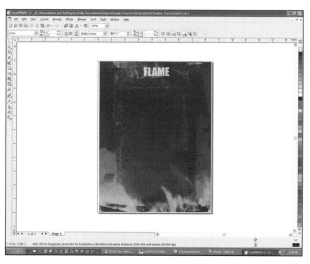

Figure 1.34 The word Flame is printed across the top of the chart in bold letters.

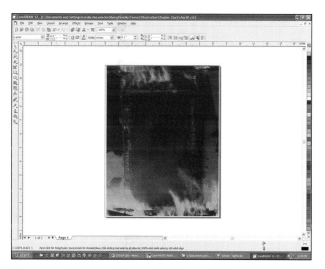

Figure 1.33 Use a flaming background for a game called *Flame*.

to learn more about creating game design documents, check out *Game Design for Teens*, another one of my books from Thomson Course Technology. It covers all aspects of designing a game.

Now that the background for the chart is set, it is time to start building the chart itself.

1. The first step is to design a frame for the text boxes in the chart. To keep with the warm temperature of the chart, create a box by using the Rectangle tool from the toolbox. Make the box yellow by left-clicking on yellow from the pallet with the rectangle still selected. Now right-click on orange to give the box an orange border. (See Figure 1.35)

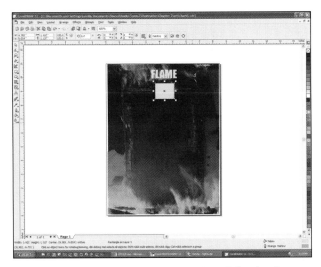

Figure 1.35 Yellow and orange work well for the design of the text boxes.

2. Give the box a thicker border by selecting 2.0 point border from the drop-down menu, as shown in Figure 1.36.

3. *Flame* is a simple game so the first screen on the chart is the *title screen*. The title screen is a screen that introduces the game to the player. Many games will play an introduction video either before or after the title screen. Videos in games are often referred to as *FMVs*, which stands for Full Motion Video. *Flame* does not have an FMV, so only the title screen text box is needed for the chart. (See Figure 1.37.)

4. The next box after the title screen is the game's *main menu*. The main menu is the central navigation page of the game. It is usually the first menu page in a game and connects the player

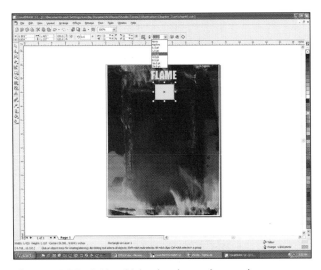

Figure 1.36 Add a thicker border to the text box.

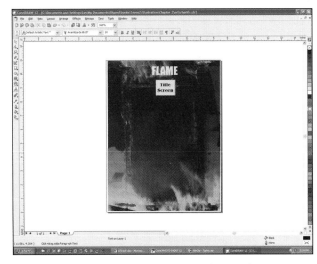

Figure 1.37 Type in **Title Screen** in the text box.

to other menu pages if there are any. Arrows show the direction of navigation through the game connecting the text boxes. Figure 1.38 shows the arrows connecting the text boxes.

5. The main menu is the hub of the game. From it the player can start a new game, continue a saved game, or change the game options. Now the chart needs to branch out with several screens from one. Figure 1.39 shows a branching chart.

Notice that the arrow to game options goes in both directions. This is to indicate that the player will be able to go from the main menu to the game options and then back to the main menu.

The first box from the main menu box on the left-hand side is the *load game* box. The load game feature is an option that allows players to continue playing a game that they started earlier. Many games are too large to play in one sitting. Some games may take

days if not weeks to complete. Allowing a player to save a game so he can resume it later is a common practice in game design.

In some games loading a new game will take the player to a new screen; in others it will just bring up a dialog window. In either case it is a separate function and should be designated as such in the game layout chart.

The middle text box below the main menu is the *new game* box. The new game option allows the player to start

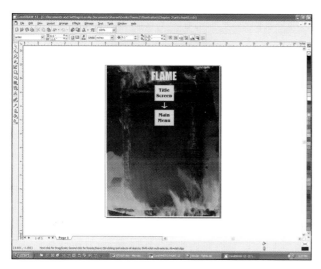

Figure 1.38 Arrows connect the text boxes.

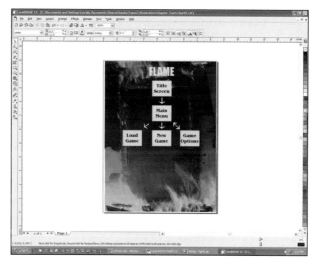

Figure 1.39 Three screens branch off of the main menu screen.

a new game. Like the load game menu, this option will usually lead to either another screen or a window.

The last text box on the right-hand side is the *game options* box. Game options are preferences that the player sets in a game like sound levels, graphics quality, animations, and other options. Once preferences are set in the game option screen or window, the player returns to the main menu. The double-sided arrow indi-cates that the player can go back and forth from the main menu to the game options.

The next set of text boxes on the chart is the play game box. This box will be expanded on other pages of the chart but only occupies one box on this chart. Play game represents the playable part of the game.

To get to the play game box the player will either have to load a saved game or create a new game. *Flame* is a char-acter-based game so the player needs to create a new character to start a new game. Notice in Figure 1.40 the placement of the play game and create character text boxes in the chart. The arrows indicate how the player navi-gates to the play game box.

There are only two outcomes of play-ing the game. Either the player will save the game in progress to resume play later or he will win or lose the game. Figure 1.41 shows the text boxes for these two outcomes.

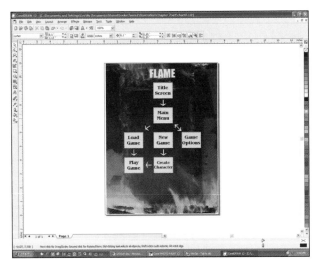

Figure 1.40 The arrows indicate how the player navigates to the play game box.

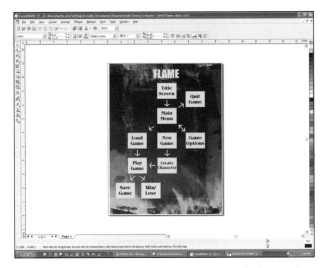

Figure 1.41 The chart shows the outcome of playing the game.

If the player saves the game, then the game will return to the main menu screen. Figure 1.42 show an arrow going from the save game text box to the main menu box.

After the win/lose box, the player will also return to the main menu but will go through one more text box on the way. That box is the *high score* box. The high score screen in games shows the players where they place among other players of a game. Figure 1.43 shows the high score box added with arrows going to the main menu screen.

Now the first page of the chart is almost finished. There is only one more text box that needs to be added and that is a way for the player to quit the game. Quit game is usually part of the main menu so the text box is added so that the arrow comes from the main menu box, as shown in Figure 1.44.

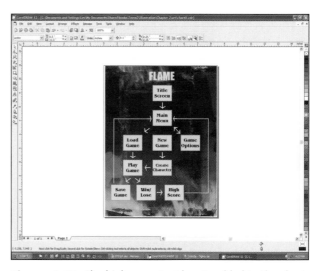

Figure 1.43 The high score text box is added to the chart.

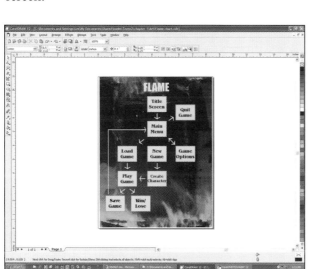

Figure 1.42 The arrow goes from the save game box to the main menu box.

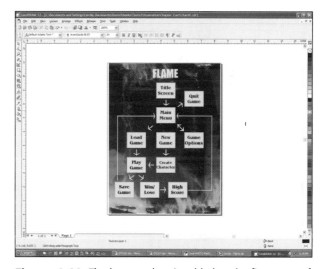

Figure 1.44 The last text box is added to the first page of the chart.

Working with 3D Modeling Programs

3D modeling programs have become the standard of the game industry. Almost all games on the market today use 3D models for creating the worlds, characters, and objects. A *3D model* is a virtual three-dimensional object in a virtual three-dimensional space. The computer calculates position, rotation, and movement of the objects in the virtual space, giving 3D models a realistic look you can't achieve using two-dimensional art programs.

At first, building game objects in a 3D program might seem a little intimidating. However, once you get used to the program, it will become an invaluable tool. 3D programs have opened a whole new world of possibilities in film, art, and gaming. Good 3D artists are in high demand in the game industry, so taking the time to learn how to create art in 3D programs is worthwhile for the beginning artist.

The CD that comes with this book contains a copy of the Personal Learning Edition of Maya. The pro-gram is a full-featured version of the professional software, but because it is designed for educational purposes, it contains an embedded watermark so you can't use the images for commercial projects. Maya is considered by many in the game industry to be the best 3D modeling and animation program on the market.

A marble column will be the example for how 3D models are created in games. The first step is to create a primitive. A *primitive* is a simple three-dimensional geometric shape. In this case, make a polygonal cylinder. A *polygon* is a flat plane of either a triangle or a rectangle bounded by points that are called *vertices*. Vertices is the plural for *vertex*, which means a single point on a polygon. Between each vertex runs a vector or line called a *segment*. Make sure the pull-down menu in the upper left-hand corner is set to Modeling. In Maya, select Polygonal Primitives from the Create menu. This will bring up a submenu. Select the small square to the right of the word Cylinder to bring up the Polygon Cylinder Options dialog box (see Figure 1.45).

Cylinders have many attributes. The Polygon Cylinder Options dialog box gives you the ability to control the size of the cylinder and the density of the polygonal mesh that will be created for it. *Polygonal mesh* is another word for the number and placement of polygons on a 3D object.

Figure 1.45 Creating a cylinder in Maya.

Hint

The greater the number of polygons in an object, the longer it will take to render that object. A good game artist will only use enough polygons to ensure the object looks good, and no more.

For this column, I created a cylinder that is 8 units high and has a radius of 0.5 units. The number of subdivisions on the height is also 8. Subdivisions around the axis are 16, and on the cap it is 1. After you enter your specifications, click Apply to create the cylinder.

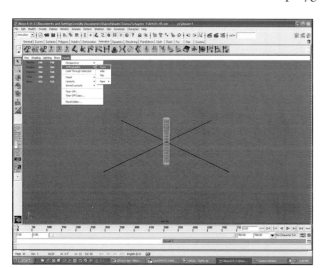

Figure 1.46 Change the view screen to the Front view.

You can change the camera view of the 3D model to make it easier to adjust some of the polygons. The current camera view is a Perspective view, which simulates how an object looks in real life. For the next step, change the view by selecting Orthographic > Front from the Panels drop-down menu, as shown in Figure 1.46. Orthographic views are like views of drafting drawings or floor plans and elevation views in design and architecture. They have no perspective but show a flat view of the model.

From the Front view it is easy to see the polygonal bands (faces or segments) around the cylinder. A cylinder makes a boring column. To add more realism to the column, you need a base and a crown for the bottom and top, respectively. Right-click on the cylinder to bring up a floating marking menu. Hold down the right mouse button and drag the cursor toward the word "vertex"; then release the button. Now

the cylinder is in what is called *Component mode*. In this mode, rather than selecting the entire object on the screen, you can select parts of the object, such as vertices, segments, or faces. By dragging a bounding box around a row of vertices, you can select all vertices within the box, as shown in Figure 1.47.

On the left side of the program window, there are several manipulator tools, which you can use to modify polygonal objects or components. The third one from the top (with the picture of a cone and an arrow) is the Move tool. The Move tool allows you to move objects or components in 3D space. Select the green arrow to move the previously selected vertices up and down in the Y axis. Move the rows of vertices until they appear as in Figure 1.48.

These vertices will make up the base of the column. You can use the Scale tool to form the base by scaling the rows of vertices. Like the Move tool, the Scale tool is a model manipulator tool. The Scale tool is the fifth tool down from the top. (It has two arrows and a cube on it.) When you select it,

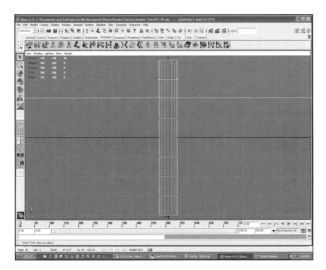

Figure 1.47 Selecting vertices in Component mode.

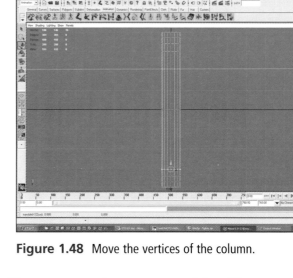

Figure 1.48 Move the vertices of the column.

a new manipulator appears. By clicking on the center (or yellow) block on the tool and moving the mouse to the right or left, you can scale the selected vertices larger or smaller in all three dimensions. Scale each row of vertices, as shown in Figure 1.49.

Repeat the same process for the bottom of the column to create an upper and lower base on the column. Now the shape of the column is finished and ready to have a surface texture applied to it (see Figure 1.50).

Most 3D objects in games use either a color or a texture to give them a real-istic look. In this case, I will use textures. *Textures* are 2D images that are applied to 3D objects. In Maya, the Hypershade tool is used to organize and apply textures to 3D objects. You access the Hypershade tool through the Window menu, as shown in Figure 1.51.

Maya creates *materials* for each texture. You use materials to adjust a texture's attributes after it is loaded in Maya. To create a material, go to the Create menu in Hypershade and choose Materials > Blinn, as shown in Figure 1.52. (Blinn is a type of material.)

A new material will appear in Hypershade. Press Ctrl+A to bring up the Attribute editor, which is used for manipulating a material (see Figure 1.53). In this case, I will use the Attribute editor to load a texture.

In the Attribute editor, click on the little checkerboard icon to the right of Color to bring up the Create Render Node dialog box, as shown in Figure 1.54.

The Create Render Node dialog box contains several options for creating textures or patterns for materials. For this column, I will use the File icon to

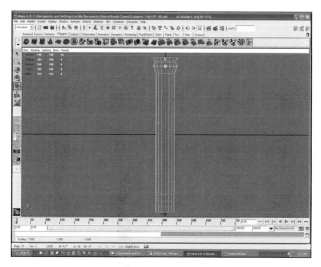

Figure 1.49 Creating the top of the column.

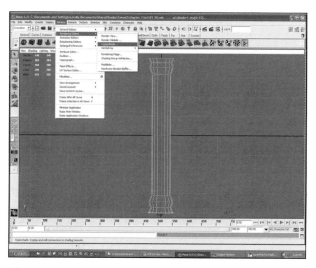

Figure 1.51 Accessing the Hypershade tool.

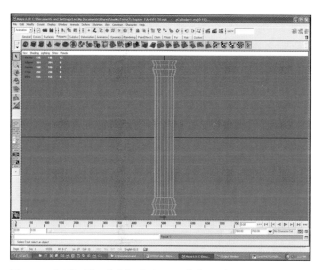

Figure 1.50 The finished shape of the column.

Figure 1.52 Creating a new material in Hypershade.

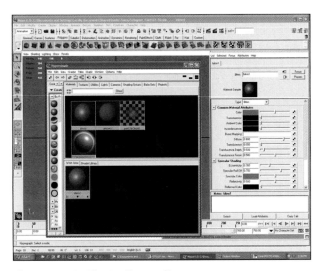

Figure 1.53 The Attribute editor.

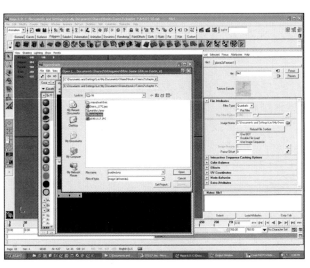

Figure 1.55 The texture-loading dialog box.

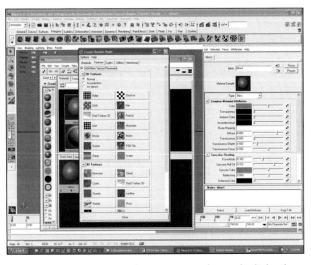

Figure 1.54 Calling up the Create Render Node dialog box.

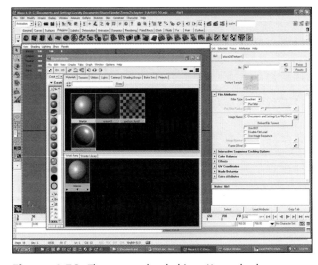

Figure 1.56 The texture loaded into Hypershade.

load a texture that was previously created in a 2D photo-paint program. Click on File to bring up a new menu on the Attribute editor. Notice that there is a file folder icon to the right of the image name. Clicking on this icon will bring up a new dialog box in which you can select the marble texture and load it into Maya (see Figure 1.55).

The texture is now loaded into Maya (see Figure 1.56). Right-click on the material in Hypershade and select Rename from the marking menu. Rename the material "marble."

Now minimize Hypershade and the Attribute editor, and then change the main view window to Perspective view. The object is still in Component mode. There are several icons below the main menu bar at the top of the program window, two of which are mode select icons (see Figure 1.57).

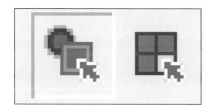

Figure 1.57 Mode select icons.

These two mode select icons control the viewing mode of the main window. The icon on the right is for Component mode, and the icon on the left is for Object mode. Return the view window to Object mode by first clicking on the Component mode icon to clear the object, and then clicking on the Object mode icon.

Now you can apply the texture to the object. If the column is selected, it will show the polygons in bright green. If the column is not highlighted in bright green, select it by clicking on it. Now bring up the Hypershade tool and right-click on the new material to bring up the marking menu. From the menu, select Assign Material to Selection. The texture will be applied to the column. Press 6 on the keyboard to see the texture applied to the column in what is known as *hardware texturing*. The 6 key is a shortcut key. Maya has a number of shortcut keys that help speed up the modeling process. We

will explain how to use a few of these keys in some of the projects in this book.

You need to adjust the texture so it looks correct on the column. Maya has several texture manipulators called *projectors*. Projectors take their name from slide projectors because they project an image onto the surface of the object. The Cylindrical Mapping projector would be the best choice for this project. You access it through the Edit Polygons menu, as shown in Figure 1.58.

Figure 1.58 Accessing the Cylindrical Mapping projector.

The Cylindrical Mapping projector is used to map an object onto a cylinder. Click the Apply button to bring up the on-screen manipulators (see Figure 1.59). Click on the center green manipulator at the top of the column and drag it down as shown in the figure. Now the object is mapped correctly.

The column could be finished now, but with only one texture it is a little boring. It would be a lot more interesting to look at if it had a second texture for the base and crown. To add a second texture, go back to Hypershade and load the second texture the same way you did the first (see Figure 1.60). This time the texture will be marble1.

The darker marble1 texture only needs to be applied to the top and bottom of the column. To select and apply a texture to only a part of an object, the object needs to be in Component mode. Press 4 on the keyboard to go back to Wireframe view, and then right-click on the object and select Faces by holding down the right mouse button and moving the cursor down toward the Faces menu on the marker menu. *Face* is the component name for a polygon. Now you can draw a bounding box around the faces that make up the bases of the column by holding the left mouse button down and dragging, as shown in Figure 1.61.

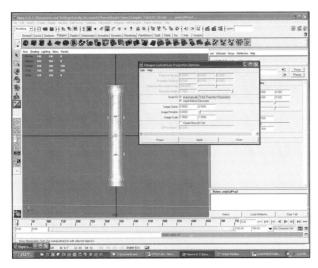

Figure 1.59 The Cylindrical Mapping on-screen manipulators.

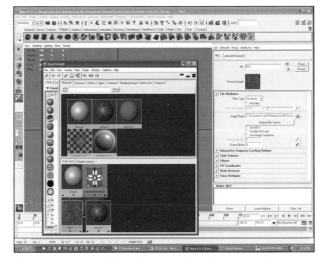

Figure 1.60 Loading the second marble texture into Hypershade.

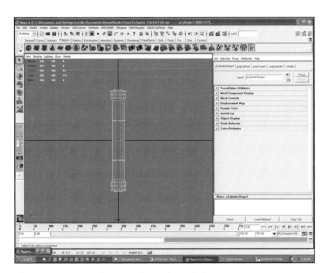

Figure 1.61 Selecting the column's bases.

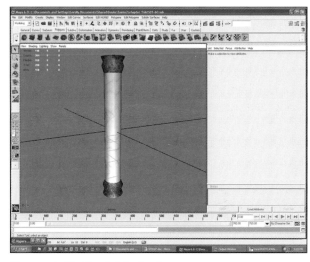

Figure 1.62 The finished column.

Apply the texture to the faces (by first selecting the faces in Component mode) with Hypershade the same way you applied it to the object earlier. Now you have a completed column, as shown in Figure 1.62.

Summary

This chapter has been an overview of the tools used in creation of art. The programs used in this chapter are contained on the CD that accompanies this book. The programs include

- Corel Painter
- Corel Photo Paint
- CorelDRAW
- Maya Personal Learning Edition

This chapter also provided brief examples of how you might use these programs in a production setting.

CHAPTER 2

2D ARTWORK IN GAMES

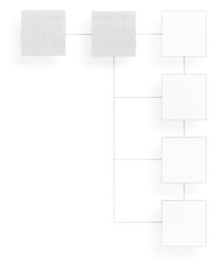

Before 3D games hit the market, games were created using 2D artwork. Even now there are many facets of game creation that require good two-dimensional artwork. The main areas for which 2D artwork is required for games include

- Textures for 3D models
- Titles, menus, legal screens, and other interface art
- Concept art

In this chapter, I will provide an overview of each type of 2D art used in games and give you some examples of how the art is created.

Learning about Textures

Textures are 2D images that are applied to a three-dimensional model to give the model surface detail. In real life every surface has a texture. Sometimes the textures are only a color, while other times they might be very complex, such as the bark of a tree. Take a quick look around and study some of the many textures you see in everyday life. You will notice on close examination that every surface has some qualities that you can fit into a few specific categories.

- Color
- Roughness
- Translucency
- Reflectivity
- Luminance

Each one of these qualities or attributes is part of what gives the surface the look and feel it has. To make a 3D model look believable in a game, the artist needs to capture the inherent qualities of the surfaces he is trying to depict by creating textures that match the surface as closely as possible. The metallic sheen of a kitchen appliance has a very different look from a weathered fencepost. The hard gray of a sidewalk is very different from the spiky look of the lawn right next to it. To better understand how you can create surface attributes in 2D artwork, take a look at each one individually.

Color in Textures

One of the most noticeable characteristics of any surface is its color. We often refer to an object by its color. We say "the red car" or "the blue sweater." Some colors are tied to emotional states. We call a person who is on a lucky streak "red-hot" or a person who is depressed "blue." We even assign temperatures to colors. Red, yellow, and orange are considered warm colors, while purple, blue, and green are thought of as cool colors.

How Light Affects Colors

To better understand color you first need to look at light. When pure light strikes an object, some of the light energy is absorbed and some is reflected. The light you see is the light that is reflected. For example, when you see a red object, you are really seeing an object that reflects red light. The object is absorbing all the non-red light and reflecting the red.

The light that your eyes process so you can see the world around you is called the *visible band* of light. The visible band of light is made up of a spectrum of colors. If you have ever seen a rainbow, you have seen the spectrum of visible light (see Figure 2.1). Rainbows are made from light bouncing off water particles in the air. Because each color has its own unique characteristics, some colors are bounced in one direction and some are bounced in another, forming bands of pure color. These bands of color are always in the same order, with red at one end and violet or purple at the other end. All the rest of the colors are between those two colors.

Figure 2.1 A rainbow in nature. © Corel Corporation.

Pure light is often called *white light*. White light contains the full spectrum of colors. When you see a white color, you are really seeing an object that reflects a full spectrum of color toward us. On the other hand, when you see a black object, you are really seeing an object that is not reflecting any band of light back to us. The black object is absorbing the full spectrum of light, while the white object is reflecting the full spectrum of light. That is why black objects tend to heat when placed in light, while white objects tend not to heat as much.

Hint

Light is a very important topic for artists. I encourage every person that I teach to learn as much as possible about the physics of light. The better an artist understands the nature of light, the better he will understand how to create realistic and believable art.

Understanding light is very important to understanding how color works. Unless you are in a completely dark room, every object sends light to your eyes (see Figure 2.2). This light not only affects the object itself, but also

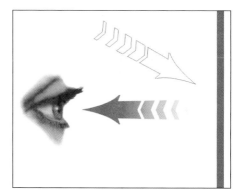

Figure 2.2 When white light strikes a red object, only red light is reflected.

other objects around it. Try an experiment. Place a white card next to a bright red object. You can see the red light from the object bouncing off the white of the card. The effect is similar to shining a red light on the card, just not as pronounced.

Any light you see that is not pure is missing part of the full spectrum of color. In some ways you can call colored light *deficient light*. Because colored light is deficient in one or more bands of color, it affects the objects it lights. Because red light does not contain blue light, objects that are blue in normal light will look very different in red light. The same thing goes for all other colored light.

Using the Color Wheel

Earlier I gave the example of the rainbow. A common tool for artists is a color wheel (see Figure 2.3). A *color wheel* is an ordered placement of colors in a circle based on their relative positions in the full spectrum of light. Remember that one end of the bands of color on a rainbow is red and the other is purple or violet. On a color wheel, these two colors are next to each other, and the other colors are arranged around the circle in order.

Some art programs actually use the color wheel as part of the color palette as seen in the upper right of the screen shot below. Corel Painter provides a good example of the color

Figure 2.3 The color wheel in Corel Painter.

wheel in a program. Load Painter and look at the color palette. Notice the color ring around the color triangle. The colors in the ring represent the different bands of color in the full spectrum of color. The inside triangle shows the current color of the spectrum from the color wheel. Look for the small ring on the color wheel. Move the ring around the wheel and notice how the color of the inside triangle changes to match the color on the wheel.

Understanding Color Saturation

Color saturation is the intensity and purity of a color. When a color is fully saturated it contains a pure band of color from the color wheel. The color is not grayed or tinted; it is the pure color at its full strength. You almost never see fully saturated colors in real life. However, every color that you see has some level of saturation.

The color palette in Corel Painter shows the fully saturated color at one corner of the inside triangle. Move the small circle inside the triangle. The right side of the triangle is the purest color. As you move the small circle away from the right, the color is less pure and more muted.

Understanding Value in Color

Color value does not refer to how expensive a color is; rather, it refers to how light or dark it is. The full *value scale* is from pure black to pure white. The value scale is represented in Corel Painter on the left side of the triangle color palette (see Figure 2.4). The lower corner of the triangle is black, and the upper corner is white. Between the two left-hand corners is grayscale without any color saturation.

All colors have values. Colors such as red and blue tend to have dark values, while a color such as yellow tends to have a lighter value. When you look at a black-and-white photograph, you are really looking at a picture of value. As an artist, I often will convert a color picture to grayscale so I can see the values of each color. If your pictures look drastically different in color than they do in grayscale, you are probably dealing with a value problem.

Roughness in Textures

Every surface you see in real life has some degree of roughness. Some surfaces, such as glass or polished metal, have such a low degree of roughness that it can only be seen using a microscope. Other surfaces, such as a rock wall or gravel, have noticeable roughness. The rougher a surface is, the more it refracts light. *Refraction* is the scattering of light when it hits an uneven surface. When light hits a surface, it bounces off the surface at a direct angle from the light source (see Figure 2.5).

Roughness is usually simulated in textures rather than built with geometry in the 3D model. Moving polygons around in a virtual world requires many mathematical calculations. The fewer polygons an artist can use to create 3D models, the faster the game will be able to run. It is impractical in most games to use polygons to define a rough texture.

Figure 2.6 shows a rough rock wall. You could create this wall using nothing more than color and geometry, but that would be an extreme waste of

Figure 2.4 The left side of the triangle is for the light-to-dark value.

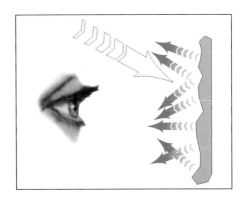

Figure 2.5 Light refracting from a rough surface.

Figure 2.6 The rough surface of a rock wall.

computer processor time that you could devote instead to more critical game needs. It would also be an extreme waste of your time. A better method would be to create the appearance of the rough rock wall in a 2D picture and paste that picture on a relatively simple object.

Translucency in Textures

In nature, not all surfaces are opaque; some surfaces are *translucent*. A translucent surface allows some amount of light to pass through it, making it possible to see through the surface. Figure 2.7 shows a good example of a translucent surface. Notice how the glass of the pyramid changes the color and detail of the building seen through it.

Some of the more advanced game engines will allow you to use translucent textures. Sometimes you will

need to create a translucent texture in a 2D paint program, but most of the time the translucency is added in the 3D art program.

Reflectivity in Textures

Reflectivity is related to roughness in textures. The more even and polished a surface is, the more it will tend to reflect light directly back to the viewer. A *reflective* surface acts like a mirror, reflecting its surroundings back to the viewer. True reflections can only be generated in the game environment; however, sometimes reflections can be simulated, as in Figure 2.8.

Even though the reflection on the door is static, it still gives the impression of a reflection. For many objects in 3D games, building true reflections is impractical. In those instances, a

static reflection will get the job done. The problem with a static reflection is that it does not move with the viewer. To solve this problem game engines often use environment maps.

An environment map is a texture map that is applied in the game engine that moves with the movement of the player and the object to simulate a moving reflection. Racing games often will use an environment map to give the racing cars a reflective appearance.

Surface Luminance in Textures

Luminance is the brightness of a color. For the purposes of this book, I will discuss luminance when dealing with a light source as seen in a game. For example, a light bulb will have a high degree of luminance when the light is turned on and no luminance when it is turned off. Like reflections, real-time luminance is a property of the game engine. Many times, though, luminance needs to be part of a 2D image. In Figure 2.9, the texture is a wall that is lit by a wall-mounted light. The wall-mounted light will be added in the 3D modeling program,

Figure 2.7 The glass of the pyramid is translucent, which allows light to pass through it.

Figure 2.8 Simulated reflections on the surface of a door texture.

but the pattern or the luminance of the light was added to the texture itself.

Figure 2.9 A lighting effect was added to the texture.

Creating Textures

To create textures for games, artists use one of two different methods. The first method is to create a texture from scratch by painting it. This method is great for artists who have a high degree of artistic ability because it allows for endless variety in the types of textures that can be produced. The only limitations are the imagination and ability of the artist. The other method of creating textures

is to use photographs. Many times a photograph of a surface is the best choice because the artist is trying to simulate a real object.

Hint

One thing I learned about working as an artist for games is that artists use whatever method they can to create the art as quickly and accurately as possible. There is no rule that states every piece of art has to be drawn by hand. If a photograph will work better, use the photograph. You will need permission to use a photograph if it isn't your property. Using a photograph without the owner's permission is illegal.

Painting Textures

For this example, we will create a weathered stucco texture using Corel Painter, which has some nice features for creating textures.

1. First open Corel Painter. Select New from the File menu to bring up the New dialog box, as shown in Figure 2.10. Set the size at 512 × 512 pixels.

Figure 2.10 The texture size is set for 512 × 512 pixels.

Hint

It is a good idea to get in the habit of making your texture's dimensions a power of two. This is of particular importance on console systems because of the limited bandwidth of the bus. It is a good rule to make the dimensions one of the following numbers: 8, 16, 32, 64, 128, 256, 512, or 1024. Texture sizes should be as small as possible but still look good in the game.

2. Next select Show Papers from the Window menu, as shown in Figure 2.11.

3. Painter will bring up the paper palette. In the upper-right-hand corner of the palette is a drop-down menu. Click on the menu to access a list of predefined

Figure 2.11 Choose Show Papers from the Window menu.

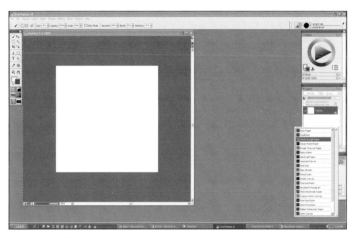

Figure 2.12 Choose Artists Rough Paper from the menu.

papers. Choose Artists Rough Paper from the list, as shown in Figure 2.12.

4. Go to the Brush Selection menu and select Air Brush. (See Figure 2.13.)

5. Now use the air brush to spray in a gradation from light aqua in the upper left corner to light violet in the lower right, as shown in Figure 2.14. Use the circular color palette to change the colors. Using a large brush size is also helpful for getting a smooth transition between colors.

6. The next step is to apply the surface texture to the image. In the Effects menu, choose Surface Control > Apply Surface Texture, as shown in Figure 2.15. This will bring up the Apply Surface Texture dialog box.

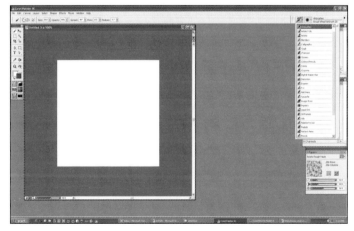

Figure 2.13 Use the Brush Selection menu to select a brush.

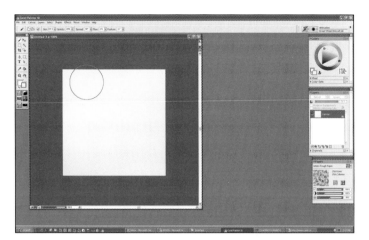

Figure 2.14 Paint a color gradation in the texture.

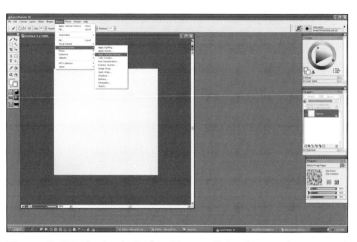

Figure 2.15 The Apply Surface Texture dialog box can be accessed from the Surface Control submenu in the Effects menu.

7. The first thing you should change in the Apply Surface Texture dialog box is the lighting. You can change the color of the light by clicking on the color square just above Lighting Color. I chose to offset the cool gray color with a warm orange light (see Figure 2.16). The mixture of a warm light source with a cool color will gray the image further, but it also adds a warm color, which will become very important later.

8. Make adjustments to the slider bars to get just the right look

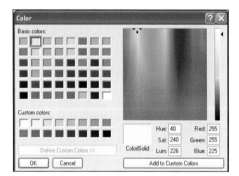

Figure 2.16 Select the lighting color.

(see Figure 2.17). Feel free to do the same or make adjustments as you like. A little experimentation with these slider bars will result in a number of dramatic

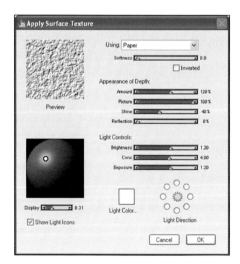

Figure 2.17 Adjust the slider bars.

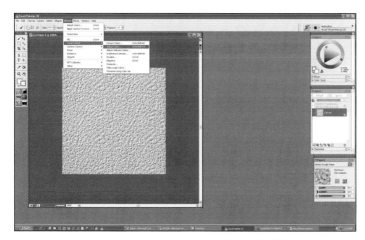

Figure 2.18 The texture is a good start, but it needs more work.

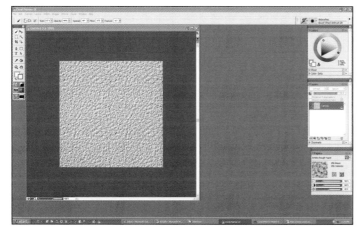

Figure 2.19 The Adjust Color dialog box can be accessed by choosing Tonal Control from the Effects menu.

changes to the surface texture. For this texture, I reduced the Shine and increased the Amount sliders. I also adjusted the three light controls.

9. Now you should have a nice-looking stucco texture (see Figure 2.18). You could finish here, but I want to add some more interest to my stucco. Right now it is too much like freshly painted stucco, and I am looking for a more weathered look with maybe a hint of moss growing on the wall.

10. Now the lighting change in Step 8 will come in handy because you have both a warm and a cool color in the texture. You can modify these colors to get the weathered look by accessing the Adjust Color dialog box, which is found under Tonal Control in the Effects menu (see Figure 2.19).

11. I didn't want to make a uniform change to the colors, so I chose Paper from the Using menu in the Adjust Color dialog box (see Figure 2.20).

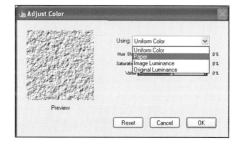

Figure 2.20 Select Paper from the Using menu in the Adjust Color dialog box.

12. Shift the Hue Shift, Saturation, and Value slider bars to get the weathered stucco look (see Figure 2.21). Notice how some colors are shifted to more of a reddish tint, while others are shifted to more of a greenish tint.

Now the texture is finished and ready to use in a game (see Figure 2.22).

Using Photographs for Textures

This texture is an example of taking a part of a picture and using it to create a repeatable texture for trim on a building. I start with a picture from www.environmental-textures.com, a great site for high quality photographs for building textures (see Figure 2.23). For this example I will use Corel Photo Paint. As I stated earlier, photo-painting software is geared specifically toward photo manipulation. I load the photo into Corel Photo Paint.

1. The first step is to crop the picture down to the area with which you want to work. You can use the Crop tool to drag a box around the area on the picture, as shown in Figure 2.24.

2. Figure 2.25 shows the cropped image. Notice that the image is not perfectly square with the edges of the cropped area. Very seldom will any picture be exactly square with the camera. The edges of the building decoration do not line up perfectly with the edges of the image. I want this texture to repeat, so it needs to be completely square with the edges of the image.

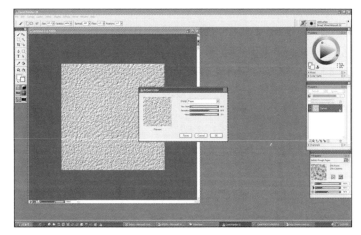

Figure 2.21 Adjust the slider bars to get the final look for the texture.

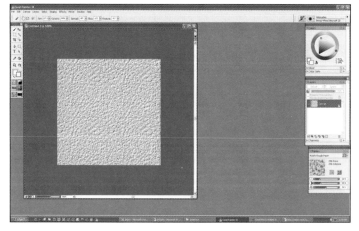

Figure 2.22 The finished stucco texture.

Figure 2.23 The base photo used to start the process of creating a texture.

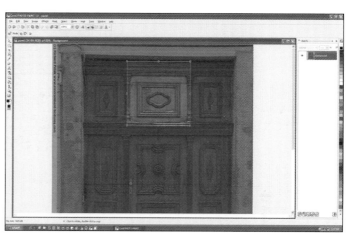

Figure 2.24 Crop to the area where the texture will be taken from the picture.

3. The easiest way to get a picture to line up with the edges of an image is to use the Distort tool. First you copy the image, and then you paste it over itself. Now you have two images, one exactly on top of the other.

4. Corel Photo Paint provides you with four different ways to manipulate the pasted image. To change the manipulation tool, all you have to do is click on the image. Try clicking on the image a few times. Notice that the handles around the image change. These handles are used for manipulating the image. The default tool is the Size tool, which is depicted by a set of black squares around the edge. After you click once inside the image, the manipulator will change to arrows that curve around the corners. This tool is the Rotate tool. The third click will bring up the Distortion tool, which is used to adjust the shape of the image by allowing you to move individual corners. The Distortion tool is repre-sented by small arrows pointed away from the picture. You can grab and move these arrows. I used these arrows to line up the picture with the edges of the image, as shown in Figure 2.25. When you have the image lined up correctly, right-click on the image and select apply.

5. Once the image is adjusted so it is even with the edges, you can combine the two images using the Combine All Images with Background option, as shown in Figure 2.26.

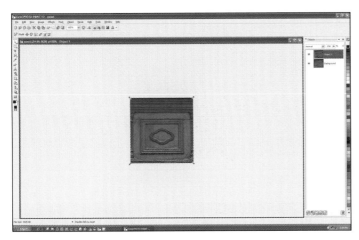

Figure 2.25 You can use the Distortion tool to line up the picture with the edges of the image.

6. The image looks like it will line up from side to side but it isn't exact. To get it to line up perfectly there will need to be some hand painting of the edges. The easiest way to see how the image will line up is to use the Offset tool. It is found in Effects > Distort > Offset (see Figure 2.27).

7. Set the tool to 50% vertical and 50% horizontal to bring the edges into the middle of the picture (see Figure 2.28).

8. The image is now offset so the former borders run through the middle of the texture. Notice that the edges do not line up exactly (see Figure 2.29). This is common with photographs. Seldom do things in the world ever match up perfectly.

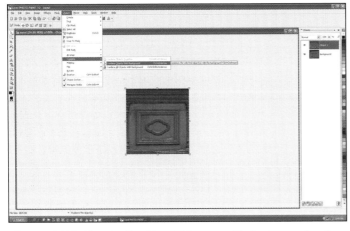

Figure 2.26 Use the Combine All Images with Background option.

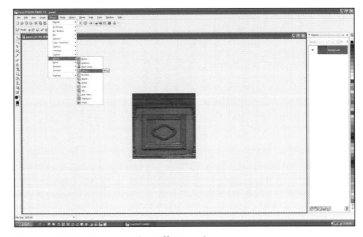

Figure 2.27 Bring up the Offset tool.

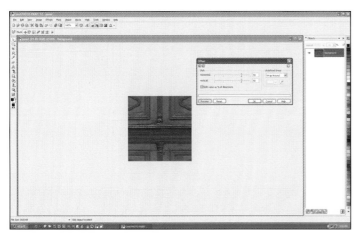

Figure 2.28 The texture after cropping.

Figure 2.29 The offset image does not line up perfectly.

9. One of the best ways to get a texture to line up is to use the Cloning Brush feature in Photo Paint. The Cloning Brush will paint using another part of the image so that one part of an image can be painted into another part. The Cloning Brush is located in the toolbox under a pull out menu (see Figure 2.30).

10. Once you have selected the Cloning Brush, go to the image. You will see a circle cursor. The circle represents the size of the brush. You can adjust the size of the brush with the size parame-

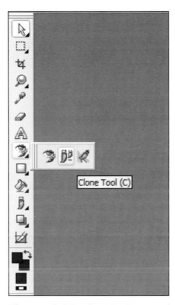

Figure 2.30 The Cloning Brush is in a pull out menu.

ter on the toolbar. Reduce the brush size to about 6 pixels.

11. The Cloning Brush is set up in two stages. The first click in the image will designate the clone source or the area from which you will paint from. The second click will determine the actual brush. For this image we will be painting from left to right. Set your source area on the left edge of the image and move directly to the right about a third of the way across the image to set the brush. Make sure the source and brush are lined up horizontally.

12. Now try painting along the seam in the middle of the picture. Notice that as you paint, the source area moves with the brush.

13. Work along some of the more blatant seams in the middle of the image (see Figure 2.31).

14. You will need to use several clone sources to get all of the seams out of the image. Figure 2.32 shows the texture with most of the seams gone.

15. Now it is time to check the tiling of the texture to see how it will look repeated over an area. A quick way to do this is to use the Tile function. The function is located at Effects > Distort > Tile, as shown in Figure 2.33.

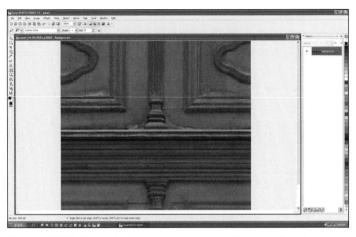

Figure 2.32 Several clone sources are used in removing the seams in the texture.

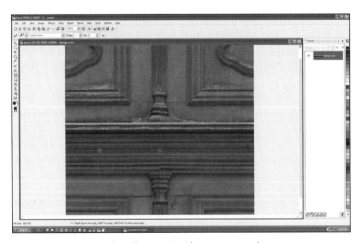

Figure 2.31 Use the Cloning Brush to remove the seams.

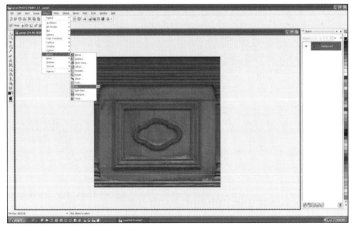

Figure 2.33 Use the Tile function to check the texture.

16. Set the tile parameters to those shown in Figure 2.34. You are using this feature to look for odd patterns created through tiling. Do not click on the OK button. When you are done, click Cancel. In this example there are no odd patterns.

Figure 2.34 Tile the image to see if there are any odd patterns created.

17. The next step will be to resample the image so that it fits a power of two number. Bring up the Resample function from the Image menu. You will need to change the measurement parameters to pixels, as shown in Figure 2.35.

Figure 2.35 Change the measurement parameters to pixels.

18. If there is a check in the maintain aspect ratio box, deselect it. Now change the height and width to 256 × 256. Click OK. The texture is now finished.

Tiling Organic Textures

Large textures take up memory in a game system, and some console game systems have very limited texture memory. To make better use of texture memory, game artists have developed a system of tiling textures. *Tiling* a texture is the process of taking a small texture and repeating it numerous times over the surface of a 3D object. For example, think about a brick wall. Most of the bricks look very similar, so there is no need to make one large texture image for the entire wall. It is much more efficient to create a small image of a few bricks and repeat it over the surface of the wall multiple times. In addition to repeating textures such as bricks, you can tile more organic images. In the following example, I will show you how a photo of a bush is adapted to a texture that tiles in two directions. If you have a similar image, you can follow along with these steps.

For this project I will be using Paint Shop Pro, a software program similar to Corel Photo Paint but a little more advanced in some of its features. Again I will be using a photograph from www.environment-textures.com.

1. The first step will be to load a source photograph into Paint Shop Pro, as shown in Figure 2.36.

2. Look at the photograph to find an area of the tree that looks fairly flat and even.

Figure 2.36 Load a source image into Paint Shop Pro.

Figure 2.38 The current picture will not tile properly because the seams between each picture would be too obvious.

3. Now use the Crop tool, third from the top of the toolbox, and drag it to define a 512 × 512 pixel area (see Figure 2.37).

4. Click on the checkmark on the toolbar to apply the crop. Tiling textures line up on all sides so there is no noticeable seam between pictures. If I tried to use the current picture as a tiling texture, the seams between each picture would be very noticeable. The texture also has some noticeable dark and light areas that will create a pattern if the tile is repeated

Figure 2.37 Select an area to be cropped.

over a large area (see Figure 2.38).

5. We will work on the pattern problem first. Paint Shop Pro has a Clone Brush that is very similar to the one in Photo Paint, with the exception that the source is selected with a right-click rather than a left-click. The Clone Brush is the 8th tool down in the toolbox. Use it to even out the light and dark areas of the texture, as shown in Figure 2.39.

6. Paint Shop Pro has an offset feature similar to Photo Paint,

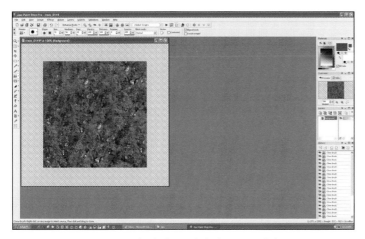

Figure 2.39 Even out the light and dark areas of the texture.

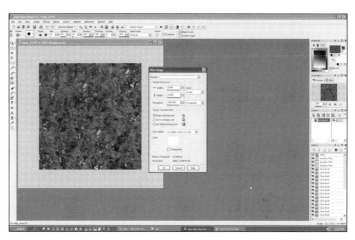

Figure 2.41 Set the page dimensions to 2048 pixels.

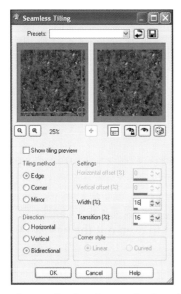

Figure 2.40 Bring up the Seamless Tiling dialog box.

but it also has a special feature for creating seamless tiles. It is in Effects > Images Effects > Seamless Tiling. Selecting it will bring up a dialog box (see Figure 2.40).

7. Set the Width (%) to 16 and the Transfer (%) to 16 and the other options as shown in Figure 2.40. Click on OK and you have a seamless tile. Wasn't that easy?

8. Paint Shop Pro has another great feature for tiling textures to see if they look good when placed together. It is called the Grid. First create a new image

by clicking on the blank page icon on the toolbar. It will bring up a dialog box (see Figure 2.41). Set the dimensions to 2048 as shown.

9. Now go to the original texture and use the Selection tool to copy the texture into the Clipboard (see Figure 2.42). Paste the copied texture into the new image, as shown in Figure 2.43.

10. Before we go any further, we need to set the size of the grid. Select Change Grid Guide and Snap Properties from the View menu (see Figure 2.44).

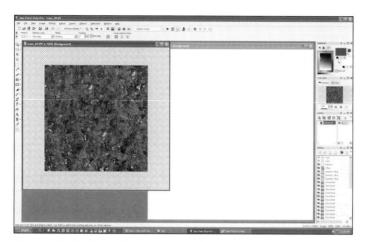

Figure 2.42 Copy the texture into the Clipboard.

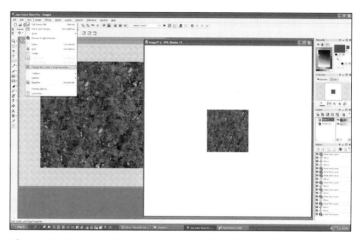

Figure 2.44 You will need to set the size of the grid.

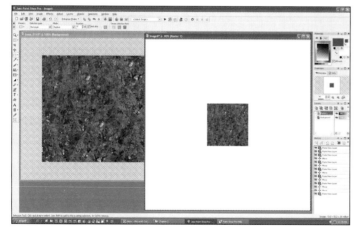

Figure 2.43 Paste the copied texture into the new image.

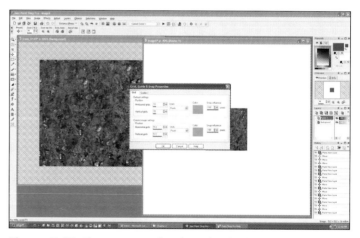

Figure 2.45 The texture and grid need to be the same size.

11. Figure 2.45 shows the grid size set to 512 × 512. The grid needs to be the same size as the texture.

12. Now in the View menu, turn on both the Grid and the Snap to Grid features (see Figure 2.46).

13. You can now move the texture in the grid and it will automatically snap into position. This is especially useful when creating 2D tile sets to see if they match up. Copy the texture into the image several times and move each texture into a grid position (see Figure 2.47).

14. Now remove the grid to see how you did. Figure 2.48 shows the final texture pattern. There is a slight pattern but overall the texture should work fine.

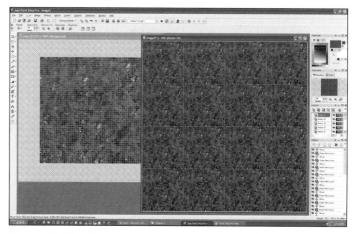

Figure 2.47 Place the texture copies next to each other.

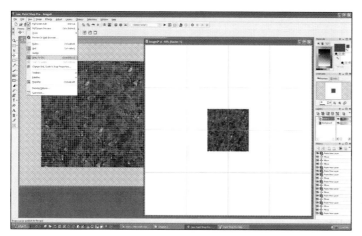

Figure 2.46 Turn on the Grid and Snap to Grid features.

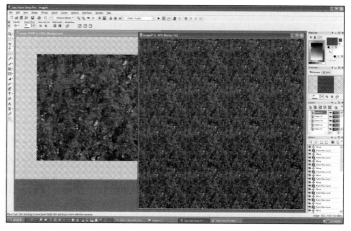

Figure 2.48 The final texture pattern with the grid removed.

Creating Game Interfaces

Significant 2D art is used in the opening and closing of most games. This art includes title screens, legal screens, navigation menus, heads-up displays, credit screens, and so on. These screens are all part of the work that an artist must create to complete a game. Collectively they are called *interface art* because they make up the art that is used for controlling and navigating a game.

A cool-looking interface can go a long way toward making a game look and feel like a professional product. Some game companies spend thousands of dollars for artists to design and create great interfaces for their games. Take a look at some of your favorite games and study how the interface was created. You will soon see that there is a lot of art created for the interface in many of these games.

Interface art can be divided into two major categories—information art and navigation art. Information art is used to inform the player of important information in a game, such as

how to play the game, who owns the game, and most importantly, who created the game. Navigation art is used to help a player move through or play a game; this might include selection menus, life meters, or load/save features.

In the following example, let's create a menu screen for loading saved games. To start with, set up the screen using CorelDRAW.

1. Open CorelDRAW.
2. Change the page view to landscape by clicking on it in the toolbar (see Figure 2.49).
3. Next, load in a background picture, as you can see in Figure 2.50, by using the Import function in the File menu.
4. Then use the Rectangle tool from the toolbox and draw a large rectangle over the top of the picture. Left-clicking the white palette square fills the rectangle (see Figure 2.51). Right-click on the palette square, marked with an X, to remove the black border.

Hint

Shapes in CorelDRAW have both an outline and a fill. When they are first drawn, the fill color is transparent. Choosing an outline and fill color is very easy. A click of the left mouse button on any palette color on the right side of the screen will fill the shape with the selected color. A right-click will change the outline color to the selected color from the palette.

5. Now round the corners by typing in the number **20** in the toolbar, as shown in Figure 2.52.
6. Now, select the Transparency tool from the 11th position down in the toolbox. It is at the end of the fly out menu and looks like a glass goblet. From there, choose the Flat option from the pull-down menu on the toolbar (see Figure 2.53).
7. Next, choose the Text tool from the toolbox and change the font to Charlesworth and the font size to 72. Click on white from the palette and type the word **Options**, as shown in Figure 2.54.

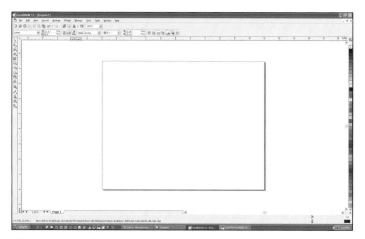

Figure 2.49 Change page view to landscape.

Figure 2.51 Create a white rectangle.

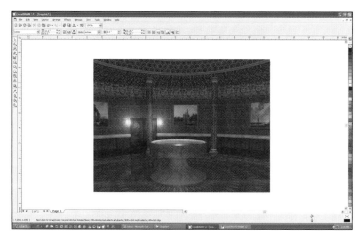

Figure 2.50 Load a background picture.

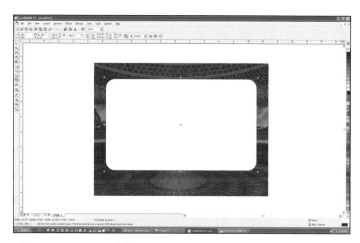

Figure 2.52 Round the corners.

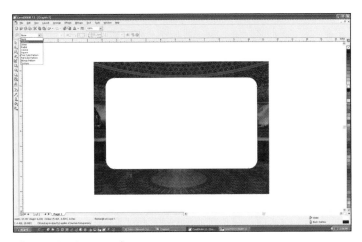

Figure 2.53 Use a flat transparency.

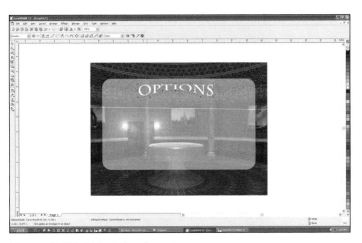

Figure 2.55 Distort the characters.

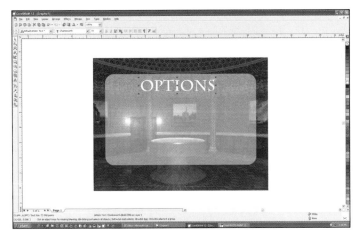

Figure 2.54 Type in the word **Options**.

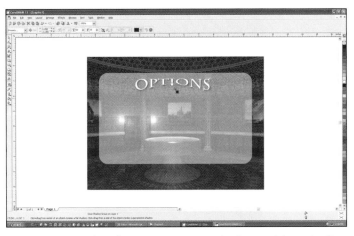

Figure 2.56 Select the Interactive Drop Shadow tool from the fly out menu.

8. From the same tool fly out as the Transparency tool, select the Envelope tool. Pull the bottom center handle up, as shown in Figure 2.55.

9. From the same tool fly out, choose the Drop Shadow tool and add a drop shadow to the type, as shown in Figure 2.56. The Interactive Drop Shadow tool works with two click-and-drag movements. The first click and drag determines the size of the shadow. The second click and drag moves the shadow. Make a moderately large

shadow and then position it so that the shadow is down and to the right of the type.

10. Now I draw a white oval, as shown in Figure 2.57.

11. I make the oval transparent, like the rectangle.

12. I then type the options in black, as shown in Figure 2.58.

13. The type is a little small so I change the size to 72 point using the toolbar (see Figure 2.59).

14. Now go back to the Envelope tool with the type still selected.

15. There is a drop-down menu in the toolbar. From it select the circle preset (see Figure 2.60).

16. Save your work. You will be using this file as one of the images. Now change the black type to transparent (see Figure 2.61). Save your work again.

17. In the game the two images will be combined to show the option selection, as shown in Figure 2.62

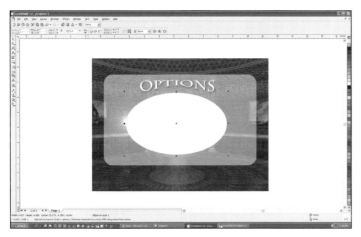

Figure 2.57 Draw a white oval.

Figure 2.58 Type the options in black.

Figure 2.59 Increase the size of the type.

Figure 2.61 Change the black type to transparent before saving.

Figure 2.60 Select the circle preset.

Figure 2.62 The selected option is indicated in black.

Creating Concept Art for Games

Concept art is not art that is actually used in a video game; rather, it is the design art that is created to visualize the game. Concept art is in the form of character designs, world designs, and storyboards.

Character designs are drawings of characters and creatures that will appear in a game. They are often in color with multiple views of the character. Designing great characters for a video game is not an easy process. It often takes artists several iterations before a final character sketch is approved to go into the game. When we were creating the new characters to go into *StarCraft: Brood War*, the artists designing the characters spent weeks working on some of them, with multiple changes and revisions.

World designs are drawings of the game environments. They might include pictures of scenes and maps of levels. Some game worlds are simple, but others are very sophisticated and complex. The game world for a fighting game might be nothing more than a simple room, but the game world for an adventure game might have an entire city with surrounding countryside that needs to be designed. As game systems advance in power, game worlds are becoming more and more complex.

Storyboards are drawings of the progression in a game. They usually are a series of pictures depicting how a game is played to give the development team a good idea of how the game will be played once it is finished. They are also used to help convey how a game should look when it is finished.

Storyboards are a great help in solving complex game play issues. While working on a platform game, I remember doing a detailed storyboard of a very complex level. The main character was a robot that could roll around the level and make small jumps. I had to design the level so it was interesting to look at but functional from the standpoint of the robot's limitations. By creating a series of storyboards, I was able to work out both the look of the level and the game play challenges within the level.

The following example will be a character illustration in oil paint on a panel. The color medium is unimportant, but oil paint has many advantages in that it does not dry quickly, allowing the artist to blend colors on the surface of the painting.

The first task is to rough in the basic forms of the character on the panel. Figure 2.63 shows the initial construction lines of the drawing.

A detailed line drawing is then created. The line drawing does not have any shading because its purpose is to

Figure 2.63 Rough in the basic construction lines of the drawing.

guide the painting. The shading will be added later in the painting. Figure 2.64 shows the base line drawing.

Figure 2.64 Create a detailed line drawing of the character.

This character is your typical run-of-the-mill knight on chicken-back. The circle behind the knight is a design element to help keep the focus on the character.

Before the artist goes to the trouble to start applying paint to the panel, it is a good idea to work out the color scheme of the painting. A small color painting is created with the basic color and value information. This small painting will then be the guide for painting the illustration. Figure 2.65 shows the small color rendering.

Figure 2.65 A small color rendering helps to plan the colors and values of the illustration.

In the first example in this chapter a mask was used to shield the painting. In this example a mask is used to protect the character from the background. The mask will protect the area where the character will later be painted. That way the background can be painted without having to work around the character. Figure 2.66 shows the background painted over the top of the character.

Figure 2.66 The background is painted over the character using a mask.

After the background is painted, the mask is removed, revealing the drawing of the character. The drawing can then be used as a guide to painting the character. Figure 2.67 shows the mask removed from the painting.

Figure 2.67 The mask is removed from the painting.

Using the small color scheme as a guide, the base colors are painted in flat tones. Figure 2.68 shows the head of the chicken roughed in color. The drawing is used as a guide for applying the tones.

Figure 2.68 The head of the chicken is painted in flat tones.

The rest of the knight and chicken is painted in flat tones like the head covering the drawing. The entire painting should now have paint on it. The advantage of painting in all the tones first before moving on to painting detail in any area is that the artist is able to see if the basic composition and values of the painting work. At this stage of the painting, if something is wrong, it is easier to change now than waiting until later when a

lot of work has gone into it. Figure 2.69 shows the painting in flat tones.

Figure 2.69 Cover the entire panel with the base flat tones.

Now that the flat tones of the painting are down, the detail work can begin. Starting at the bottom of the painting, the rocks are painted because the chicken will stand on top of them, and it is easier to paint the rocks in and then the feet on top of them. Figure 2.70 shows the rocks with the beginning of the chicken's feet on top of them.

The knight is then painted. The guy is all encased in armor. The armor is decorated with etched metal. To achieve the look of etched metal, the basic colors and values of the armor

are painted and then the etching is applied with a fine brush in a darker color. The knight's lance is also painted behind the chicken's head. See Figure 2.71 for the results of the work.

Figure 2.70 The rocks are brought to life beneath the characters.

Figure 2.71 The knight is painted next.

Following the same procedure as used on the knight's armor, the chicken's barding is also painted, as shown in Figure 2.72.

Figure 2.72 The barding is painted with the same technique as the armor.

The nice aspect of painting in oils when doing the chicken's feathers is that the lighter white paint can be brushed into the darker gray paint. The feathers then can be painted relatively quickly with good effect. Figure 2.73 shows the detailed work around the chicken's head. Some orange is added to a few of the feathers to tie them into the environment. In nature, the environment would reflect light on the feathers. Adding orange simulates the reflected light.

Figure 2.73 Paint the detail of the chicken's head.

Working from left to right, the lower feathers and legs of the chicken are painted. See Figure 2.74.

Figure 2.74 Continue to paint the chicken, working on the lower body and legs.

Now the only thing left is to paint the tail feathers. Like the other feathers, yellow and orange are added to tie the character in with the environment. Figure 2.75 shows the finished character illustration.

Figure 2.75 Finish the illustration by painting in the tail feathers.

Summary

Even though three-dimensional art is used in almost all current games on the market, two-dimensional art still plays a major role in the creation of a game. Even the most advanced 3D games use significant amounts of textures for 3D models within the game. 2D art is also used in the creation of interface art and concept sketches.

Understanding light and color is very important in developing textures for games. Textures also simulate shininess, roughness, transparency, and luminance.

The chapter gave examples of the following:

- Making 2D textures
- Making a texture from a photograph
- Making an organic seamless texture tile
- Creating a game menu screen
- Creating a character concept illustration

Corel Painter is a good tool for creating textures when you use its paper texture features. Corel Photo Paint and Paint Shop Pro have several powerful tools for preparing photographs for textures and for creating tiling textures. CorelDRAW is a good choice for creating menus. And, sometimes traditional media like oil paint is the best choice for creating art for games.

CHAPTER 3

2D ANIMATION

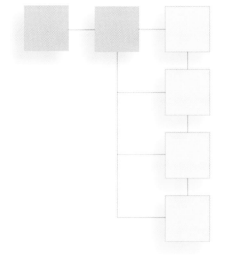

W hen I first started creating games, all animation was done in 2D or what is sometimes referred to as cell animation. The term *cell animation* comes from the motion picture industry. It refers to how animation was once created on clear plastic pages called *cells*. These cells were laid over background art and photographed one at a time.

How Does Animation Work?

Animation is the process of taking a series of drawn or rendered pictures that successively show motion.

Displaying them to the viewer in rapid succession gives the illusion of motion. When this happens, the slight differences between pictures give the illusion of movement. This process of showing pictures in rapid succession is the same method used in motion pictures, videos, and television. A motion picture camera does not record movement; it records a series of still images called frames. A *frame* is a single image in a series of images used in film video and animation. If a motion picture camera is recording a scene from an action car-chase movie, each picture of the cars will be slightly different. The first frame of the car

chase might be of the cars in the distance coming toward the camera. Each successive frame will have the cars a little closer to the camera. When all the frames are played back in order, the cars will actually appear to move toward the camera.

In motion pictures and television, the frames are presented so quickly that the normal human eye does not register that they are individual frames. In motion pictures, the normal rate of pictures projected on the screen is 24 frames per second, although some will go as high as 70 frames per second. TV and video run at 30 frames per second. Frame rates in games are not set because often the speed of the computer and the complexity of the program determine the frame rate. However, most game developers target 60 frames per second. Games that drop below 30 frames per second are harder to play because the controls often seem sluggish.

Hint

The number of frames per second is very important to the animator. The most common mistake of beginning animators is they make the difference in movement between frames even. They do not take into account that faster movements have greater differences between frames, while slower movements have lesser movements between frames. However, movement between frames should not be sporadic, causing the animation to have a jerky appearance. Differences in movement rates should be smooth.

Artists use animation to make things move in video games. In 2D animation each movement is drawn by hand. This is a very time-consuming process that requires several artists working on a single project.

Creating a Simple 2D Animation

For this example I will use Corel Painter to create a simple animation.

1. Animations in Corel Painter are set up the same way as new pictures. Choose New from the File menu (see Figure 3.1).

2. In the New dialog box, select the Movie radio button (see Figure 3.2). Change the frame count to 16 and the image size to 512×512. Click on OK.

3. Corel Painter automatically saves animations, so the Enter Movie Name dialog box will appear, as shown in Figure 3.3. Name the animation Ball and click on Save.

4. The New Frame Stack dialog box allows you to set up Painter's onion skin feature. Onion skin is a simulation of the velum used by traditional animators to see multiple drawings. Set the levels to 4 and the color depth to 24, as shown in Figure 3.4. Click on OK to continue.

5. Now the Animation window will appear. In addition to the Animation window, there is also a Frame Stack window. *Frame stack* is the term used in Corel Painter for the series of frames in an animation. The Frame Stack window has controls for advancing frames forward and backward. The current frame is on the right with the red arrow above it.

6. Now you need an image to animate in the frame. Corel Painter has some preset images you can use. To call up the Image Portfolio, select Show Image Portfolio from the Window menu, as shown in Figure 3.5.

7. Drag the marble image from the Image Portfolio to the animation area (see Figure 3.6).

8. Now position the marble as high in the upper-left corner as possible (see Figure 3.7). You will be animating the marble to drop from the left side of the screen and bounce to the right. Moving an item is the simplest form of animation because all you are doing is changing the

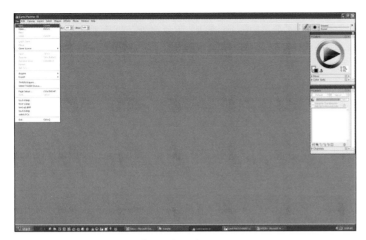

Figure 3.1 Select New from the File menu to set up a new animation.

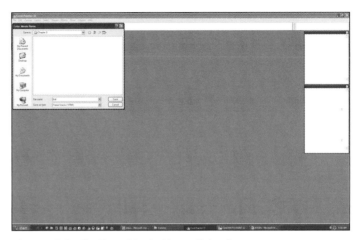

Figure 3.3 The Enter Movie Name dialog box.

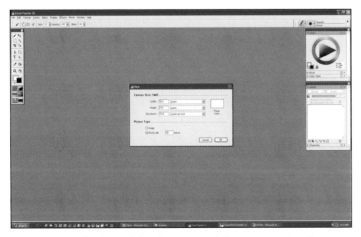

Figure 3.2 The New dialog box, set to bring up an animation.

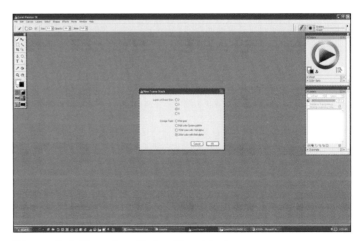

Figure 3.4 The onion skin level is set to 4.

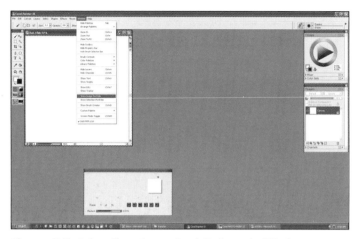

Figure 3.5 Select Show Image Portfolio from the Window menu.

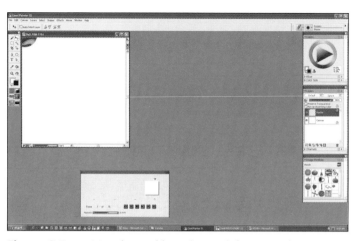

Figure 3.7 Position the marble in the top-left corner of the screen.

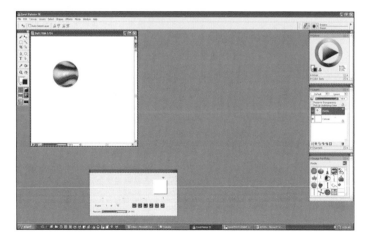

Figure 3.6 Move the marble image to the animation area.

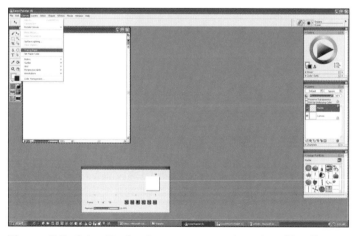

Figure 3.8 Select Tracing Paper to turn on the onion skin effect.

position of the item from frame to frame. Later, you will work on moving a character.

Hint

Game artists seldom move objects on the screen in game animation. Typically, movement of objects and characters is done in the game and is part of the game computer code.

9. To bring up the onion skin effect to see the four levels of animation you selected at the beginning, you need to select Tracing Paper from the Canvas menu, as shown in Figure 3.8.

10. Next click the Advance One Frame button in the Frame Stack window. (It's the second button from the right.) Notice that the marble remains in the same position. If you look at the Frame Stack window, you will see frame 1 has the marble in the upper-left corner. The marble is an object that floats above the animation background. When a frame is advanced, all floating objects are combined with the background of the previous frame. The floating object is then transferred to the current frame.

11. Drag the marble down and to the right, as shown in Figure 3.9.

12. We will have the marble hitting the ground, represented by the bottom of the image, on frame 5. As the marble descends, have it move a little faster by dragging it down and spacing it a little farther apart in each succeeding frame, as shown in Figure 3.10. Notice that you can see the past frames almost as if you were looking through tracing paper.

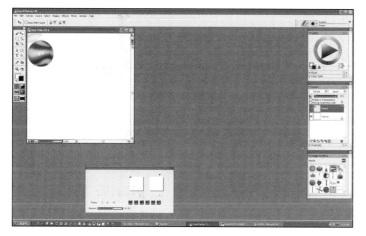

Figure 3.9 The marble is moved to a new position in frame 2.

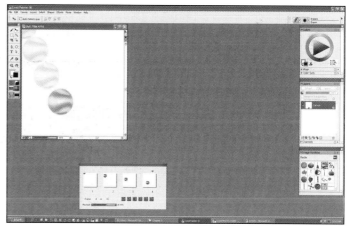

Figure 3.10 Separate the marble a little more in each succeeding frame.

13. Animation is about timing. As the marble drops, it accelerates toward the ground. As it hits the ground, some of the energy from the falling marble is transferred to the ground and the rest is redirected in the bounce of the marble. This slows the marble. In frames 5 through 10, the marble won't be separated as far because it is moving slower. Frame 5 is different because you need to slow the impact of the marble with the ground. Select Scale from the Effects > Orientation > Scale menu (see Figure 3.11).

14. In the dialog box click on the Constrain Aspect Ratio to turn it off. Now change the horizontal scale to 110 percent and the vertical scale to 90 percent (see Figure 3.12). The marble needs to be squashed just a little to show that it is hitting a hard surface. While this is only one frame, it is noticeable and will enhance the animation. When you're done, drop the layer by selecting Drop from the Layers menu.

15. Go to frame 6 and drag a new marble over. We want to keep the marble the same relative size. It is easier to do that if the marble always starts at the original size. In frame 6 we want to stretch the marble to enhance the look springing from the ground. Go to Effects > Orientation > Rotate to bring up the Rotate dialog box. Rotate the marble –15 degrees, as shown in Figure 3.13.

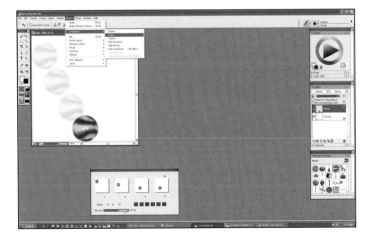

Figure 3.11 Select Scale.

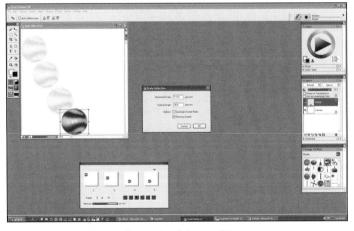

Figure 3.12 Change the scale of the marble.

16. Now scale the marble 90 percent horizontally and 110 percent vertically to get the stretch look. Rotate the marble –15 degrees to put it back where it was (see Figure 3.14). Again drop the layer so it won't carry over to the new frame.

17. Go to frame 7 and drag the marble over again and place it, as shown in Figure 3.15.

18. Continue to move the marble up and to the right, decreasing the distance of movement slightly from frame to frame until you get to frame 12 (see Figure 3.16).

19. The marble will start to accelerate on its descent. Increase the distance moved by the marble between each succeeding frame as it descends off the frame (see Figure 3.17). Drop the marble layer at frame 16. Do not advance the animation to 17 because this is a 16 frame animation. Painter automatically creates new frames if you advance the frame.

Congratulations! You just finished an animation. Press the Play arrow, as shown in Figure 3.18, to see how you did. You can set the frame rate using the slider bar.

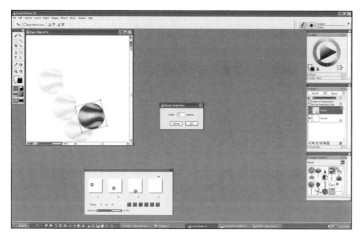

Figure 3.13 Rotate the marble –15 degrees.

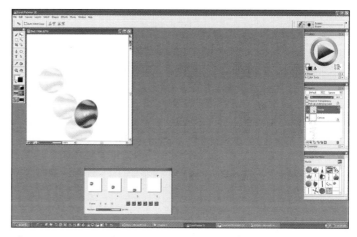

Figure 3.14 Stretch the marble in the direction of the bounce.

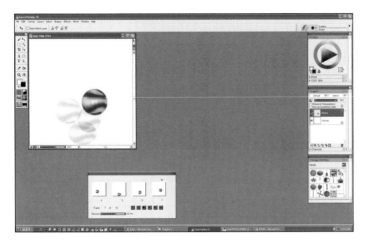

Figure 3.15 Place a new marble in frame 7.

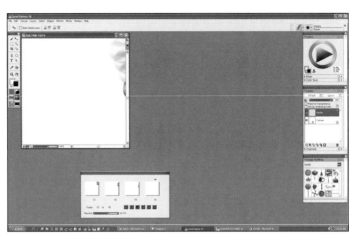

Figure 3.17 The marble will increase in speed as it descends.

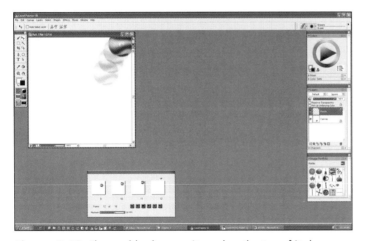

Figure 3.16 The marble slows as it reaches the top of its bounce.

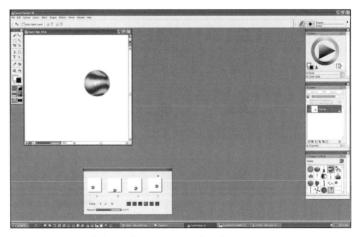

Figure 3.18 Click on the arrow to play the animation.

Creating Character Animation

Animating a character is a complex task. There are many things to consider when an animator simulates the movement of a person or creature. In this book we will not have the space to go over every aspect of good character animation. Instead we will focus on the basics. I highly recommend that you experiment with the concepts in this book. You should also study great animated videos or DVDs to see how animators create the illusion of movement. Try going through a video or DVD frame by frame; you will be able to see the differences in each frame.

Comparing Motions

If you are serious about animation, you should take a look at one of my other books, *The Animator's Reference Book*, also by Thomson Course Technology PTR. In this book models were photographed from four different angles while performing common game actions. You can use the book to compare motions to see how one motion differs from another. The book is also good for studying how balance is maintained and body movement differs.

Motions vary a great deal. A skip motion is very different from a run motion. A sneak motion is very different from a casual walk. Even walk motions vary depending on the speed. Compare the two photos in Figure 3.19. When the model is carrying a heavy duffle bag, he leans forward. This is to balance the added weight of the duffle bag. The more the bag weighs, the more the model will have to lean forward to balance the weight.

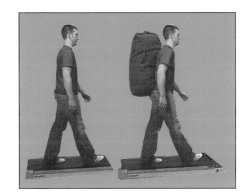

Figure 3.19 The model has to lean forward to balance the weight of the duffle bag.

Weight and Gravity

A common problem with beginning animators is that their characters lack any feeling of weight. In Figure 3.19, you could see how carrying the duffle bag changed the way the character walked. Closer study reveals that carrying the duffle bag affected more than just the model's balance. It also affected the effort the model had to make to move. Weight puts more stress on the muscles and joints. This extra stress is evident in the way the model had to move to carry a heavier object.

Even without carrying an object the model still has weight. The sense of weight is most evident in the model's feet, when walking barefoot. When one foot is holding the weight of the model while the other is in the air, the one on the ground will be more compressed and flattened than the one in the air.

Moving weight takes energy. The body supplies this energy in the form of muscle movement. There is really no stress on the arms when casually walking, but there is a lot of stress on the legs. The muscles in the legs will tend to show greater degrees of flexing than the arms.

Observe how weight and gravity affect the human body in motion. Even though some of these effects are subtle, mastering them can bring a huge improvement to animation.

Arcs in Animation

The human body uses a system of bones, joints, and muscles to cause movement. The system always moves in an arc because the joints that anchor the bones to each other act as pivot points.

The concept of arcs has been around for some time in animation. Understanding how to trace these arcs, however, has not been an easy process. Figure 3.20 shows the arc of the head and hand in a typical walk sequence. Notice how the motion of movement between frames in the sequence swings in an arc.

One way to achieve a believable exaggeration in 2D animation is to exaggerate the arcs of human motion. This type of exaggeration will seem natural to the viewer because it fits with the natural movement of the character.

Internal Animation

The game artist generally will not deal with movement of a character or object across the screen. The game programmer usually does that work, although the game artist may need to show the programmer how far to move a character from frame to frame. What the artist is more likely to deal with is the character's or object's *internal animation*. Internal animation is the movement within a character or object itself rather than the movement across a screen. For example, if a character is walking, the movement of the legs is an internal animation, whereas the progress the character makes across the screen is not. When an artist animates a character walking in a game, he will animate the character walking in place. This is very important because if the artist moves the character, it will make it a lot more difficult for the programmer to move the character in the game.

Character Animation

Many animations in computer games are *cycled animation*. A cycled animation is a looping animation that ends where it starts. For example, most walking and running animation in a game is one full step repeated several times. In the industry it is referred to as a walk or a run cycle. In the following example, we will create a walk cycle for a character.

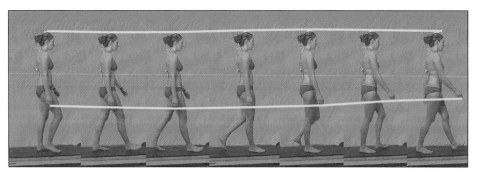

Figure 3.20 All human movement tends to be in arcs.

1. To start this animation, we need to bring up an animation window in Corel Painter, as we did in the last example. (See Figure 3.21.)

2. Set the dimensions to 256 × 256 and the frames to 12. Click Movie and then OK. Save the movie as *walk* in the Enter Movie Name dialog box, as shown in Figure 3.22.

3. Set the layers to 4 and the color depth to 24 bit, as shown in Figure 3.23.

4. For this animation we will start with a character. I loaded a picture of the character from a drawing that I created earlier. You can find this drawing on the CD. Randy is already in the process of taking a step. (See Figure 3.24.)

5. We now select Randy using the Box Selection tool on the left-hand side of the screen. Drag the box selection around Randy, as shown in Figure 3.25.

6. Once the character is selected, it is an easy process to click on the selected character and drag him over to the animation window. He is now a floating object and can be positioned anywhere on the page. Place him in the middle of the page, as shown in Figure 3.26.

7. It is easier to draw an animation if it is larger on screen. At the bottom of the animation window there is a blue bar. This is the magnification control. Slide the bar to the right until it is set to 200%.

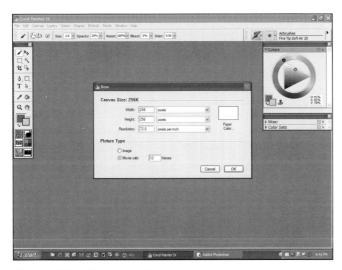

Figure 3.21 The New animation window.

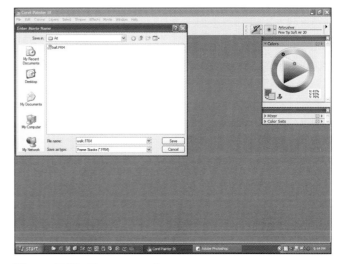

Figure 3.22 The save movie menu.

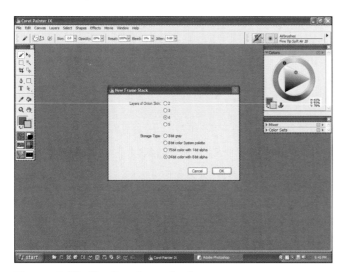

Figure 3.23 The New Frame Stack menu.

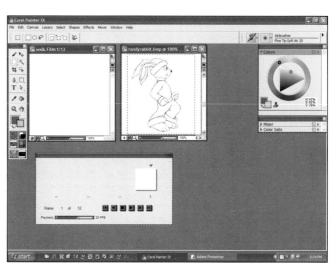

Figure 3.25 Select the character.

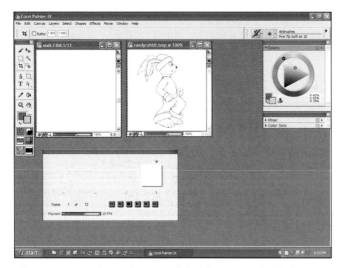

Figure 3.24 A base drawing of the character is loaded as a guide.

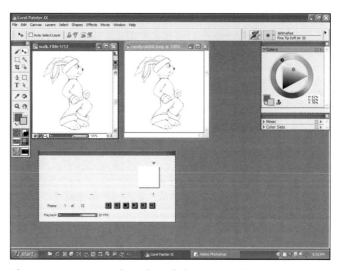

Figure 3.26 Move the selected character to the animation window.

8. Now grab the lower right-hand corner and enlarge the window to hold the animation.

9. Use the animation controls to increment the frame forward one frame. The drawing of Randy is now flattened onto the first frame. We will want to change Randy for the second frame so the floating drawing needs to be deleted. Select Delete Layer from the Layers menu, as shown in Figure 3.27.

10. Next, turn on the Tracing Paper feature located in the upper right-hand corner of the animation window, as shown in Figure 3.28

11. Now we can see the first drawing through the second frame so that we can use it as a guide for drawing the second frame of the animation. We draw the second frame with Randy's feet and hands moved to a new

position. Notice that we also are raising the character slightly in this frame to give him a bounce as he walks. (See Figure 3.29.)

12. Continue to draw new frames of the animation of Randy's walk using the drawings below it as a guide to each drawing, as shown in Figure 3.30.

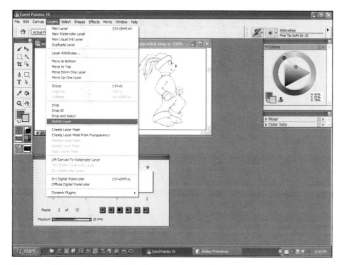

Figure 3.27 Delete the floating layer from frame two.

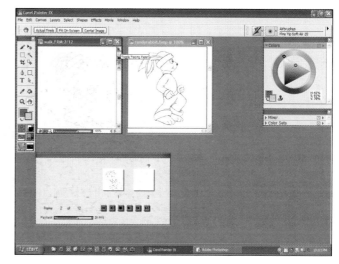

Figure 3.28 Turn on Tracing Paper.

Figure 3.29 Frame two of the animation is drawn.

Figure 3.30 Draw one through four of the animation sequence.

Hint

One of the biggest challenges of animation is timing. In a walk cycle the rate of movement is fairly constant, meaning that the act of walking generally does not have uneven movement. In most cases the animator can divide the distance of movement between each frame evenly. In a 12-frame animation, frame 1 and 7 will look much the same with the only exception being that the left and right sides of the character are reversed. (See Figure 3.31.)

The same thing will be true for frame 2 and 8; frame 3 and 9; frame 4 and 10; frame 5 and 11; and finally frame 6 and 12. If the artist does a good job with the first half of the walk cycle, the second half becomes easier because the first half can be used as a template. Look at Figure 3.32 and notice the similarities between frames.

13. Continue drawing each frame. Once you have reached the last frame and have compared each frame as in Figure 3.32, review the motion by incrementing through the animation one at a time. Be careful to only go to 12. Corel Painter will automatically add unwanted frames if you increment beyond 12. (See Figure 3.33.)

14. Press the Play button. The animation will run fast but you will be able to see your work. (See Figure 3.34.) You can slow the animation by adjusting the frame slider on the animation menu.

Figure 3.31 Frame 1 and frame 7.

Figure 3.32 Similarities between frames of animation.

Figure 3.33 Review your animation one frame at a time.

Figure 3.34 Playing the animation.

Summary

In this chapter we looked at 2D animation. We covered the following concepts.

- Defining animation
- How animation is drawn
- Squash and stretch in animation
- Weight and balance in animation
- Animation arcs
- Animation cycles
- Similarities between frames in a walk animation
- How to create a walk cycle

You should have a beginning understanding of creating 2D animation with Corel Painter. Many draw and paint programs have animation features that are similar to Painter. Try a few out and see which you like best.

CHAPTER 4

INTRODUCTION TO 3D

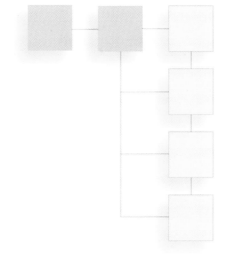

Most of the art you create as a game artist will probably be in a 3D art program. These programs are very complex because creating believable 3D models is not a simple process. In the next several chapters I will attempt to simplify model creation so it is easy to follow. Each exercise in this book will build on the previous exercises so that when you finish, you should have a good foundation to continue learning about 3D art and how it is used in games.

The 3D Art Program

Although the programs and processes are complex, they are not necessarily hard. The biggest challenge with most of the professional 3D programs is getting to know the many features. Of the many 3D art programs available, I have chosen Maya for use in this book. I chose Maya not because it is the simplest—far from it!—but because it is considered to be the standard in the industry. By learning Maya, you will have a head start on gaining the skills necessary for becoming a real game artist, I hope.

The first step in starting with 3D is to understand the 3D program. We are using Maya as the 3D program for this book, and the Personal Learning Edition of Maya is included on the CD. If you haven't already installed the program on your computer, do so now so you can follow along with the demonstrations in the book.

Maya is a very deep and powerful art creation tool. It is the same tool used by professional motion picture artists to create the amazing 3D creatures and settings in many of the most popular movies and video games.

The first look at the Maya interface can be a little overwhelming. The sheer number of menus and icons seems endless, and it would take volumes of books to explain every feature in Maya. Don't worry right now about learning every feature. The step-by-step instructions in this book are designed to help you understand the features of the program that are needed to create each project. As you work with Maya, you will become accustomed to the features.

Learning how to use Maya is kind of like moving to a new city. When you first arrive, you don't have any idea where anything is. You don't know where to go to buy groceries or where to get your dry cleaning done. You may know a few roads to and from your new home, but you know little else. As you begin your stay in the new city, you first find the businesses and services that are essential for your existence, such as the phone company and the utility company. You also locate places to buy food and other necessities. After a while you start to become more accustomed to your surroundings and find better stores

and services that fit your needs more closely.

Like moving to a new city, the first thing that you need to know about Maya is how the program is set up and where the essential tools are located. From there you can move forward in creating 3D digital art. The more you use Maya, the more accustomed you will become to the tools.

Figure 4.1 shows the Maya interface screen as it comes up for the first time.

The interface screen can be broken down into several component parts to help give clarity to how the program works. Figure 4.2 shows the area of the screen called the Panel.

The Panel is where you build the model. Notice that it has its own menu in the upper left-hand corner. This menu is called the Panel menu.

Figure 4.3 highlights the area to the far left of the screen. This area houses the toolbox and the Quick Layout buttons. The toolbox is in the upper section of the area and it contains model manipulation tools. An icon represents each tool. The lower part of

the area has icons that are used to change the view layout of the Panel.

Figure 6.4 shows where the Main menu is located. This is where many of Maya's features are located.

Figure 4.5 shows the Status line. This line contains many icons. It also contains a selection menu on the far left of the screen. This selection menu changes the Main menu to configure it to specific functions, like Modeling and Animation, among others. The Status line also contains many common functions. It allows for controlling the selection mask and setting various options. On the far right of the screen are several icons that change the sidebar. The sidebar is the area directly to the right of the Panel.

The area shown in Figure 4.6 directly below the Status line is called the Shelves. The Shelves contain icons and tabs. Each tab has different icons, and each icon has a different function in Maya. The tabs are used to group functions for specific tasks.

Figure 4.7 shows the area of the screen called the Sidebar. This area contains several editor elements and consists of

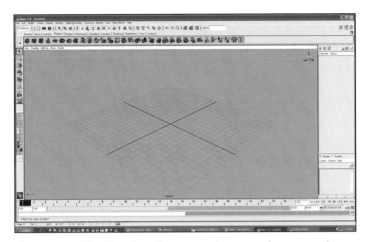

Figure 4.1 The Maya interface screen has many features and options.

Figure 4.3 The highlighted area contains the toolbox and the Quick Layout buttons.

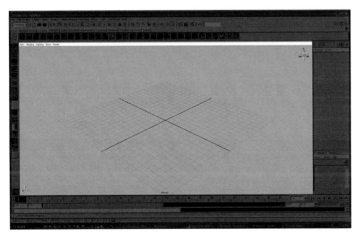

Figure 4.2 The Panel is the work area of the interface.

Figure 4.4 Many of Maya's features are located in the Main menu.

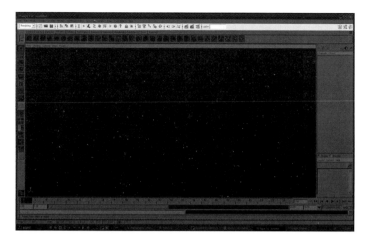

Figure 4.5 The Status line is directly below the Main menu.

Figure 4.6 The Shelves contain icons that call up specific functions.

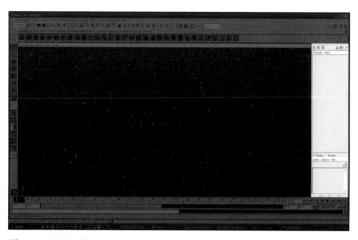

Figure 4.7 The Channel Box and Layer Editor are part of the Sidebar.

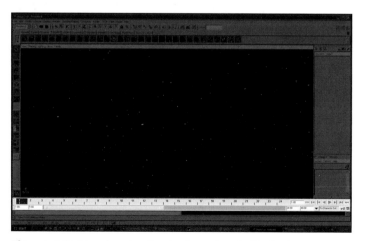

Figure 4.8 Maya's animation tools are located in the lower part of the screen.

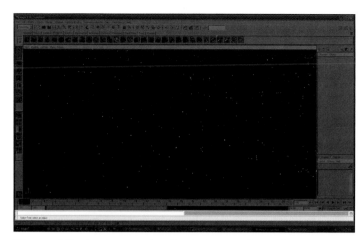

Figure 4.9 The Command and Help lines are located at the bottom of the screen.

two parts. The top part is the Channel Box, which is used to edit object attributes. The bottom part is the Layer Editor, which is used to edit 3D layers.

Figure 4.8 highlights the lower part of the Maya screen. This is where Maya's animation tools are located. It includes the Time slider on the upper portion of the highlighted area and the Range slider on the lower portion of the highlighted area. The right side of the highlighted area contains several tools for playing and viewing animations.

At the bottom of the screen shown in Figure 4.9 are three text windows. The one on the upper-left side of the highlighted area is the Command line. This is where special scripts can be entered. The text window directly to the left of the Command line is the area that shows the results of each command. Below the Command line is the Help line. This window is used for help messages.

See, that wasn't so bad. Now that you know the basic parts of the Maya screen, it's time to put some of that knowledge to work.

Building 3D Worlds

One of the basic elements in game art is the game world. A *game world* is the environment in which the game takes place. The game world could be tracks in racing games or stadiums in sports

games. Sometimes they are extensive, like in adventure games, while other times they might be very small, like in a puzzle game.

Game worlds can have a huge impact on a game. Their main purpose is to set the stage for the action, but they are becoming more interactive themselves. In many games, characters can pick up objects and use them just as they would in real life.

Building a 3D Castle

You will start by building a castle with four turrets, one in each corner. This will be a simple castle because it is your first project, but it will form the base of what could be a very unique building, depending on how far you want to take the design.

1. The first part of the castle you will build will be the turret or tower. Start by opening Maya. When Maya first comes up, it will display a window that offers several tutorials to help you learn how the program works. You can click out of the tutorial window for now. I suggest you take a look at the

tutorials later. They have some very valuable information on the program that will be helpful as you progress in your 3D studies. To the left-hand side of the status bar is a drop-down menu. Make sure it is set to Modeling.

2. You will start by using a primitive object. In this case, you are building a turret so you should use a cylinder. To bring up the Polygon Cylinder Options dialog box, select Polygon Primitives > Cylinder from the Create menu, as shown in Figure 4.10.

3. You want the base of the turret to be about 8 units high and about 4 units in diameter. Set the radius to 2 and the height to 8 in the Polygon Cylinder Options dialog box (see Figure 4.11). Then set the subdivisions around the axis to 32, the subdivisions on height to 6, and the subdivisions on the cap to 5. Click on either Create or Apply to create the cylinder. The Create button will create the cylinder and close the dialog box. The Apply button will create the cylinder and leave the dialog box open.

4. You now have a cylinder to work with, but it is in the wrong position. By default Maya will always create an object centered on the exact center of the grid. You can easily adjust the object with the Channel Box. The Channel Box is activated by clicking on the Channel Box icon on the far right side of the status bar (see Figure 4.12). The Channel Box is used to alter or modify an object after it is created.

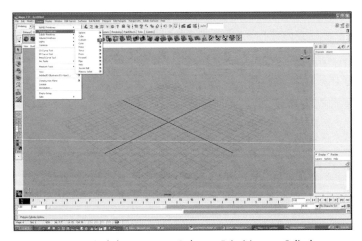

Figure 4.10 Find the Create > Polygon Primitives > Cylinder menu.

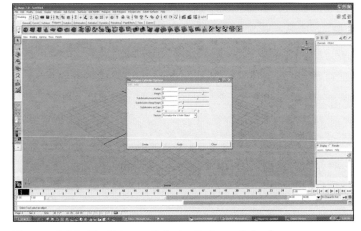

Figure 4.11 The Polygon Cylinder Options dialog box.

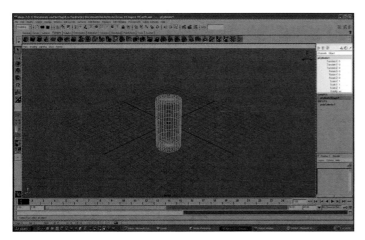

Figure 4.12 The Channel Box in Maya is on the right side of the screen.

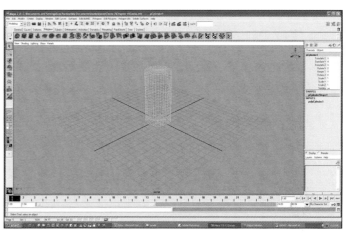

Figure 4.13 Type **4** in the Translate Y box.

5. Your cylinder is 8 units high. You want to bring it up level with the grid, so you need to move it up 4 units in the Y direction. In the Channel Box, type **4** in the Translate Y box and then press Enter (see Figure 4.13). The cylinder will now be positioned where you want it.

6. Some artists like to work with multiple views of an object on the screen at the same time. Maya supports almost every screen configuration common in 3D development. Personally, I prefer to work in only one view at a time and change the view when I need to see the object from another view. In some cases it is easier to work with an object in Orthographic view than in Perspective view. In Orthographic view, everything is square with the camera and there is no perspective. It is similar to a drawing created in a drafting program. Select the Front view from the Orthographic option under the Panels menu, as shown in Figure 4.14.

7. Now that the view is from the front, it is easy to see the bands of polygons that make up the sides of the cylinder. Use the Marking menu to change the cylinder from Object view to Vertex view by right-clicking on the object and selecting Vertex.

8. The next step is to shape the tower. Start by selecting the row of vertices three down from the top, as shown in Figure 4.15. Draw a bounding box around the vertices to select the row. To draw a bounding box, click with the left mouse button to the top left of the selection area and drag the mouse with the button down around the selection area.

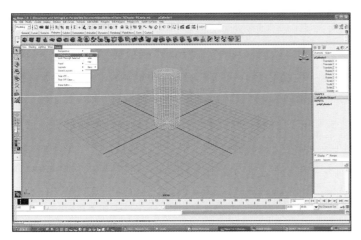

Figure 4.14 Change views in the Panels menu.

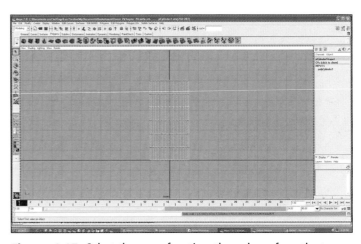

Figure 4.15 Select the row of vertices three down from the top.

9. Once the vertices are selected, you can manipulate them using the tools on the left side of the screen. Select the Scale tool (the one that looks like a box with two arrows around it). A manipulator will appear on the screen. You want to size the tower in all three dimensions. The middle yellow block on the Scale tool scales in all three dimensions, so pick that one. Press and hold the mouse button on the yellow block and slide the mouse to the left until your screen matches Figure 4.16.

10. Now continue to scale each row of vertices until it matches Figure 4.17. The cylinder should now look a lot like a rook from a chess set.

11. The tower is starting to take shape. Next you need to build the top. Change the Selection mode to faces using the Marking menu. Right-click on a vertex and drag the mouse toward Face in the Marking menu. Select the top row of faces and change the view to the Perspective view.

12. Sometimes it is easier to work on a model if you only have to deal with the area on which you want to work. You are finished with the lower part of the tower, so you really don't need it hanging around and getting in your way. Select Isolate Select > View Selected from the Show menu, as shown in Figure 4.18.

13. Now select every other face on the outer ring of the tower top, as shown in Figure 4.19.

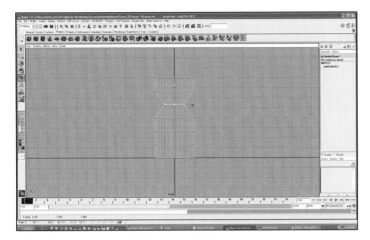

Figure 4.16 Scale the third row of vertices.

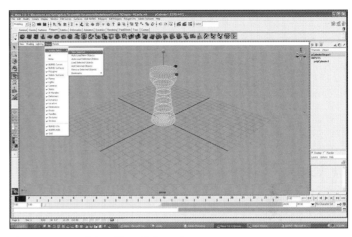

Figure 4.18 Select View Selected.

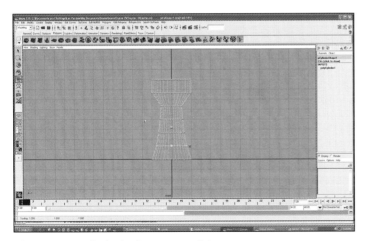

Figure 4.17 Scale the lower part of the tower.

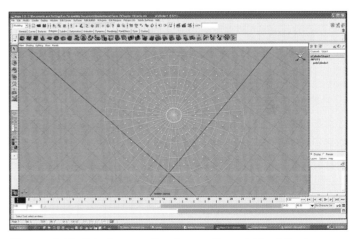

Figure 4.19 Select every other face on the outside of the tower top.

14. You want to keep the faces together, so before you go any further, you need to set the software to Keep Faces Together. The menu item is found in the Tool Options submenu in the Polygons menu, as shown in Figure 4.20. If Keep Faces Together is on, there will be a check mark by it.

15. Next select Extrude Face from the Edit Polygons menu, as shown in Figure 4.21.

16. When you use the Extrude Face tool, it will automatically bring up a special Manipulator tool. You will use that tool on another project, but for this one you only want to move the faces up. Click on the Move tool from the Manipulator tools on the left side of the screen. Now click on the green up arrow, hold down the mouse button, and pull up the faces until they match Figure 4.22. Press the 5 key so you can better see your work. The 5 key changes the shading from wire frame to flat shaded.

17. Now select all the faces from the second ring in from the outside, as shown in Figure 4.23.

18. Change the view to the Front view.

19. Now extrude the ring of faces downward one unit, as shown in Figure 4.24.

20. You don't want your characters to get wet while they are guarding the castle, so you need to build a roof over the top of the tower. Change the view to the Top view and select the third ring in of the rings of faces, as shown in Figure 4.25. Be careful not to select any faces except for the three remaining rings.

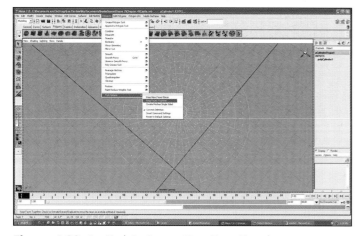

Figure 4.20 Set Tool Options to Keep Faces Together.

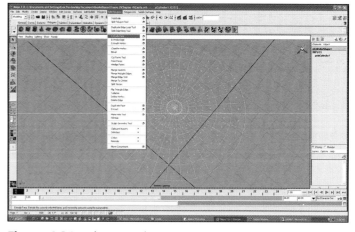

Figure 4.21 Select Extrude Face.

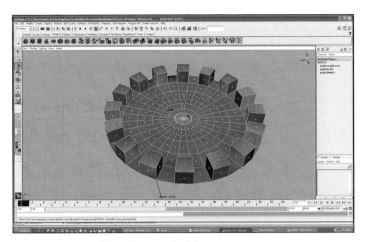

Figure 4.22 Pull up the extruded faces.

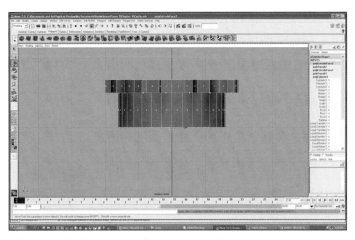

Figure 4.24 Extrude the faces downward.

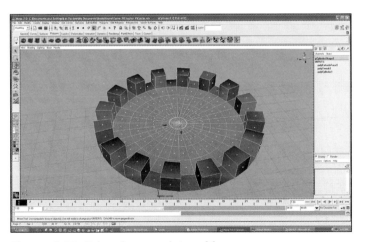

Figure 4.23 Select the second ring of faces.

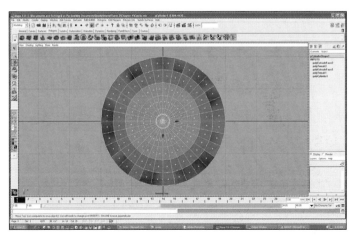

Figure 4.25 Select the inner rings of polygons.

21. Now switch to the Front view again and pull the faces upward 2 units, as shown in Figure 4.26.

22. Next go back to the Top view and select the two inside rings of faces (see Figure 4.27).

23. Use the Scale tool to expand the two rings of faces until they are slightly larger than the diameter of the tower top, as shown in Figure 4.28.

24. The next step is to create the peaked roof. Select the inside ring of faces, as shown in Figure 4.29.

25. From the Front view, pull the faces upward to start the peaked roof (see Figure 4.30).

26. Now you need to go back to the Vertex Selection mode to get the peak. Return to the Top view and change the Selection mode to Vertex in the Marking menu.

27. Select the centermost vertex, as shown in Figure 4.31.

28. Go back to the Front view and pull the center vertex upward, as shown in Figure 4.32. Now you have a peaked roof. Your characters won't have to get wet

from the rain—unless of course the wind is blowing.

29. You could stop here, but notice that the bottom roofline looks unnatural, like it has no depth. Select the faces in the roof and extrude them upward to form an edge around the bottom of the roof (see Figure 4.33). Scale the roof out a little to make the edge look better.

30. Next go back to the Perspective view. You want to see how your tower is looking with the lower part that you hid earlier. Go back to the Show menu and select View Selected again.

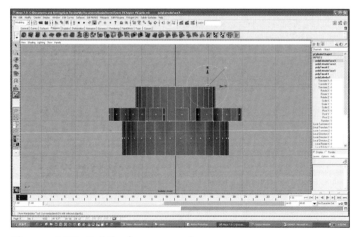

Figure 4.26 Pull the faces upward.

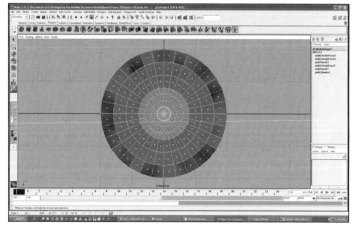

Figure 4.27 Select the two inside rings of faces.

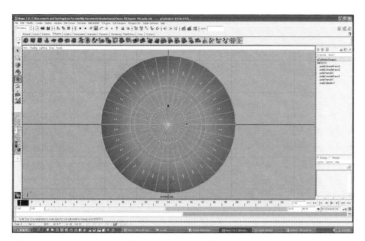

Figure 4.28 Expand the two rings of faces.

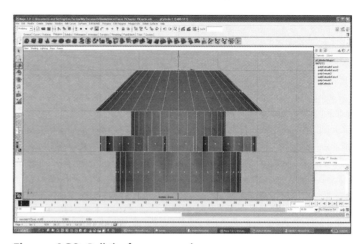

Figure 4.30 Pull the faces upward.

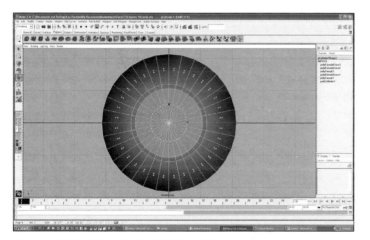

Figure 4.29 Select the inside ring of faces.

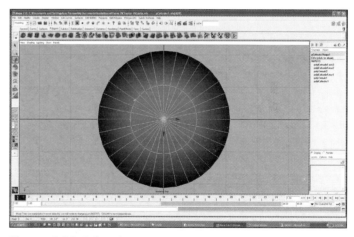

Figure 4.31 Select the center vertex.

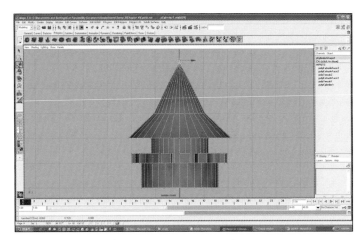

Figure 4.32 Pull the center vertex upward.

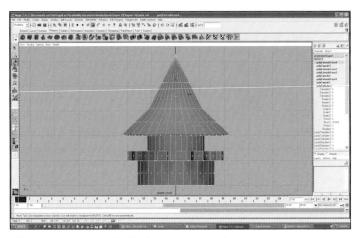

Figure 4.33 Extrude the faces in the roof upward.

Notice that the option has a checkmark by it. When it is active, it has a checkmark; when it is not, it does not have a checkmark by it.

31. The roof does not look peaked enough. Change the object back to Vertex mode and shape the roof until it looks like Figure 4.34.

Building the Walls

You now have the geometry for a nice medieval-looking tower. But one tower does not a castle make. You need to build some walls for your castle. It won't be much of a castle if there are no walls.

1. Before you can build the walls, you need to place the tower at the corner of the castle. In the Channel Box, enter **12** in both the Translate X and Translate Z fields (see Figure 4.35).

2. You now have one tower in one corner of the castle. You still have three other corners that need a tower as well. It would sure be nifty if you didn't have to rebuild each tower. Well, guess what? You don't. Maya has this neat little feature called Duplicate Object. With the object selected, press Ctrl+D on the keyboard and voila—you

have a new tower. The new tower is selected and is directly over the old one.

3. Type a minus sign in front of the 12 in the Translate X box. Now the duplicated tower will be in position on the other end of the castle (see Figure 4.36).

4. Repeat the process twice more to duplicate two more towers, and position them on the other corners of the castle (see Figure 4.37). The coordinates for tower three are X -12, Y 4, and Z -12. The coordinates for tower four are X 12, Y 4, and Z -12.

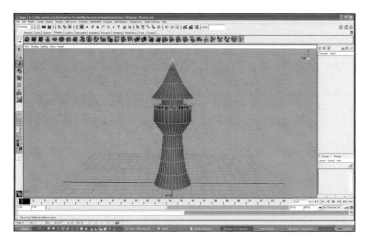

Figure 4.34 Shape the roof.

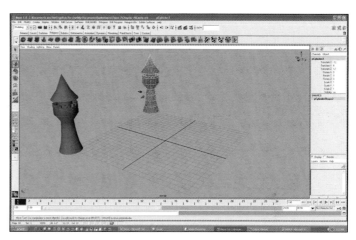

Figure 4.36 The duplicate tower.

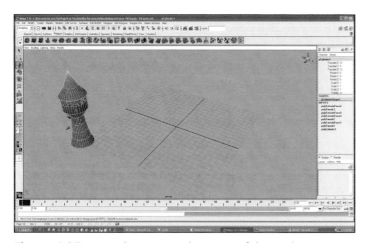

Figure 4.35 Move the tower to the corner of the castle.

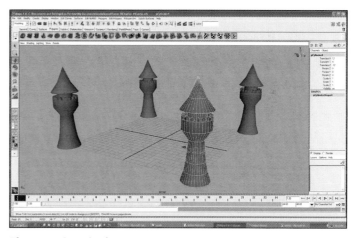

Figure 4.37 The four towers are positioned at each corner of the castle.

5. Now that the towers are in position, you can hide them so they won't be in the way while you build the walls. Select all four towers and then press Ctrl+H to hide the towers; alternately, you can select Display > Hide > Hide Selected from the Main menu.

6. Now select Polygon Primitives > Cube from the Create menu (see Figure 4.38).

7. Set the options to match the ones shown in Figure 4.39.

8. Now you have the polygon cube you will use to make a wall. Move it up four in Translate Y and over 12 in Translate Z so it fits between the two towers on that end of the castle (see Figure 4.40).

9. Now go to the Side view and shape the wall similarly to how you did the tower, except instead of scaling in all three dimensions, only scale in the X direction (see Figure 4.41). Select the box on the left of the Scale tool and slide it toward the center box.

10. Go to the next row of vertices and continue shaping the wall to match Figure 4.42.

11. Select the inside top four vertices and size them in the X direction to match Figure 4.43.

12. Now go back to the Perspective view and change the View mode to Faces by right-clicking on the object and sliding the cursor toward Face.

13. On the top of the wall, select every other face. Extrude the faces upward, as shown in Figure 4.44.

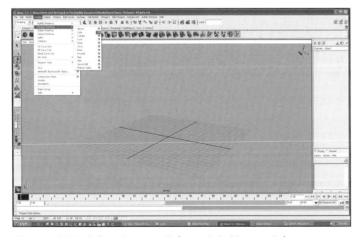

Figure 4.38 Select Create > Polygon Primitives > Cube.

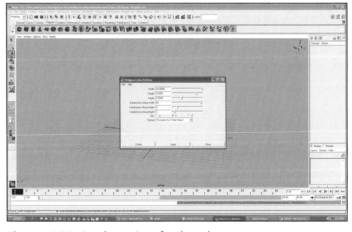

Figure 4.39 Set the options for the cube.

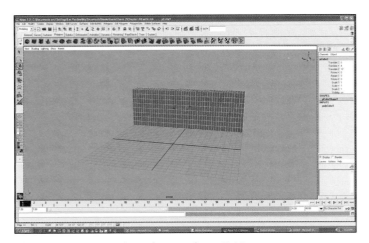

Figure 4.40 Move the polygon cube to Z 12.

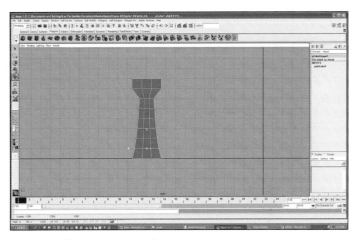

Figure 4.42 Shape the wall.

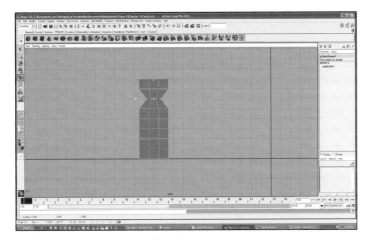

Figure 4.41 Scale the wall in the X direction.

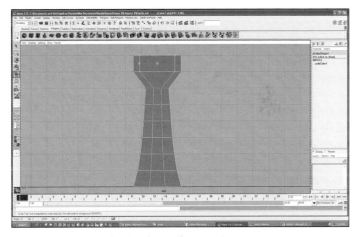

Figure 4.43 Size the inside top four vertices.

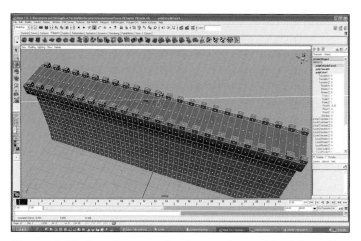

Figure 4.44 Extrude every other face on the outside of the wall top.

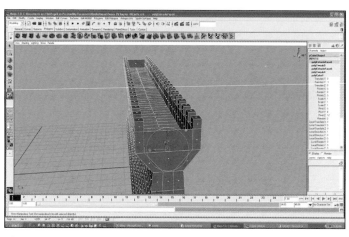

Figure 4.45 Extrude center faces downward.

14. Next select the center row of faces and extrude them downward 1 unit (see Figure 4.45).

15. Now the general shape of the wall is finished. You need to duplicate the wall for all four sides of the castle. Select the wall and press Ctrl+G. This will center the pivot of the wall to the X–0, Z–0, and Y–0 position (see Figure 4.46). Ctrl+G is actually the Group function, but it works here to center the pivot because grouping by default puts the center of the group in the center position.

16. Now duplicate the wall and rotate it 90 degrees.

17. Next duplicate the wall and rotate it 180 degrees.

18. Finally duplicate the wall and rotate it 270 degrees (see Figure 4.47).

19. Now you need to bring back all the towers to see how the walls and towers fit together (see Figure 4.48). To see how the entire castle will look, go to Display > Show > Show Last Hidden.

20. Now you are beginning to see the completed castle. There is still some work to do, but it is starting to take shape. Notice that the walls run into the towers. This is fine for the lower areas, but it looks out of place at the top. You need to fix that area. Select three of the wall sections and three of the towers and delete them, leaving one wall connected to one tower. It is easier to fix one section and duplicate it than it is to fix all of the sections (see Figure 4.49).

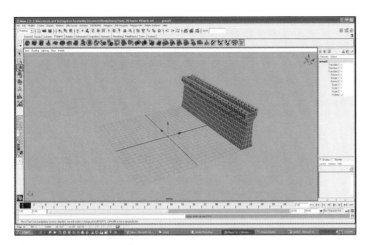

Figure 4.46 Center the pivot.

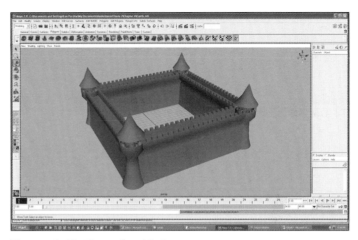

Figure 4.48 The walls with the towers.

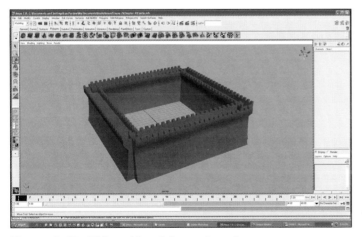

Figure 4.47 All four sides of the castle walls.

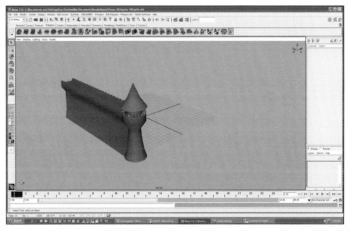

Figure 4.49 Delete the unneeded wall and tower sections.

21. Now change the View mode back to Wire Frame by pressing the 4 key at the top of the keyboard. This will help you see the inside of the intersection of the tower and the wall.

22. Notice that the wall extends into the tower. Select the wall section and change the View mode to Faces. Make sure only the wall is selected.

23. Go to either the Front or Side view, whichever shows the wall entering the tower, as shown in Figure 4.50. Select the faces shown in the figure.

24. Next press the Delete key to remove those faces (see Figure 4.51).

25. Now change back to Perspective view and swing the view around so you are looking at the tower from just above the wall. Press the 5 key to go to Flat Shaded mode.

26. Select the tower faces that block the entrance from the wall. You may need to swing your view around to get the faces on the inside of the tower wall. (see Figure 4.52).

27. Delete the faces, as shown in Figure 4.53.

28. Select the edges of the tower and extrude them to close the holes created by deleting the faces earlier, as shown in Figure 4.54.

29. You are going to need to fix the tower wall so that it can connect with the wall coming from the other direction. Change the Selection mode to Object and rotate the tower 90 degrees in the Y axis using the Channel Box, as shown in Figure 4.55.

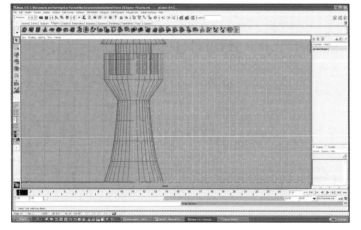

Figure 4.50 Select the unneeded polygon faces of the wall.

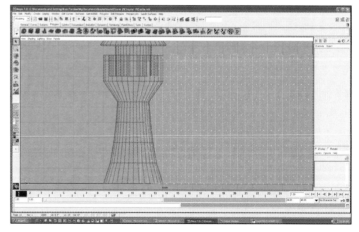

Figure 4.51 Delete unwanted faces.

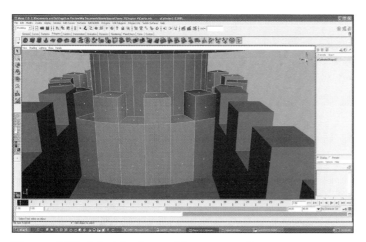

Figure 4.52 Select the faces of the tower wall.

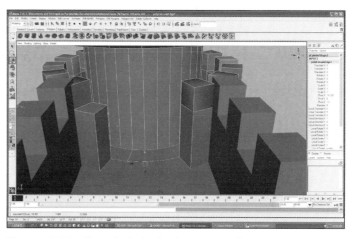

Figure 4.54 Close the holes in the tower wall.

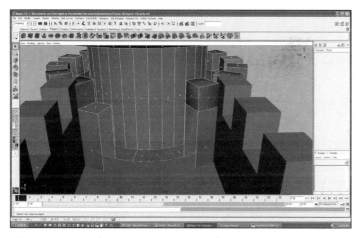

Figure 4.53 Delete the selected tower faces.

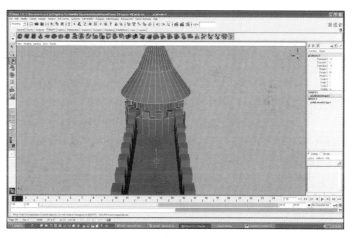

Figure 4.55 Rotate the tower 90 degrees.

30. Delete the wall and extrude the edges like you did earlier in Steps 26 through 28, then rotate the tower back to 0 in the Y axis using the Channel Box (see Figure 4.56).

31. The tower is now ready to connect to the wall, but the wall still needs some work to get it to connect to the tower correctly. The biggest problem is getting the rampart floors to match up. Right now they overlap, which will cause problems later when the castle is textured. Select the face of the wall floor

that overlaps with the tower, as shown in Figure 4.57.

32. Now select from the Edit Polygon menu the Split Polygon function.

33. The Split Polygon tool is used for dividing polygons. It requires at least two clicks of the mouse to work. First click on the center of the top edge of the wall floor, then on the bottom edge of the same polygon. Hold the second mouse click down and slide the cursor to the left until it snaps to the corner vertex, as shown in Figure

4.58. Press Enter to complete the function.

34. You will need to split the polygon four more times, as shown in Figure 4.59.

35. Holding down the V key will snap one vertex to another using the Move tool. Select a newly created vertex. Hold down the V key and use the Move tool to move the vertex toward one of the tower vertices. Do this for each of the new vertices until your work looks like Figure 4.60.

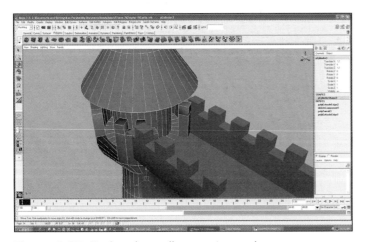

Figure 4.56 Fix the other wall connection on the tower.

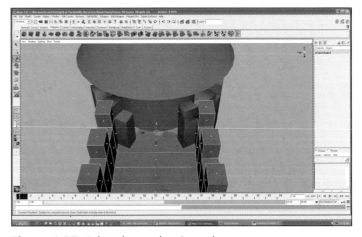

Figure 4.57 Select the overlapping polygon.

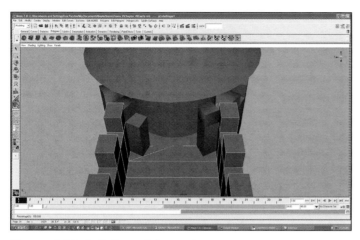

Figure 4.58 Split the wall floor polygon.

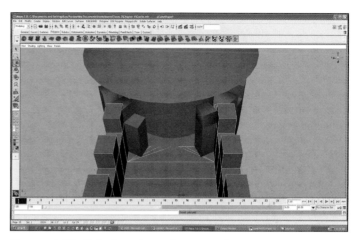

Figure 4.59 Split the polygon four more times.

36. You will need to do the same procedure for the other end of the wall. Rotate the wall 180 degrees in Object mode. Delete the unneeded faces and then split and line up the wall with the tower (see Figure 4.61).

37. Now the wall and tower are ready to duplicate and rotate and this time they will work correctly so your characters can walk all around the castle walls. Group the tower and wall by pressing Ctrl+G and duplicate and rotate the wall and tower the same way you did earlier (see Figure 4.62).

The castle walls are now finished, but what good is a castle if there is no entrance? The castle needs an entrance for your characters to get in and out because helicopters had not been invented back when castles were used.

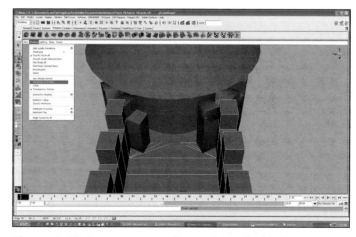

Figure 4.60 Snap to vertex to line up the wall with the tower.

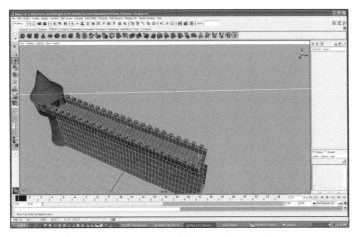

Figure 4.61 Fix the other end of the wall to match the tower.

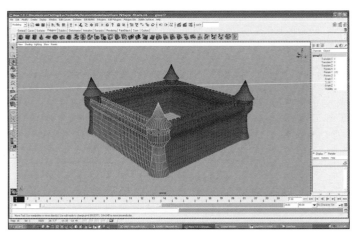

Figure 4.62 Duplicate and rotate the wall and tower.

Building the Gate House

We will be using one of the castle walls to create a gate house where your game characters can enter and exit the castle. Hide everything except the section of wall that you want to use for the entrance.

1. Go to the Top view and select the wall faces as shown in Figure 4.63.

2. Go back to the Perspective view and extrude the faces out from the wall .5 of a unit, as shown in Figure 4.64.

3. We need to do a little patch-up work on the wall between it and the extruded section. Select the vertices along the outside edge of the extruded section and snap them over to the next set of vertices, as shown in Figure 4.65.

4. Do the same thing for the other side of the extruded section.

5. Now create a new primitive cylinder, as shown in Figure 4.66. Make sure to change the options to those shown in the figure.

6. Delete all of the faces of the bottom half of the cylinder and all but the outer ring of faces on both ends of the cylinder (see Figure 4.67).

7. Select the inner edges of the cylinder, as shown in Figure 4.68.

8. Extrude the edges and snap them to the opposite side of the cylinder (See Figure 4.69).

9. The vertices need to be merged, so select the vertices of the cylinder and use the Merge Vertices function, as shown in Figure 4.70.

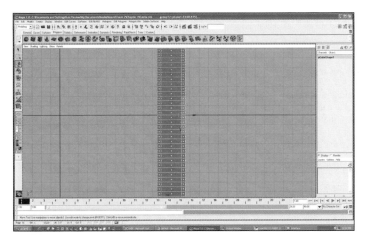

Figure 4.63 Select the wall faces to create the gate house.

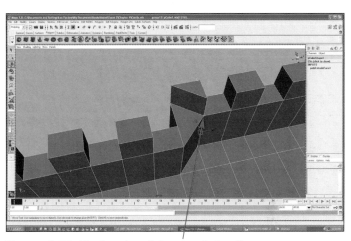

Figure 4.65 Fix the edge of the extruded wall.

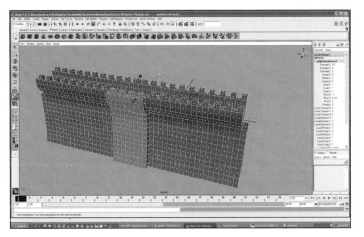

Figure 4.64 Extrude the faces of the gate house.

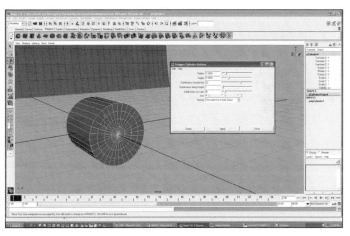

Figure 4.66 Create a new polygon cylinder.

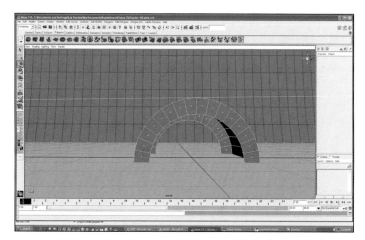

Figure 4.67 Delete the bottom and inner faces of the cylinder.

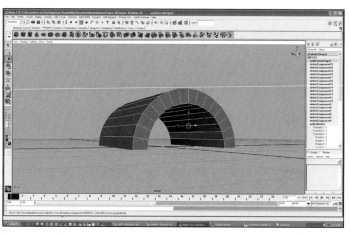

Figure 4.69 Snap the extruded edges to the other side of the cylinder.

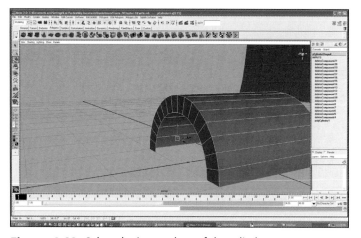

Figure 4.68 Select the inner edges of the cylinder.

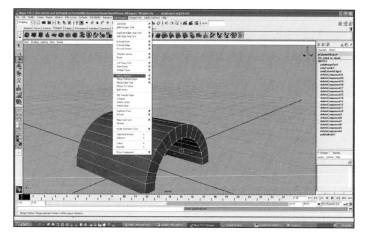

Figure 4.70 Merge the snapped vertices to those they were snapped to.

10. Move the half cylinder 2 units up in the Y axis so that it forms the upper part of the castle entrance (see Figure 4.71).

11. Select the bottom edges of the half cylinder, as shown in Figure 4.72.

12. Extrude the edges down four times, moving them −.5 units in the Y axis (see Figure 4.73).

13. Now move the new geometry 12 units in the X axis to place it in the wall, as shown in Figure 4.74. Notice that it is not as wide as the wall.

14. Change the X scale number in the Channel Box to 2 to make the portcullis wide enough for the wall (see Figure 4.75).

15. Now delete the faces of the wall inside the portcullis, as shown in Figure 4.76.

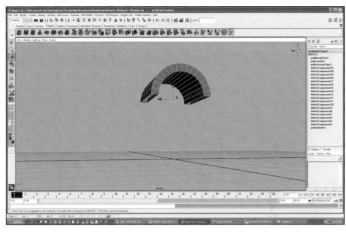

Figure 4.72 Select the faces at the bottom of the half cylinder.

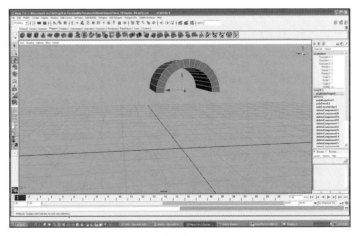

Figure 4.71 Move the half cylinder up.

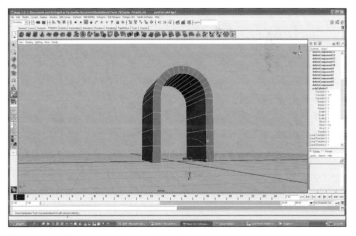

Figure 4.73 Extrude the edges down.

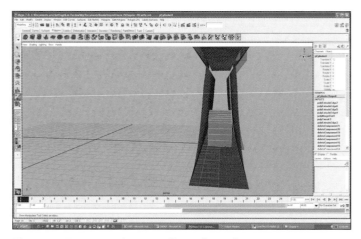

Figure 4.74 Move the portcullis to the wall.

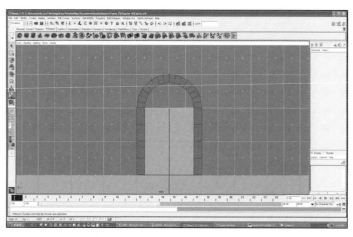

Figure 4.76 Delete the bottom two rows of wall faces within the portcullis.

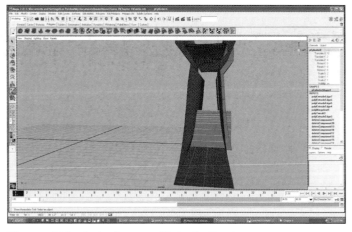

Figure 4.75 Scale the portcullis in the X axis.

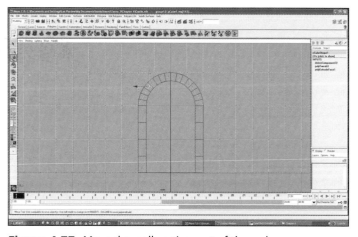

Figure 4.77 Move the wall vertices out of the archway.

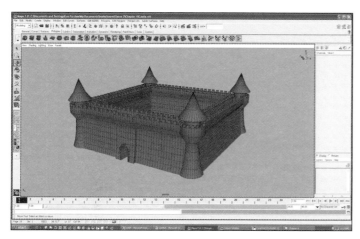

Figure 4.78 View the finished castle geometry.

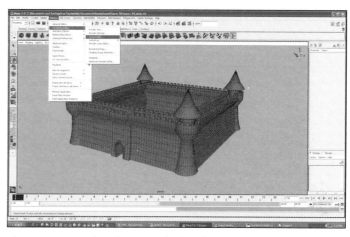

Figure 4.79 Select the Hypershade editor.

16. Change the Selection mode to Vertex and move the wall vertices up, as shown in Figure 4.77, to clear the archway. You will need to switch to Wire Frame view mode to see where to put the vertices.

There you go. You now have a castle (see Figure 4.78). You can even have your characters walk in and out of it. It does look a little bland though without any rock textures.

Texturing the Castle

Now the geometry is finished, and you are ready to add the surface textures. Your tower and wall look pretty good, but they are flat shaded so they aren't very interesting. By adding a surface texture to the models, you can give them an almost lifelike look.

For this example, I will be using two textures for the wall and the tower. You could use many more, but for this lesson two textures will be enough to get you started. The two textures are on the CD that came with this book; their names are wall.bmp and roof.bmp.

1. You will need to work in the Hypershade editor to bring your textures into Maya. Bring up Hypershade by selecting it from the Rendering Editors submenu in the Window menu, as shown in Figure 4.79.

2. Create a new material in Hypershade by selecting Materials > Blinn from the Create menu, as shown in Figure 4.80.

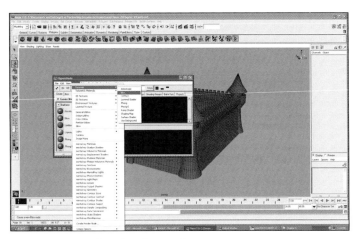

Figure 4.80 Select the Blinn option.

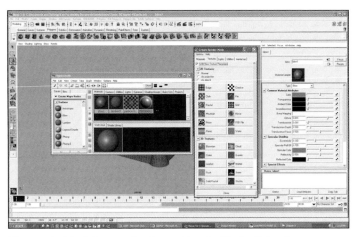

Figure 4.81 Bring up the Create Render Node dialog box.

Hint

You will notice that Maya supports a number of material types. Each type has its own purpose. The many different game engines do not always support all material types found in Maya. Make certain that the game engine supports the material type you want to use. Most game engines support blinn materials, so I will use those in this book. Blinns are used primarily for metallic surfaces, but they have a wider range of editing capabilities than Lamberts and Phongs, so they are often used as good all-around materials for games.

3. You will be using a texture from the CD, so select the new material in Hypershade and then press Ctrl+A. This will bring up the Attribute editor.

4. Click on the Checkerboard icon to the right of Color to bring up the Create Render Node dialog box (see Figure 4.81).

5. In the Create Render Node dialog box, select File. The dialog box will disappear, and the file will appear in the Attribute editor. Now all you need to do is load the texture file into the material.

6. Look for the small file folder icon next to the Image Name box. Notice that the Image Name box is empty. Click on the file folder to bring up the Open dialog box (see Figure 4.82).

7. You will need to browse the CD and look for one of the two texture files. They are in the Chapter 4 directory in the Resources directory. Choose the wall.bmp file and click on Open.

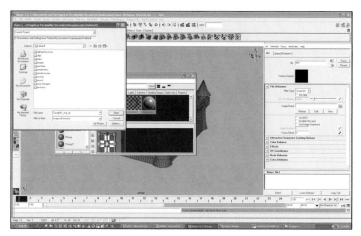

Figure 4.82 Bring up the Open dialog box.

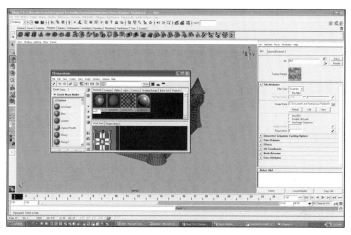

Figure 4.83 Rename the material "wall."

8. Now that the texture is loaded, go back to Hypershade and rename it "wall" by right-clicking on the material and selecting Rename from the menu that appears (see Figure 4.83).

9. Now repeat the same process for loading the roof texture (see Figure 4.84).

10. You will need the Hypershade editor to apply the textures to the model, but the window is so large it is hard to see your model. It will be much easer to work with if you don't have the editor cover up the model. Exit out of the editor by clicking on the red X in the upper-right corner.

11. Now click on the Two-Panel view. It is the third view icon from the top, just under the Manipulator icons on the left side of the screen.

12. You can now change the first panel to Hypershade by selecting it from the Panels menu, as shown in Figure 4.85.

13. That's much better. You can see both Hypershade and the model. Select the wall and apply the wall material to it by right-

clicking on it in Hypershade and selecting Apply to Selected from the menu (see Figure 4.86). Press the 6 key to change the view of the model to Textured view so you can see the material on the model.

14. The wall material is a tile material, so you will want it to repeat several times. The easiest way to tile a texture is to have it repeat once for every polygon. In Maya that process is called *unitizing*. With the wall selected, select Unitize UVs from the Polygon UVs menu, as shown in Figure 4.87.

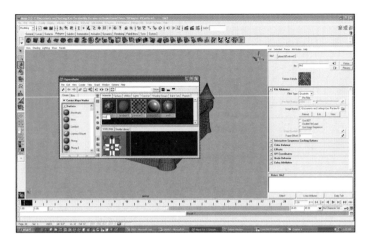

Figure 4.84 Load the roof texture.

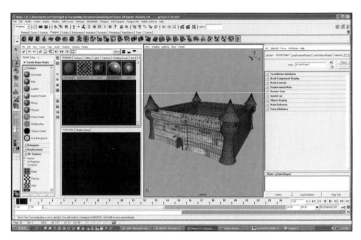

Figure 4.86 Apply the wall material to the wall.

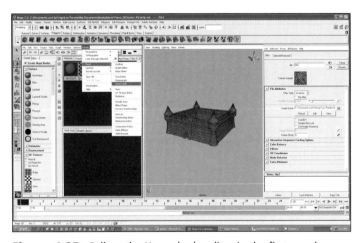

Figure 4.85 Call up the Hypershade editor in the first panel.

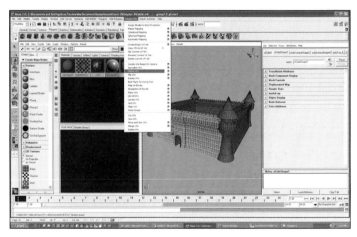

Figure 4.87 Unitize the material on the model.

15. Now go to the Side view and do the same thing with the lower part of the tower, as shown in Figure 4.88.

16. Next apply the roof texture to the upper part of the tower.

17. Unitize the textures (see Figure 4.89).

18. Apply the wall texture to the portcullis and unitize those textures as well (see Figure 4.90).

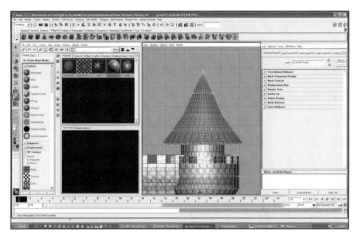

Figure 4.89 Unitize the roof textures.

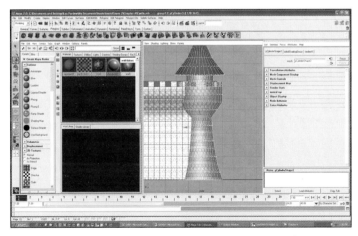

Figure 4.88 Apply the wall texture to the lower part of the tower.

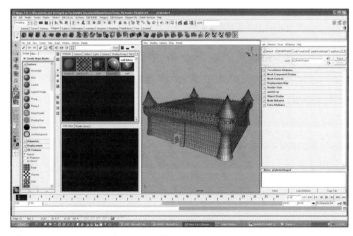

Figure 4.90 Map the portcullis.

Finishing the Castle

Now the wall and the tower are mapped (see Figure 4.91). All you have to do to finish the castle is map the other towers and walls.

The castle is not complete because you only have the outside wall. A good castle will have some buildings inside the wall and some towers attached to the building. Using the knowledge you have gained in this chapter, you should be able to complete these details with no problem. Give it a try and good luck.

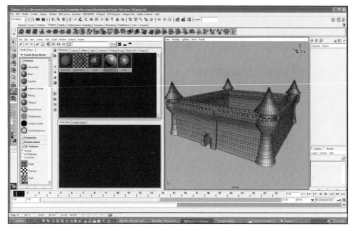

Figure 4.91 The tower and wall are mapped.

Summary

This chapter covered how to build exterior objects in Maya. You had a chance to gain some experience with the 3D program by building simple objects with polygons. In this chapter you used many tools and functions in Maya, including the following:

- Create Primitives
- Move objects and components
- Extrude faces and edges
- Delete faces
- Group objects
- Duplicate objects
- Merge vertices
- Hypershade
- Apply material
- Unitize UVs

Practice what you have learned to build a variety of outdoor buildings. Try building a small village around your castle—this could be the set for your first video game.

CHAPTER 5

BUILDING GAME INTERIORS

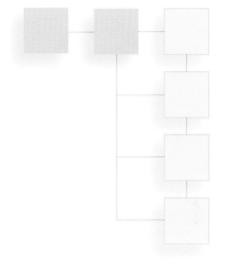

In the last chapter you built a castle. A castle from the outside is a grand and inspiring site that will inspire a game player to try to get inside it. In fact, many games are created almost entirely from inside views of buildings or dungeons. Therefore, you should spend some time learning about building game interiors.

A *game interior* is any enclosed play area in a game. The main difference between building a model of an interior and a model of an exterior is that unless they are huge caverns or halls, interiors can get a little cramped and difficult to see. When you build an

exterior object, you can view it from almost any angle because you are on the outside looking in. When you build an interior, it is meant to be viewed from the inside looking out.

Interiors are typically viewed much closer to the camera than exteriors are. Closer viewing generally means you need to give your models more detailed textures because the camera will often come right up to a wall or an object. If the textures are too small they will appear blocky when the camera gets close to them. In addition to larger, more detailed textures, an interior will generally need more detail in the geometry.

Building the Interior

In this chapter you will build a two-story domed room with columns and a balcony. This model will be more complex than the model in the previous chapter. It will also require more textures. I have included the textures on the CD under the Chapter 5 directory, so put the CD in your drive if you haven't already done so. As with all the 3D exercises in this book, you will be using Maya, so bring up the program and let's get started.

1. Bring up the Polygon Cylinder Options dialog box and set the options to those shown in Figure 5.1.

2. Translate the cylinder up 8 units and change the view to Side view so it looks like Figure 5.2.

3. You will create a round room, and the cylinder will form the basic shape. Now you need to adjust the cylinder to give it the desired features of your two-story room. Change the Selection mode to Face and select the row of faces shown in Figure 5.3.

4. Scale the row of faces inward just a bit, as in Figure 5.4.

5. You will use this row of faces to make some wainscoting on the wall. Change the Selection mode to Vertex. Using the Scale tool, pull together the vertices above and below the faces you scaled in the last step until they look like Figure 5.5.

6. Next you need to build the balcony. Change the Selection mode back to Face and select the faces in the fifth row from the top. You will be using them to create the balcony. Make the

faces smaller by scaling them in the Y direction and then move them to the position shown in Figure 5.6.

7. If you haven't changed that option, it should still be on. If it's not, turn it on by selecting Tool Options from the Polygons menu. Use the Extrude tool to create the balcony. Select Extrude Face from the Edit Polygon menu and then scale the balcony inward, as shown in Figure 5.7. In an earlier chapter you turned on the Keep Faces Together option.

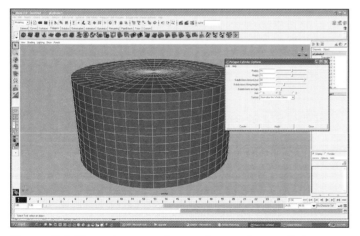

Figure 5.1 The option screen for creating a polygon cylinder.

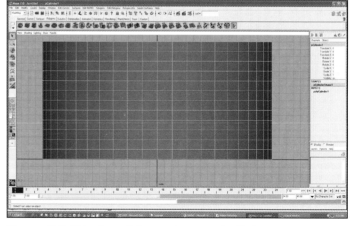

Figure 5.2 Side view of the newly created cylinder.

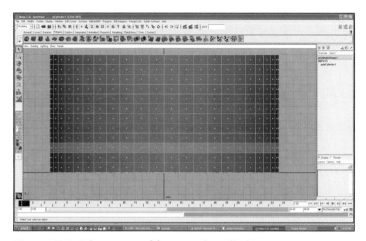

Figure 5.3 Select a row of faces on the cylinder.

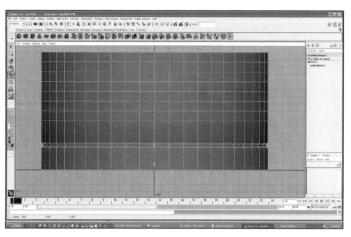

Figure 5.5 Move the vertices together to make the wainscoting.

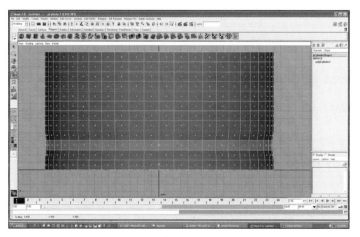

Figure 5.4 Scale in the row of faces slightly.

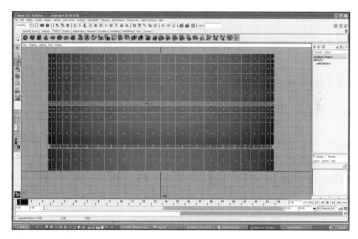

Figure 5.6 Scale the faces for the balcony and move them into position.

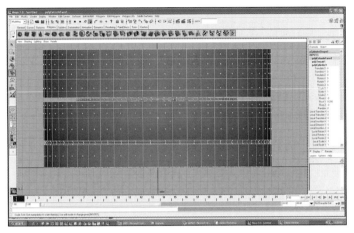

Figure 5.7 Extrude the faces to form the balcony.

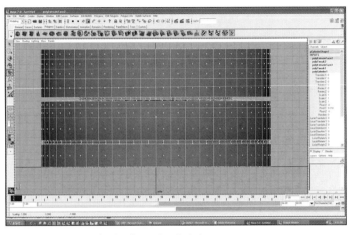

Figure 5.8 Extrude the faces in slightly.

8. Pull the faces up using the Move tool so the top of the balcony is parallel with the ground.

9. You are going to need some railing around the balcony so your characters don't just walk off it. Use the Extrude Face tool again and scale it in just a bit, as shown in Figure 5.8.

10. You will come back later to finish the balcony. For now you can continue building the rest of the room. In the Side view, select the faces at the top of the cylinder, as shown in Figure 5.9.

11. Choose View Selected from the Show menu.

12. Now select the third ring of vertices from the outside and move them down to form a lip around the edge of the dome, as shown in Figure 5.10.

13. Expand the ring using the Scale tool until it is just below and inside the second ring of vertices, as shown in Figure 5.11.

14. Now you need to build a dome roof to the room. Select all the vertices on the inside of the third ring of vertices. Your room should now look like Figure 5.12.

15. Pull the selected vertices upward, then scale them outward until they match what is shown in Figure 5.13.

16. Next, deselect the outer ring of selected vertices. Pull the remaining vertices upward. Continue working your way inward, pulling vertices upward until they match the dome shown in Figure 5.14.

17. Bring the rest of the room back by going to Isolate Selected > View Selected in the Show menu on the Panel menu.

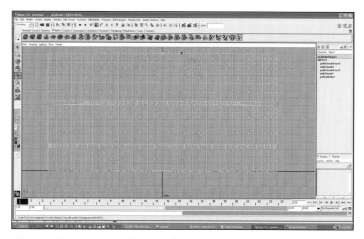

Figure 5.9 Select the faces at the top of the cylinder.

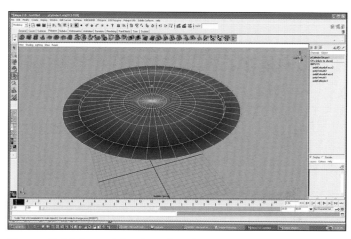

Figure 5.11 Expand the ring of vertices.

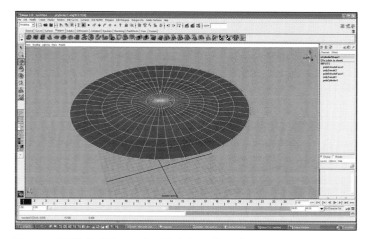

Figure 5.10 Pull down the third ring of vertices.

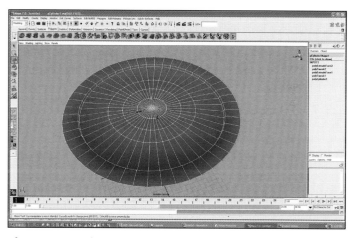

Figure 5.12 Select the inside vertices.

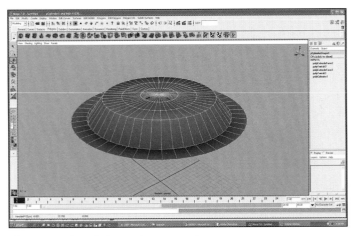

Figure 5.13 Pull the vertices upward.

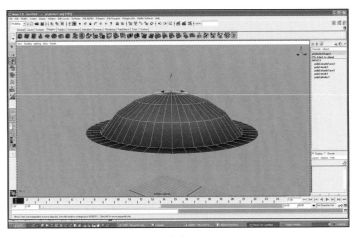

Figure 5.14 The upper dome of the room.

18. Now select and isolate the bottom of the room similar to the way you selected the top earlier, as shown in Figure 5.15.

19. You are going to place a large chalice-shaped pool at the bottom of the room. You can use the floor geometry to create the pool. Select the center vertex and the inner ring of vertices.

20. Pull the selected vertices upward, as shown in Figure 5.16.

21. Select the next ring of vertices outward from the ones you just moved.

22. Move these vertices upward until they match Figure 5.17.

23. Scale the ring of vertices inward until it is directly above the inner ring of vertices, as shown in Figure 5.18.

24. Now select the next ring of vertices outward from the last ring selected.

25. Move the ring up until it is level with the last ring.

26. Scale the ring in until it is just outside of the last ring, as shown in Figure 5.19.

27. You now have the basin and the upper lips of the chalice-like pool. Select the next ring of vertices outward from the last set.

28. Scale this ring of vertices until it is directly below the outer ring of the lip of the pool. Use Figure 5.20 as a guide.

29. Select the next ring of vertices from the last ring selected and scale it about halfway between the outer ring and the pool, as shown in Figure 5.21.

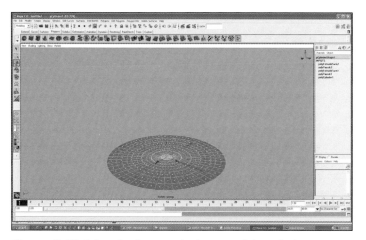

Figure 5.15 Select the faces at the bottom of the cylinder.

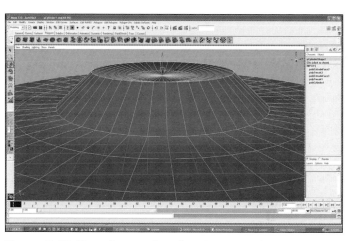

Figure 5.17 Move the next ring of vertices upward.

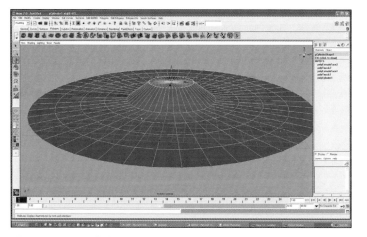

Figure 5.16 Pull the inner vertices upward.

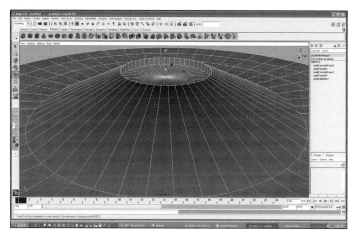

Figure 5.18 Scale the ring of vertices.

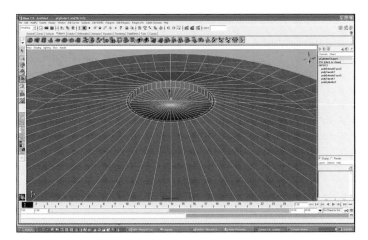

Figure 5.19 Scale the next ring inward.

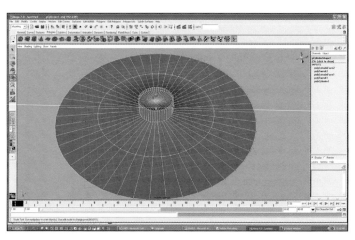

Figure 5.21 Scale the next ring inward about halfway between the other rings.

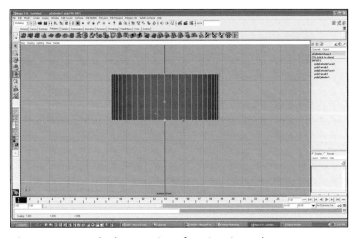

Figure 5.20 Scale the next ring of vertices inward.

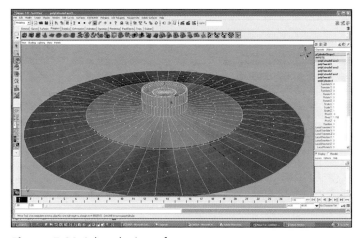

Figure 5.22 Select the inner faces.

30. To finish building the pool and the platform it sits on, you will need more vertices. You can create them by extruding them out of your current geometry. Change the View mode to Face and select all the faces except the outer ring. Check your work to make sure it matches Figure 5.22.

31. Select Extrude Faces from the Edit Polygons menu and move the faces upward to form the platform.

32. Next select the faces of the pool, as shown in Figure 5.23.

33. Now extrude the faces and move them upward three times. (Refer to Figure 5.24.)

34. You now need to shape the base and inside of your chalice pool. Change the Selection mode back to Vertex. Scale and move the vertices until they match those in Figure 5.25.

35. Bring back the rest of the geometry and check the scale of the pool with the room. It should look like Figure 5.26. You might have to adjust a few things to get the pool to fit in the room correctly.

Hint

You could have built the chalice pool out of a separate piece of geometry, but whenever possible I prefer to use the geometry of the room. If an object is built out of the room's geometry it will remove any possibility of there being a seam between the two pieces of geometry. Not all objects should be built out of the room geometry, as you will see when you build the columns to support the balcony. In those cases, you need to pay special attention to make sure the two objects intersect past each other.

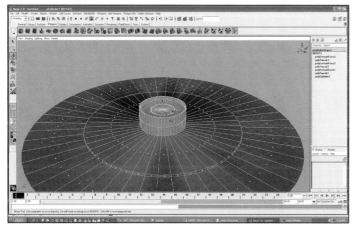

Figure 5.23 Select the faces of the pool.

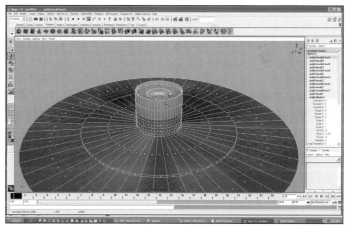

Figure 5.24 Extrude the pool faces upward three times.

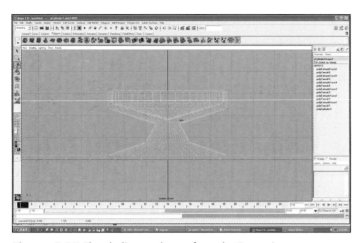

Figure 5.25 The chalice pool seen from the Front view.

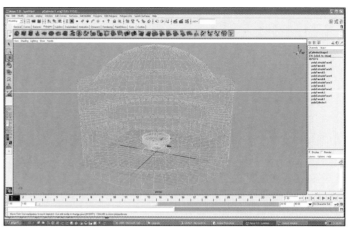

Figure 5.26 Check the pool with the rest of the room.

Building the Columns

So far, so good. You now have the beginnings of a room built from your original cylinder. If you haven't already, this would be a good time to save your work. It is always a good idea to save your work often. You never know when something might happen and all your hard work will be lost.

Now you can continue building your room. You will need some supports for your balcony, so you will build some columns to hold it up.

1. Bring up the Polygon Cylinder Options dialog box, as you did for the room. Change the settings to match those shown in Figure 5.27.

2. Hide the room so you can work on the column by itself.

3. Adjust the vertices in the column to match those in Figure 5.28.

4. You will only build one column right now. After you texture it, you will duplicate the column and move the duplicates to form several supports. Unhide the room so you can continue to work on it.

5. You need to have a way into and out of the room. Create doors for the room on four sides at the base and on the balcony. Using the grid as a guide, select the faces of the room's wall.

6. Extrude the faces and pull them outward one unit from the room, as shown in Figure 5.29. Repeat this process for the four doors in the bottom and the balcony.

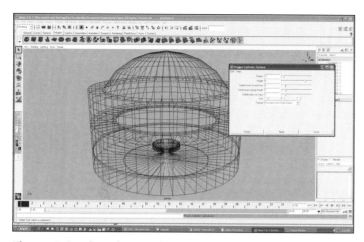

Figure 5.27 The Polygon Cylinder Options dialog box.

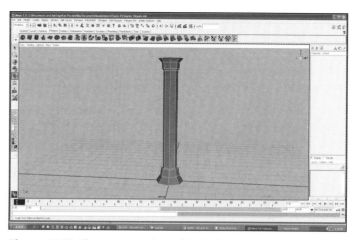

Figure 5.28 The support column for the balcony.

7. The room's walls are rounded, but you don't want to have a rounded door. With the faces still selected, use the Scale tool to flatten the door. Go to a Side view of the room and pull the perpendicular box toward the center box. Be careful not to pull it past the center box or you will flip the face, which will cause problems later (see Figure 5.30).

8. Repeat the process for creating the door for the other three sides of the room at the base.

9. Now create four doors on opposite sides of the balcony directly above the doors below. You want these doors to be smaller than the ones on the ground floor. Refer to Figure 5.31 to see how the finished doors should look.

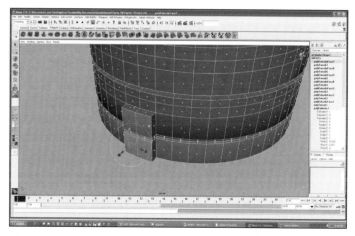

Figure 5.29 Select the group of faces to form a door.

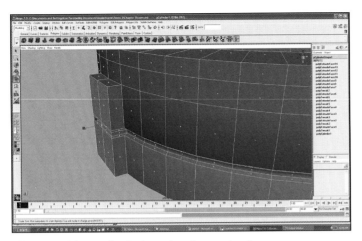

Figure 5.30 Use the Scale tool to flatten the door.

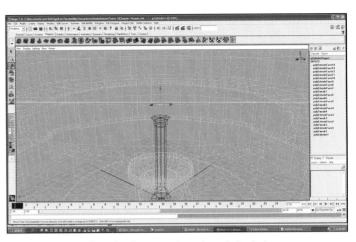

Figure 5.32 Select the faces at the edge of the balcony.

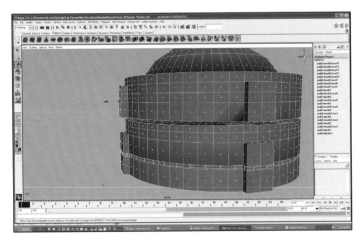

Figure 5.31 The room with doors.

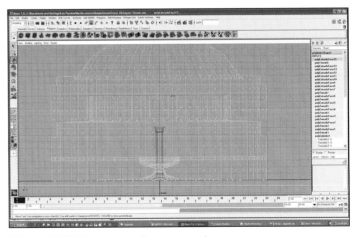

Figure 5.33 Extrude the faces upward.

10. Now you need to create some balcony railings so your characters will not fall into the pool below. Select the faces at the edge of the balcony, as shown in Figure 5.32.

11. Extrude the faces upward, as shown in Figure 5.33.

Face Normals

The geometry for the room is almost complete, but you have one more thing to deal with before you move on to applying the textures. Because you created the room from a cylinder, all the faces are pointed in the wrong direction. By default all Maya primitive geometry has the normals facing outward. If you exported this room into a game right now, you would be able to see the room from the outside but not from the inside because all the faces are pointing out.

You can see the direction of the faces in Maya by selecting Polygon Components > Normals from the Display menu, as shown in Figure 5.34.

Maya shows the direction a face is facing with a line coming out of the middle of the face, perpendicular to it. Notice in Figure 5.35 that the room looks like a porcupine, with all the face normals pointing outward.

You need to correct this problem. Maya has a tool that will reverse the normals of an object. Select Normals > Reverse from the Edit Polygons menu, as shown in Figure 5.36.

Now you will notice that there are almost no face normals visible from the outside of the room, except for the few around the top of the room where the face normal lines are showing

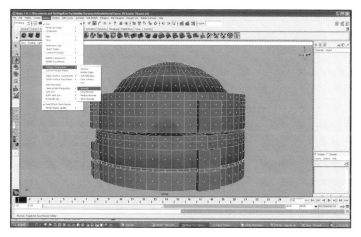

Figure 5.34 Select Normals from the menu.

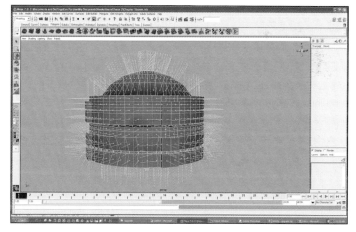

Figure 5.35 Normals are facing outward.

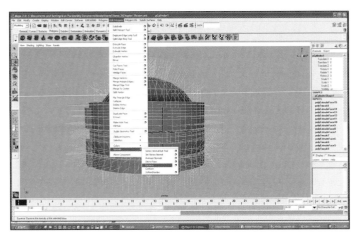

Figure 5.36 The Reverse Normals tool.

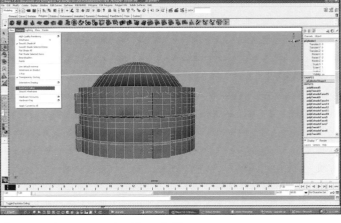

Figure 5.37 Turn on Backface Culling.

through. These are actually pointing in the correct direction, but the lines are so long that the ends are poking through the room geometry.

To better understand how faces work in a game, select Backface Culling from the Shading menu, as shown in Figure 5.37.

As you can see, all the face normal lines are pointing inward. In a game, it takes processor time to render a polygonal face. Most game engines will automatically cull the back side of all faces to reduce rendering time.

Texture Mapping

Now that the room is built, it is time to see how it will look with some textures.

1. Start with the column. Change the view to two panels, with the Hypershade on one side and the Perspective view on the other.

2. Hide the room so only the column is showing, as in Figure 5.38.

3. All the textures for this project are on the CD. Create two new

materials and load the bluemarble and colbase textures from the CD. (I covered creating and naming materials in Chapters 1 and 4; you can review those chapters if you need a refresher on this.)

4. Rename the new materials, as in Figure 5.39.

5. Apply the new materials to the model of the column by either dragging the material to the selected faces or right-clicking on the material and selecting Assign Material to Selection

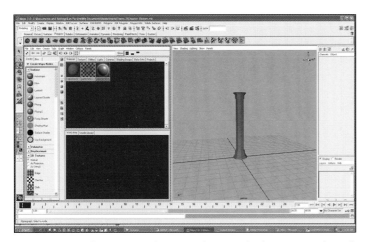

Figure 5.38 The two-panel view with Hypershade on one side and Perspective view on the other.

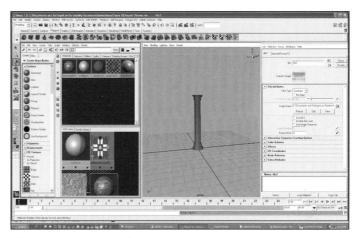

Figure 5.39 Rename the new materials.

from the menu. Use the Cylindrical Mapping tool. Apply the materials to the column; apply the base to both the top and bottom of the column. The tool has several handles that allow you to manipulate the texture after it is applied. To avoid stretching the bluemarble texture, click on the center square of the tool and drag it toward the center of the column. Refer to Figure 5.40 to see how the column should look. Make sure to press the 6 key to turn on

hardware texturing so you can see the textures.

6. Notice that the column looks faceted; you want it to look round. You can give the column a rounded look without having to add more geometry. Go back to Object mode. In the Edit Polygons menu, select Normals > Soften/Harden, as shown in Figure 5.41.

7. Set the tool to all soft and then apply it to the object. All of the facets should disappear, and the column should look like Figure 5.42.

8. Now that the column is textured, move the column in the Z axis until it is under the balcony about 12 units. Duplicate it. Press Ctrl+G to group the duplicate and center the pivot on the 0 axis.

9. Next, rotate the duplicate column 45 degrees around the middle axis.

10. Continue duplicating the column and rotating it around the axis in 45-degree increments until you have eight columns supporting the balcony, as shown in Figure 5.43.

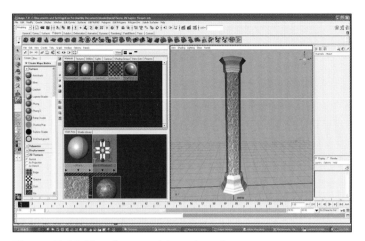

Figure 5.40 Map the materials to the column.

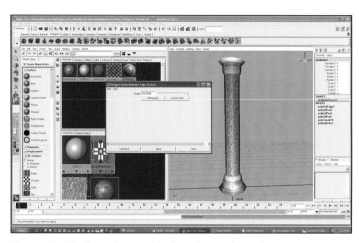

Figure 5.42 The column with the edges softened.

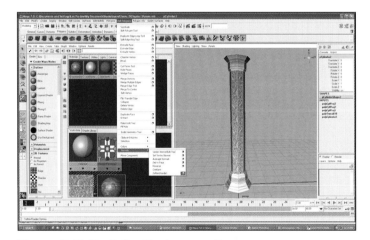

Figure 5.41 The Soften/Harden menu item.

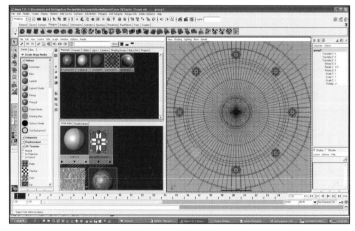

Figure 5.43 The eight columns, as seen from the Top view.

11. It would be easier to texture the rest of the room if you didn't have the columns obstructing your view of the interior faces. Go to the Hypergraph in the Window menu and select all of the columns, as shown in Figure 5.44. Press Ctrl+H to hide the columns.

12. At this point save the file again. This time rename it dome01, as shown in Figure 5.45. I often save different versions of my work in progress. The advantage of saving in this manner is that if you don't like the work,

Figure 5.45 Save the file as dome01.

you can always go back to an earlier version and take a different path.

13. You are now ready to apply materials to the room. Load all the remaining texture files for this lesson into Hypershade, creating materials for each one and naming each one, as shown in Figure 5.46.

14. The first thing to which you should apply a material is the pool. Change the view to Face mode and select all the pool's faces except the ones at the bottom of the pool, as shown in Figure 5.47.

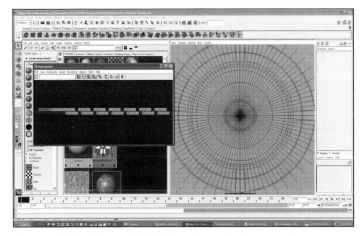

Figure 5.44 Select and hide the columns in Hypergraph.

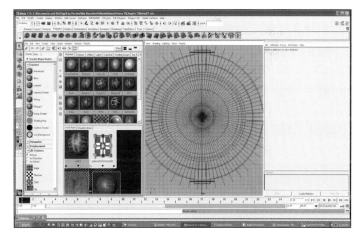

Figure 5.46 The textures loaded into Hypershade.

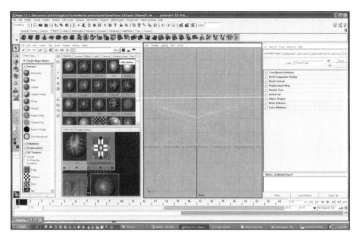

Figure 5.47 Select the faces of the pool.

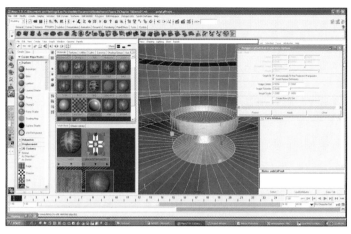

Figure 5.48 Map the pool with the marble2 material.

15. Apply the marble2 texture and Unitize the texture (see Figure 5.48).

16. Select the faces at the bottom of the pool and apply the flrtl3 material using the Planar Mapping tool, as shown in Figure 5.49. Make sure to take note of the image scale set at 10.

17. The pool needs to contain some water. You create the water by selecting the faces at the very top of the building and duplicating them. The Duplicate Faces function is in the Edit Polygons menu. Select the small square next to the Duplicate Faces option to bring up the Duplicate Face Options dialog box.

18. Make sure the check box for Separate Duplicated Faces is checked and click on the Apply button.

19. Move the newly duplicated faces down to the pool and use the Scale tool to flatten them, as shown in Figure 5.50. Rotate the faces in the X axis 180 degrees.

20. Apply the water material to the new faces.

21. You want to make the water transparent. In Hypershade, go to the water material and bring up its Attribute editor by pressing Ctrl+A.

22. Find the Transparency slider and move it about halfway to the right, as shown in Figure 5.51.

23. Next work on the floor of the room. Select the ring of faces next to the pool and apply the flrtl2 material to them.

24. Unitize the faces. They should now look like Figure 5.52.

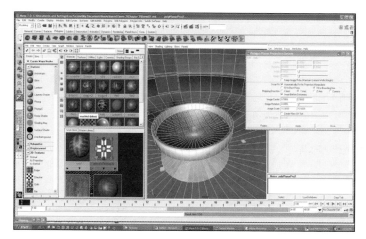

Figure 5.49 Map the pool bottom using the Planar Mapping tool.

Figure 5.51 Use the Transparency slider to make the water material transparent.

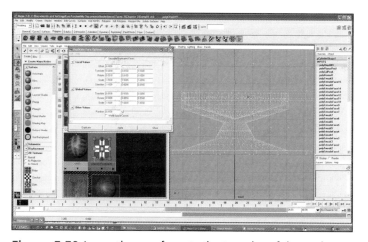

Figure 5.50 Lower the new faces to the top edge of the pool.

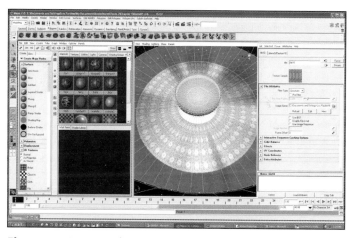

Figure 5.52 Unitize the tile material on the floor of the room.

25. Now select the small ring of faces that you extruded earlier to form a platform around the pool.

26. Apply the wlltl2 material to the selected faces and unitize them, as shown in Figure 5.53.

27. You will use flrtl1 for the next ring of faces. Apply it and unitize it the same way you did for the other two rings. It should now look like Figure 5.54.

28. Notice that this texture is a little different. It is not a complete texture; rather, it is a half texture. To make it complete you need to flip some of the faces. Select every other face around the ring.

29. In the Edit Polygons menu, choose Texture > Flip UVs to bring up the Polygon Force UV Options dialog box.

30. Set the options as shown in Figure 5.55 and click on Apply.

31. The last section of the floor is the area next to the doors. You will use the flrtl3 material for this section of the floor. Select the faces next to one of the doors.

32. Apply the flrtl3 material and Unitize it so it looks like Figure 5.56.

33. Now repeat the process for the areas next to the other three doors.

34. Now that the floor is textured, you can move on to the walls. Start with the doors. Select the faces that make up the doors to

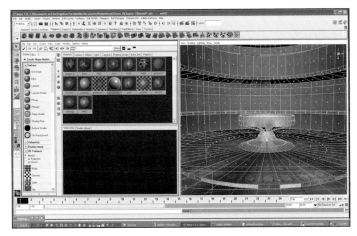

Figure 5.53 Apply the tile material to the next ring of faces.

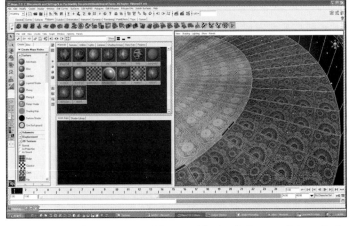

Figure 5.54 The next ring of faces with the flrtl1 material applied.

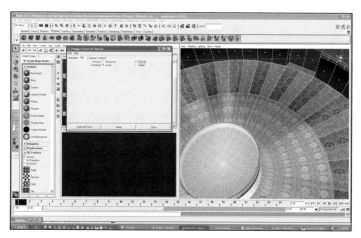

Figure 5.55 Flip the selected faces.

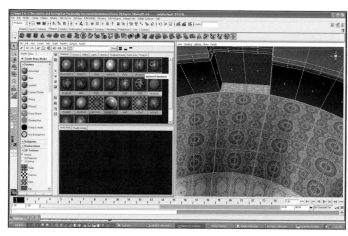

Figure 5.56 Apply the flrtl3 material to the floor area near the door.

the room. Use the Planar Mapping tool to project the map and then apply the door material to the selected faces, as shown in Figure 5.57. Repeat for each door. You will need to map some in the Z axis and some in the X axis.

35. Select the first row of faces at the base of the wall. Make sure you don't select the faces of the doors that you mapped earlier. Refer to Figure 5.58 to check your work.

36. Apply the wllsclp material to the selected faces and unitize them.

37. You will notice that the material will be lying on its side. You need to rotate it so it is correct. To rotate it you first need to change the Selection mode from Face to UVs. You can do this without having to reselect them by changing your Selection mode for the selected faces in the Edit Polygons menu. In the menu, choose Selection >

Convert Selection to UVs, as shown in Figure 5.59.

38. Now bring up the Rotate UVs Options dialog box. It is located in the Edit Polygons menu under the Texture option.

39. Set the rotation amount to 90 and click on Apply until the material is lined up correctly on the wall, as shown in Figure 5.60. Note that the materials near the doors will have to be rotated separately from the rest of the walls.

Figure 5.57 Apply the door material to the door faces.

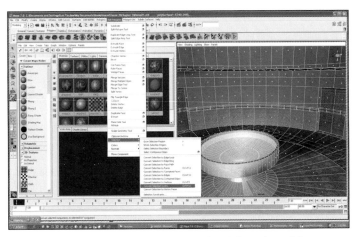

Figure 5.59 Convert the Selection mode of the selected faces to UVs.

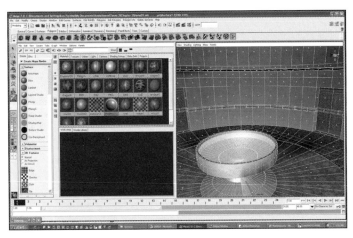

Figure 5.58 Select the faces at the base of the wall.

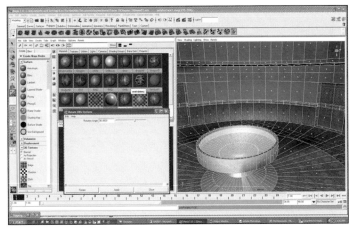

Figure 5.60 Rotate the texture until it is lined up correctly.

40. Now you must continue to move up the wall. Select the three rows of faces that form the top of the wainscoting on the wall, as shown in Figure 5.61. Apply the colbase material to the selected faces and unitize them as shown. Rotate them the same as you did the other wall texture.

41. Select the next two rows of the wall's faces, moving upward.

42. Apply the wall material to these wall faces. Unitize and rotate the faces to match Figure 5.62.

43. Next, apply the dragon3 material to the top of the wall. Unitize the material and rotate it as needed. Refer to Figure 5.63 to check your work.

44. You will be applying the flrtl3 material to the bottom of the balcony. Select the faces for the bottom and the first row of faces on the inside lip of the balcony.

45. Apply the flrtl3 material and unitize all the selected faces. It should now look like Figure 5.64.

46. The next step is to apply the rail material to the rail of the balcony. You use the Cylindrical Mapping tool for the job. Select all the faces for the balcony rails.

47. Use the Cylindrical Mapping tool and then apply the rail material, as shown in Figure 5.65.

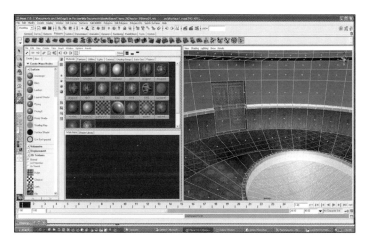

Figure 5.61 Select the faces of the top of the wainscoting.

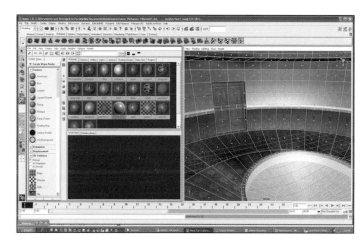

Figure 5.62 Apply the wall material to the wall.

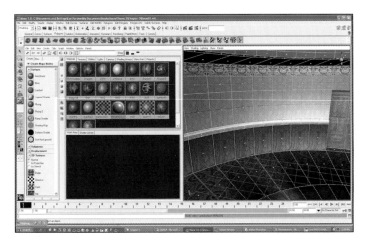

Figure 5.63 Add the dragon3 material to the top of the wall.

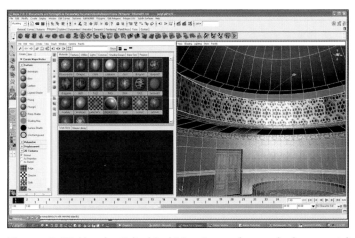

Figure 5.65 Use the Cylindrical Mapping tool to apply the material to the rail of the balcony.

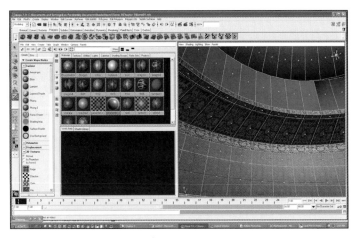

Figure 5.64 Apply the flrtl3 material to the bottom of the balcony.

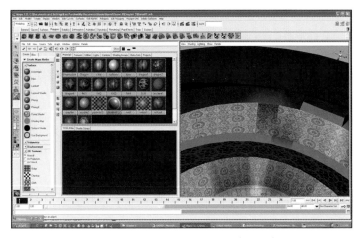

Figure 5.66 Apply the flrtl1 material to the floor of the balcony.

48. Use the flrtl1 material to map the floor of the balcony, much like you did for the floor of the room. It should look like Figure 5.66.

49. Apply the wall material to the wall, as shown in Figure 5.67. Unitize and rotate the material as needed.

50. Now apply the wall material to the walls around the door, as shown in Figure 5.68. Some of the textures will be upside down when unitized and some will not. Rotate those that are incorrect.

51. Now apply the flrtl3 material to the floor area near the doors, much like you did for the floor on the ground floor of the room. See Figure 5.69 for reference.

52. Now apply the door material to the door, as shown in Figure 5.70.

53. Next apply the dragon material to the top of the wall, much like you did on the lower section of the room.

54. Apply the flrtl3 material to the lower part of the roof, the same way you did for the bottom of the balcony. Refer to Figure 5.71 to check your work.

55. Select all the faces of the dome and apply the marble material to them.

56. Unitize the faces. Your design should now look like Figure 5.72.

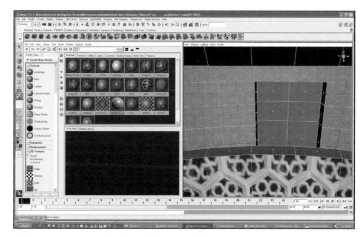

Figure 5.67 Apply the wall material to the wall.

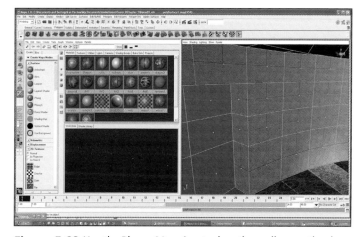

Figure 5.68 Use the Planar Mapping tool on the walls near the door.

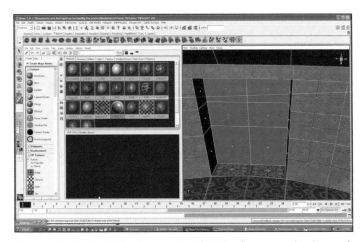

Figure 5.69 Apply the floor material to the floor near the doors of the balcony.

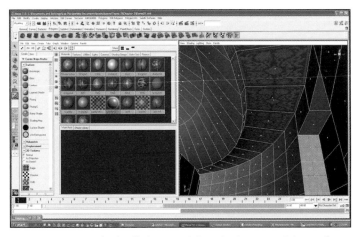

Figure 5.71 Apply the flrtl3 material to the bottom of the roof.

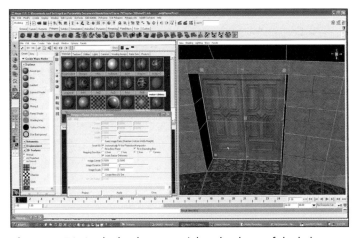

Figure 5.70 Apply the door material to the doors of the balcony.

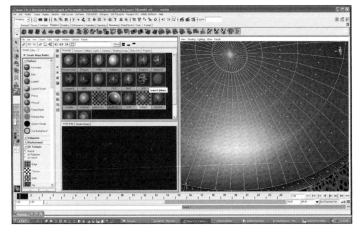

Figure 5.72 Apply the dome material to the faces of the dome.

57. Now there is just one more thing to finish before you are done. If you noticed, there is no handrail on the balcony railing. To fix that, select the faces of the top of the railing and extrude them up just a bit.

58. Now select the newly extruded faces of the rail and apply the colbase material. Unitize the faces.

59. Apply the whtmrbl material to the top of the rail and unitize it as well.

The room is now textured. It looks a lot different with the textures than it did with just the geometry of the model. Unhide the columns you created earlier by selecting Show > Show Last Hidden from the Display menu.

The geometry of the room should look like Figure 5.73.

Notice that the columns don't quite reach the balcony. Select the top faces of the column and move them upward to connect with the balcony, as shown in Figure 5.74.

Figures 5.75 and 5.76 show two more views of the finished room.

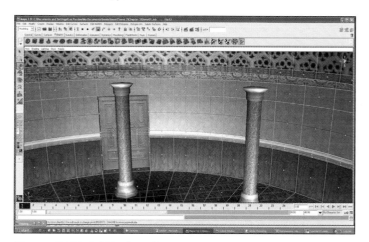

Figure 5.73 Unhide the columns.

Figure 5.74 Move the tops of the columns to connect with the balcony.

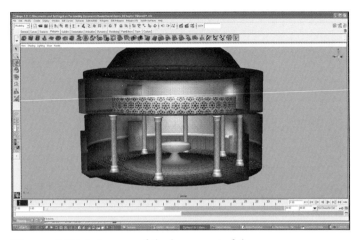

Figure 5.75 A close-up of the lower part of the room.

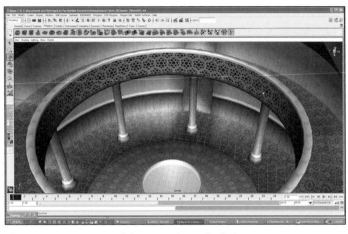

Figure 5.76 A view of the room from the balcony.

Summary

In this chapter you learned how to create a domed two-story room with a balcony and a pool. Here's a listing of the important topics we covered.

- Using the Manipulator tools to shape primitive geometry
- Using Extrude Faces to add new faces to a scene
- Using the Duplicate Faces tool
- Using the Change Selection function
- Using the Cylindrical Projection tool
- Using the Flip and Rotate UV tool
- Using Hypershade to organize materials

Now that you have finished creating a room, try creating a few more. Add some rooms to this model, connecting the doors.

Chapter 6

Lighting and Reflections

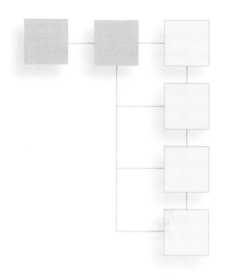

An important part of developing realistic game environments is developing qualities and attributes that you see in normal life. How an environment is lit will play a big role in how realistic that environment will look. Another important factor of an environment is its reflective nature. A shiny object should reflect what is around it.

Real-time lighting and reflections require intensive calculations. You must use them sparingly in games, or they will bog the game speed down and make the game difficult to play. In this chapter you will examine real-time lighting and reflections. In addition to real-time, you will also look at other methods of lighting and reflections that don't require as much calculation. These methods give the game a great look while freeing the processor to render more important game elements.

Real-Time Lighting

Real-time lighting is used in a game to illuminate the game geometry; it is updated every frame so it simulates the real world. Real-time lighting has traditionally been the realm of the programmer, but more and more artists are being asked to design the lighting for a game.

When designing the lighting for a game, you need to understand two important things—where and what. By where, I mean the location of the light. By what, I mean the type of light. Before you get into placing a light, you need to understand the types of lights used in games. Some of the more common lights are

- Point lights
- Directional lights
- Ambient lights
- Colored lights

Point Light

A *point light* is similar to the light given off by a light bulb. The light projects in all directions and is brightest near the source. The light from a point light diminishes with distance. Look at the light in Figure 6.1. Notice that the light gives off a strong highlight on the ball. The area around the light is brightest; the areas on the corners of the plane are darker.

Point lights are good for lighting a room or a local area outside where artificial light is used, such as a streetlamp at night.

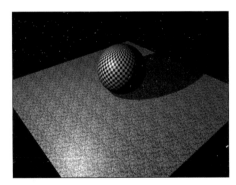

Figure 6.1 A point light is used to light a scene.

Directional Light

Directional lights simulate the light of the sun. The sun is a bright light source that is millions of miles away. Its light rays are almost exactly parallel to each other as they hit the Earth's surface. A directional light illuminates everything evenly. Look at Figure 6.2, and notice how the light on the plane is even. There is no darkening with distance from the light.

Directional light is the most widely used light source in games because it is one of the easiest to calculate. It is also a light that you are comfortable with because you see it every day in real life.

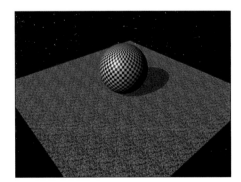

Figure 6.2 A directional light is used to light a scene.

Ambient Light

An *ambient light* is a general light source that lights all surfaces in all directions evenly. It is usually combined with a point or directional light to give a scene a more natural appearance. Ambient light is the result of light bouncing off one surface and then another. Most light in a home that comes through the windows is ambient light unless the sun is shining directly through the window. Because the nature of light is to bounce from one surface to another, shadows are not completely black. You might have noticed that the shadows in Figures 6.1 and 6.2 are almost completely black, which gives them a very unnatural look. In real life, light bounces off everything so almost all shadows have some light bouncing into them. Look at Figure 6.3, and notice that the shadows are much softer and the ball looks three-dimensional. The ambient light simulates the reflected light normally seen in real life.

Almost every scene needs to have some ambient light to make it look realistic. The only exception is a game set in deep space, where there is little or no reflected light.

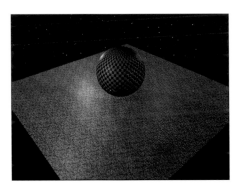

Figure 6.3 An ambient light is used to light the shadow areas.

Colored Light

A *colored light* is not really a light; rather, it is an attribute of all the lights I have already discussed. Colored light is any light source that has a specific color. The scene in Figure 6.4 is lit

with four separate colored lights. They are all point lights, but each has a different color.

Almost every light source is a colored light. A fluorescent light is usually slightly blue, while a normal incandescent light bulb is yellow. The rays of the sun tend to be a little on the yellow side, unless it is setting, and then they can be very red and orange. When you are lighting a scene, use a light that fits the nature of the scene. For example, when you are doing an interior room, give it a slightly yellow light to simulate the incandescent light source.

Preset Lighting

Because real-time lighting is so processor intensive, most games use a system of lighting that is set up prior to the game running. This system is often referred to as *vertex lighting* because it is controlled from the vertices of the polygons. The concept behind vertex lighting is a simple one. The game engine can lighten and darken a texture based on information stored in the model. The lighting takes the form of a gradient, which is a ramp from one color to another.

Figure 6.5 shows an example of a gradient. One corner is light blue, and the opposite corner is darker blue, almost purple. The colors blend evenly from one side to the other.

Figure 6.5 An example of a gradient.

There are basically two ways to set up vertex lighting in a model—prelighting and applying a color directly to a vertex. *Prelighting* is a process in Maya where the lighting is calculated and applied to the vertices automatically. All the artist has to do is set up the lighting for the scene, and Maya will calculate the vertex lighting automatically. To apply color directly to vertices, the artist simply needs to select the vertices and then apply a color to them. Let's take a look at how both processes are used to create lighting for games.

Figure 6.4 Four colored lights are used to light this scene.

For this example, you will use the room you created in Chapter 5. Before you create the lights, however, you need to create some lamps and windows for the room. Bring up Maya and let's get started.

1. The first step is to create a cylinder. Bring up the Polygon Cylinder Options dialog box and adjust the attributes to those shown in Figure 6.6.

2. For this example, you want the lamps to be six-sided, but you need more polygons so you need to subdivide the cylinder.

The Polygon Subdivide Face Options dialog box is located in the Edit Polygons menu. Bring up the dialog box and set the Subdivision Levels to 1, as shown in Figure 6.7.

3. Before you go any farther, you need to create a template so you can adjust the polygons of the cylinder to match those of the texture. A *template* is an object that is used as a guide for creating your model. It is not used as part of the model. There are many ways to create templates;

I will go over some of them in this book. Create a polygon plane inside the cylinder, as shown in Figure 6.8.

4. Now you are ready to load the texture for the lamp. Create a new material in Hypershade and load the lamp texture file, as shown in Figure 6.9.

5. Apply the lamp material to the texture template plane.

6. Press the 6 key so you can see the textures.

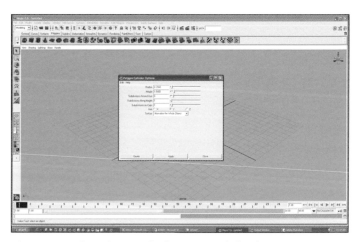

Figure 6.6 The Polygon Cylinder Options dialog box.

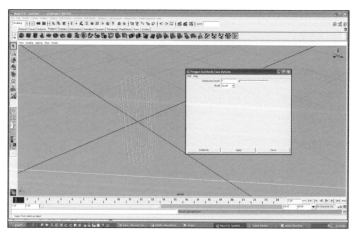

Figure 6.7 Subdivide the cylinder.

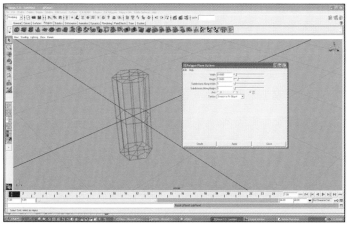

Figure 6.8 Create a plane for a texture template.

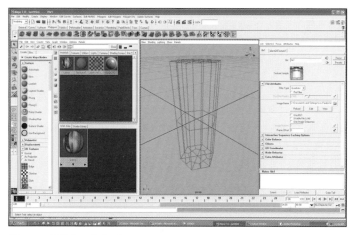

Figure 6.9 Load the lamp texture.

7. Under the Shading menu on the Panel, turn on both the X-Ray and Wire Frame on Shaded options, as shown in Figure 6.10.

8. Scale the width of the template to match the panel size of the lamp, as shown in Figure 6.11.

9. Select the middle vertices of the cylinder and pull them up, as shown in Figure 6.12.

10. On the top of the cylinder, select all the interior vertices and the corner vertices on the edges, as shown in Figure 6.13.

11. Snap the vertices down so they are even with the one you raised earlier. You can do this by holding down the V key and selecting the green arrow on the Move tool to only move along the Y axis. The green arrow will turn yellow to show that it is active. Pull the yellow arrow down until the selected vertices snap to the lower vertices. Your model should now look like Figure 6.14.

12. You don't need the template any longer, so hide it and turn off X-Ray shading.

13. Now you need to project the material so it matches the template you created earlier. Select the faces of the front-facing lamp panel.

14. Use the Planar Mapping tool to project to the selected faces, as shown in Figure 6.15.

15. Project the material using the Planar Mapping tool, as shown in Figure 6.16.

16. Rotate the lamp cylinder around the Y axis 60 degrees, as shown in Figure 6.17.

17. Project the material to the panel facing you, the same way you did in Step 15.

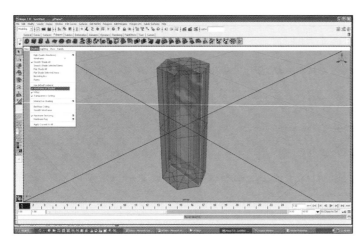

Figure 6.10 Turn on the options under Shaded options.

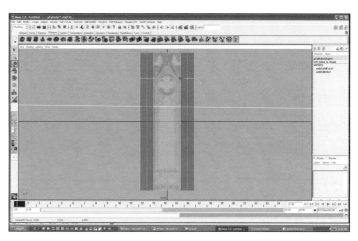

Figure 6.12 Adjust the lamp vertices.

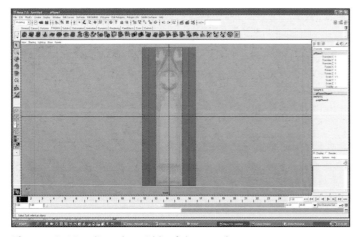

Figure 6.11 Adjust the width of the template.

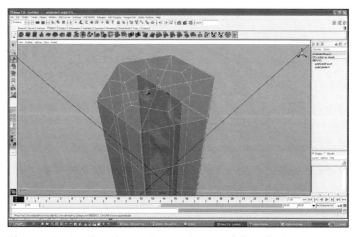

Figure 6.13 Select the vertices at the top of the cylinder.

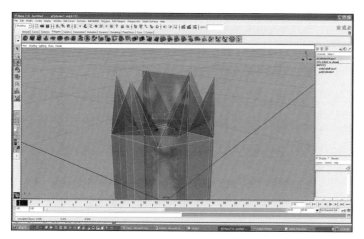

Figure 6.14 Move the selected vertices down.

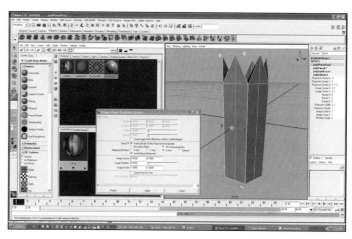

Figure 6.16 Project the material using the Planar Mapping tool.

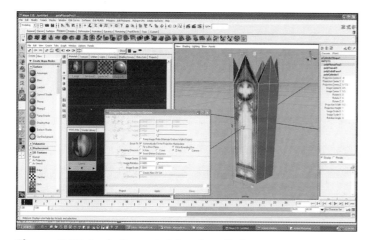

Figure 6.15 Apply the material to the cylinder.

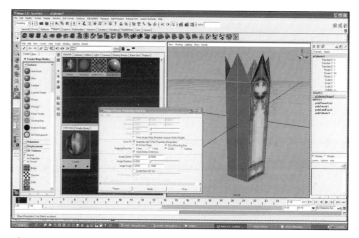

Figure 6.17 Rotate the cylinder.

18. Continue rotating and projecting the lamp material until it is projected on all sides, as shown in Figure 6.18.

19. Now you need to apply a color to the faces on the top and bottom of the cylinder. Create a new material and give it a black color by clicking on the swatch next to color in the Material Attribute editor. When the palette comes up, change the color to black and label the new material Black.

20. Now apply the black material to all of the faces on the top and bottom of the cylinder, as shown in Figure 6.19.

Save the lamp to a file so you can use it later.

Adding the Lamp

Now you have a lamp that you can add to the room you created earlier. Bring up the room from Chapter 5. You will add the lamp and create windows to the room for your light sources.

1. In the File menu, go to Import, as shown in Figure 6.20.

2. Import the lamp file you just saved.

3. Adjust the position of the lamp using the Channel Box, as shown in Figure 6.21.

4. Press Ctrl+G to group the lamp and center the pivot of the lamp and then duplicate it by pressing Ctrl+D.

5. Rotate the duplicated lamp -17 degrees around the Y axis to place it on the other side of the doorway, as shown in Figure 6.22.

6. Select both lamps.

7. Press Ctrl+G to center the pivot.

8. Duplicate the two lamps and rotate them 90 degrees to the next doorway, as shown in Figure 6.23.

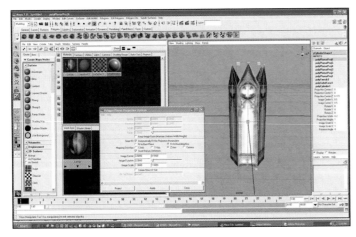

Figure 6.18 The finished lamp.

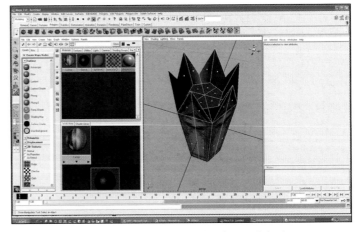

Figure 6.19 Apply black to all the other faces of the lamp.

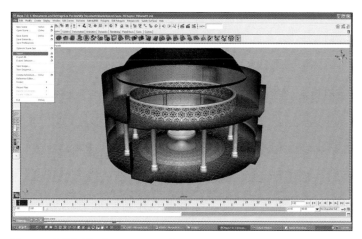

Figure 6.20 The Import menu item.

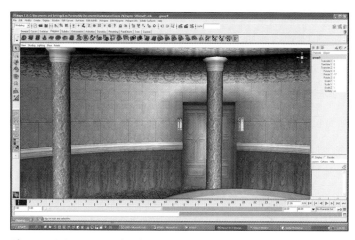

Figure 6.22 Rotate the duplicated lamp.

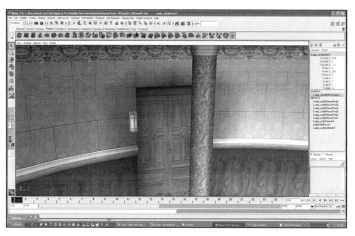

Figure 6.21 Move the position of the lamp using the Channel Box.

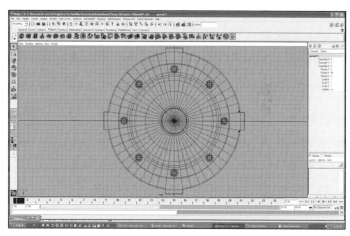

Figure 6.23 Rotate the lamps to the next doorway.

9. Repeat the process of duplicating and rotating the lamps until they are in front of the other two doorways. The lamps should now be by each doorway, as shown in Figure 6.24.

10. Now create four windows along the balcony. Rotate the room 45 degrees in the Y axis so the windows are facing the X and Z directions. Go to the Side view and select the four faces in the center of the room. (You will actually be selecting eight faces because there are four faces on each side of the room.) Look at Figure 6.25 for reference.

11. Extrude the faces.

12. Use the Move tool to move the extruded faces outward, as shown in Figure 6.26. Repeat the process four times for a window along both sides of the Z and X axes.

13. Create a new material using the window texture from the CD. Use the Planar Mapping tool to project then apply the material onto the faces, as shown in Figure 6.27.

Now you have the geometry in place for your light sources, but you are not done with the scene yet. Notice the stretched textures around the window. You need to fix the textures there.

The extruded faces around the window already have the wall texture applied to them. They only need to have their UVs adjusted. The easiest way to adjust the UVs is to use the Planar Mapping tool and map each face, changing the axis of the projection as needed.

Once you have all the windows looking correct, you will be ready to add the vertex lighting to the scene. Rotate the room back to 0 in the Y axis.

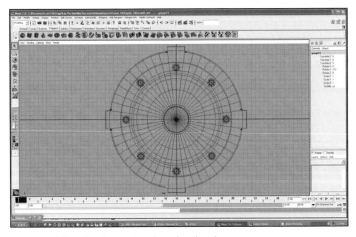

Figure 6.24 The lamps in place by the doorways.

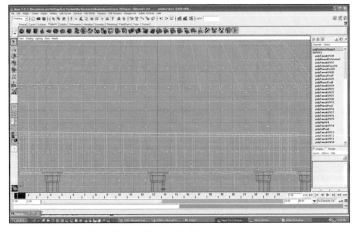

Figure 6.25 Select faces for a window.

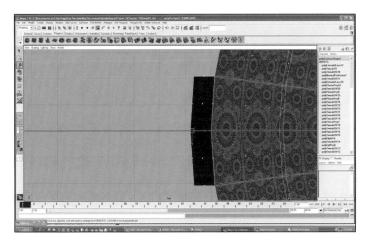

Figure 6.26 Extrude the windows outward.

Figure 6.27 Project the window material on the faces of the window.

Prelighting a Scene

1. You create lights in Maya the same way you create polygonal primitives. Bring up the Create Point Light Options dialog box by selecting Lights > Point Light from the Create menu, as shown in Figure 6.28.

2. Set the intensity of the light to 5 and the Decay Rate to linear.

3. Click on the rectangle box next to Color to bring up the Color palette.

4. Move the color selection circle in the palette to a warm yellow color, as shown in Figure 6.29.

5. Select a dark, cool blue color for the shadow color, as shown in Figure 6.30.

6. Click on Create to create a light in the scene. Lights are represented by a sunburst in Maya.

7. Move the light to just in front of one of the lamps. Refer to Figure 6.31.

8. Remember how you duplicated the lamps and placed them near the doorways? You can do the same thing with the point light. Place one light in front of each lamp, as shown in Figure 6.32.

9. You will also use the pool as a light source. A luminescent pool is a cool thing. Bring up the Create Point Light Options dialog box again.

10. Adjust the colors, intensity, and drop-off to those shown in Figure 6.33.

11. Place the new light just above the pool, as shown in Figure 6.34.

12. Now you are ready to prelight the room. Bring up the Polygon Prelight Options dialog box by selecting Colors > Prelight from the Edit Polygons menu, as shown in Figure 6.35.

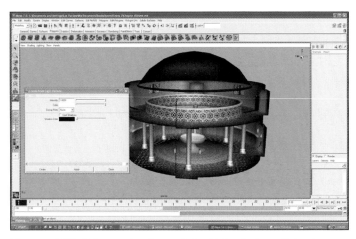

Figure 6.28 Bring up the Create Point Light Options dialog box.

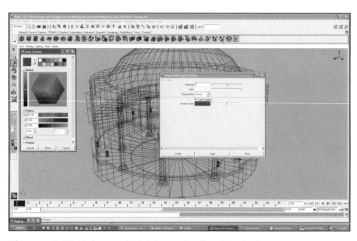

Figure 6.30 Select a dark blue color for the shadow.

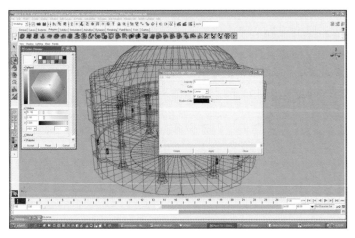

Figure 6.29 Select a warm yellow color from the palette.

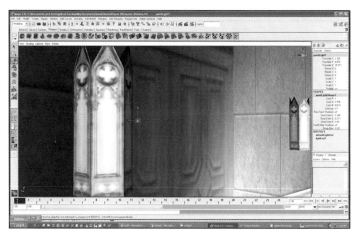

Figure 6.31 Place the light in front of one of the lamps.

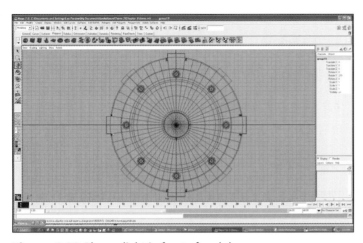

Figure 6.32 Place a light in front of each lamp.

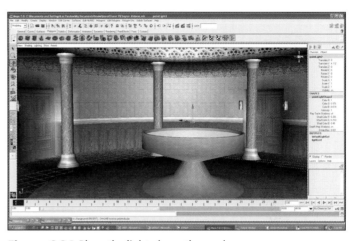

Figure 6.34 Place the light above the pool.

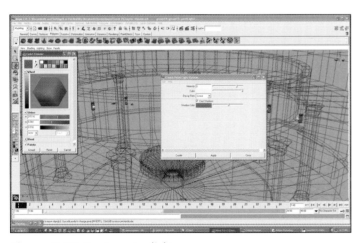

Figure 6.33 Create a new light.

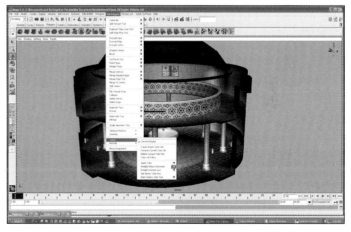

Figure 6.35 Bring up the Polygon Prelight Options dialog box.

13. Check the options shown in Figure 6.36.

14. Go to Edit > Select All to select all elements of the scene. Click on the Prelight button. It will take Maya a few seconds to calculate the lighting.

15. When Maya is finished calculating the lighting, the image will change from the Wire Frame view to the Shaded view. If you want to see how the shading looks, go to the Lighting menu of the view screen and select Use No Lights. Your scene should look like Figure 6.37.

The room will appear dark. This is because the prelighting is to establish shadows. When the room is in a game, real-time lighting will also illuminate the room.

Applying Color

Applying color to vertices is like prelighting, except that it is done evenly to selected vertices. Often after prelighting a scene, the artist will go in and adjust vertex colors to give the scene a better look.

1. You will want the lamps to be brighter, as if they are lighting the room. Select all the lamps and bring up the Polygon Apply Color Options dialog box from the Edit Polygon > Colors > Apply Colors menu, as shown in Figure 6.38.

2. Change the colors to those shown in Figure 6.39.

3. Click on the Apply Color button. The lamps should look bright, as shown in Figure 6.40.

4. Next you need to light the upper part of the room. Select the faces of the room from the balcony upward, as shown in Figure 6.41.

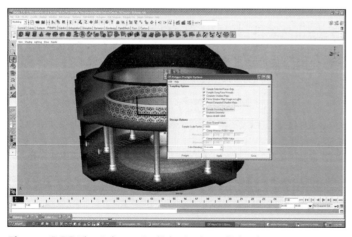

Figure 6.36 The Polygon Prelight Options dialog box.

Figure 6.37 The room after prelighting.

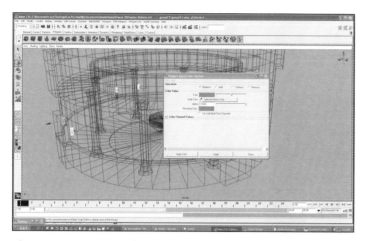

Figure 6.38 Bring up the Polygon Apply Color Options dialog box.

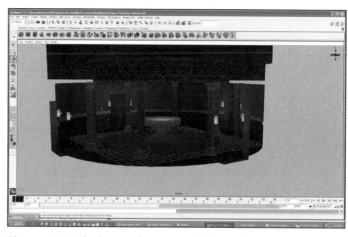

Figure 6.40 The lamps after you apply the color to the vertices.

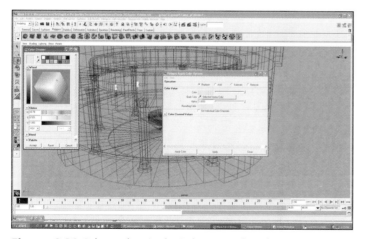

Figure 6.39 Select colors in the Polygon Apply Color Options dialog box.

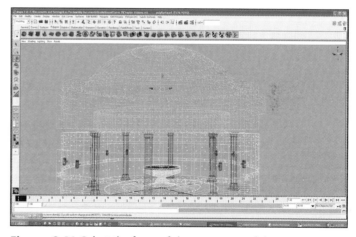

Figure 6.41 Select the faces of the upper part of the room.

5. Use the View Selected function to only see those areas on which you want to work.

6. Now apply color to the upper part of the room evenly using the Apply Color tool. Change the Selection mode to Vertices and select all the vertices.

7. Bring up the Polygon Apply Color Options dialog box and adjust it to match Figure 6.42.

8. Once you have an even lighting on the room, you can go in and adjust individual vertices to give the lighting a more realistic look. Start with the windows. Select the vertices of the window.

9. Use the Apply Color tool and apply color to the selected vertices, as shown in Figure 6.43.

10. Usually a bright window will cast light into a room. The light will be brighter near the window. You can simulate this effect by selecting the vertices of the rail and floor where the light would fall and lightening them by applying a lighter color, as shown in Figure 6.44.

11. Repeat the process for the other windows. The model should now look like Figure 6.45.

12. Bring back the lower part of the room to see how your lighting looks. Refer to Figure 6.46 to compare your room with the example.

You now have a basic understanding of lighting and prelighting. Experiment with the lighting tools in Maya to get more familiar with them. Try building a few simple rooms and lighting them in different ways.

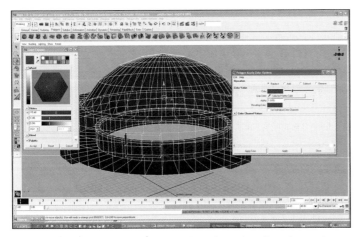

Figure 6.42 Adjust the values in the Polygon Apply Color Options dialog box.

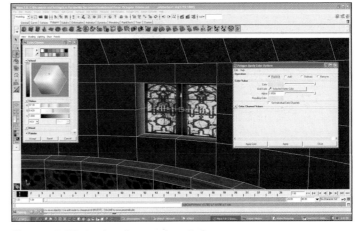

Figure 6.43 Apply colors to the window.

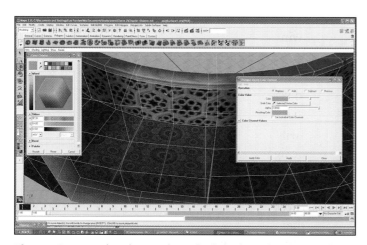

Figure 6.44 Apply color to where the light from the window falls.

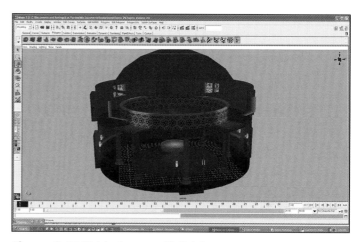

Figure 6.46 Finished room with lighting.

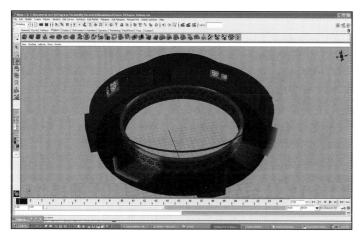

Figure 6.45 The upper part of the room.

Real-Time Reflections

A shiny surface looks shiny because it reflects its surroundings. The only way to get a true reflection on a surface in a game is to calculate it based on the angle of the surroundings and the game view, and then render the calculated image on the surface. This usually has to be done for each ray of light; the process is called *ray tracing*. Ray tracing is impractical for real-time game rendering because it takes up too much processor time. In the absence of true reflections, game developers have come up with a few tricks that simulate reflective surfaces.

Specularity

Specularity is a surface property that helps define an object as shiny or dull. Look at Figure 6.47. There are several slid-

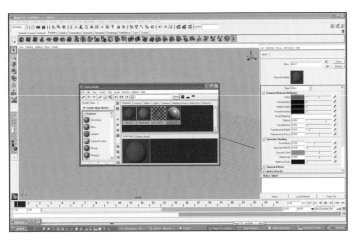

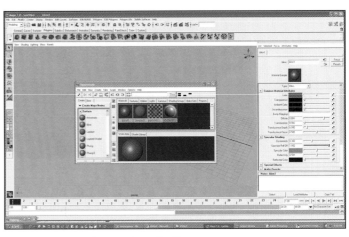

Figure 6.47 No specular roll off.   **Figure 6.48** High specular roll off.

er bars for specular properties in the Attribute editor of a Blinn material. In Figure 6.47, I have moved the Specular Roll Off slider all the way to the left. Look at the image of the material—it is dull.

Now look at Figure 6.48, in which I have moved the slider all the way to the right, increasing the specular roll off. Notice how the material looks shiny.

The material is not reflecting its surroundings, but by changing the way the material reflects highlights, you can give the material a simulated shiny look. Adjusting the specular

qualities of the material is the basic way game developers add shininess to surfaces.

Environment Maps

Some surfaces need more than just a specular highlight to look right. A shiny car, for example, needs to reflect its surroundings. One way developers have created the look of reflections without the time-consuming process of ray tracing is by using an environment map. An

environment map is a texture that gets rendered onto a surface as a reflection. The texture is usually a close approximation of the environment the object is in, and it can be changed from time to time as an object moves. Figure 6.49 shows an example of an environment map.

Figure 6.49 An environment map.

Rendered Reflections

Another trick for achieving reflective qualities in games is to build the reflection geometry. This method only works on flat surfaces such as floors, but it is very effective in giving a scene a realistic reflection. Take a look at how this is done.

1. In Maya, load the lamp model you created earlier.

2. Use the Channel Box to translate the model up .5 so the bottom of the lamp is flush with the grid, as shown in Figure 6.50.

3. Create a single polygon plane under the lamp, as shown in Figure 6.51.

4. Create a new Blinn material and load the tile texture into that material.

5. Project the material using the Planar Mapping tool in the Y axis.

6. Apply the new material to the plane.

7. Set the projection width and height to 1 in the Channel Box, as shown in Figure 6.52.

8. Bring up the tile material in the Attribute editor.

9. Adjust the Transparency slider to the right, as shown in Figure 6.53.

10. Now select the lamp in Object mode.

11. Select Mirror Geometry from the Polygons menu, as shown in Figure 6.54. In the Polygon Mirror Options dialog box, select the –Y radio button.

12. Click on the Apply button, as shown in Figure 6.55.

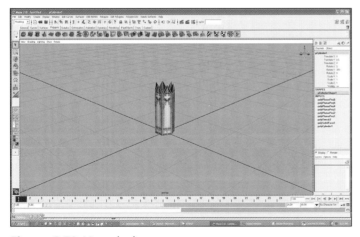

Figure 6.50 Move the lamp up.

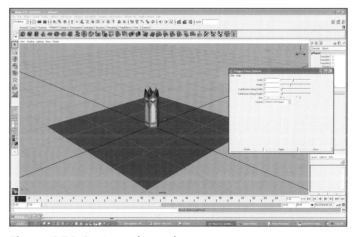

Figure 6.51 Create a polygon plane.

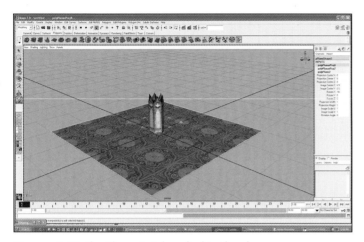

Figure 6.52 The tile material applied to the plane.

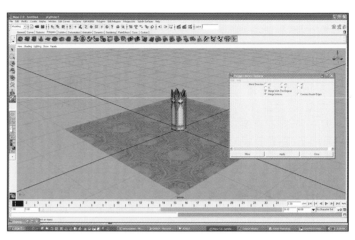

Figure 6.54 Select Mirror Geometry from the Polygons menu.

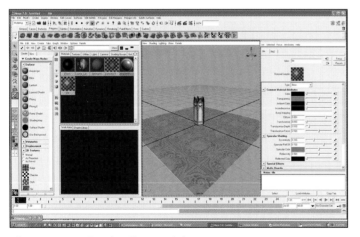

Figure 6.53 Give the tile material some transparency.

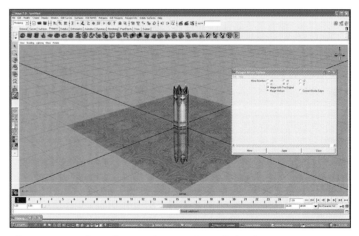

Figure 6.55 The Polygon Mirror Options dialog box.

The lamp now looks like it is reflecting off the surface of the plane (see Figure 6.56). This process is effective, but it is also costly because not only does the environment need to be duplicated, but all objects, characters, and special effects need to be mirrored as well. Usually the game artist will have to create a different model for the reflection that has substantially fewer polygons than the original to work well.

Summary

In this chapter you learned about lighting and reflections. The techniques covered in this chapter were

- Point lights
- Directional lights
- Ambient lights
- Colored lights
- Prelighting
- Applying vertex colors
- Specularity
- Environment maps
- Reflection geometry

These techniques are very useful for a game artist interested in creating believable game worlds. Practice building a few game environments to experiment with the principles you have learned.

Figure 6.56 The lamp now appears to be reflected in the tiles.

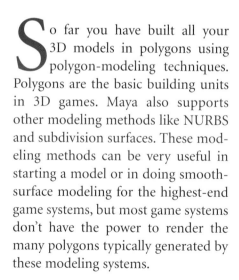

CHAPTER 7

BUILDING ENVIRONMENTS IN NURBS

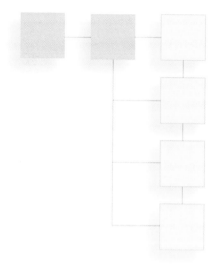

So far you have built all your 3D models in polygons using polygon-modeling techniques. Polygons are the basic building units in 3D games. Maya also supports other modeling methods like NURBS and subdivision surfaces. These modeling methods can be very useful in starting a model or in doing smooth-surface modeling for the highest-end game systems, but most game systems don't have the power to render the many polygons typically generated by these modeling systems.

Even though your end product has to be in polygons, this doesn't mean that using other methods of modeling is not useful. In this chapter you will explore some NURBS modeling techniques for building a racecourse. This chapter will by no means be an in-depth exploration of NURBS. It will, however, give you a starting point for exploring NURBS modeling on your own.

What Are NURBS?

NURBS stands for *Non-Uniform Rational B-Splines*, which is a technical way of saying curves. A *spline* is a curve that is calculated mathematically. Because it is a mathematical curve,

it can be manipulated using math. The nice part about 3D programs is that the computer does all the math, and all the artist has to do is manipulate a series of points called *control vertices* (CV, for short). A control vertex is an editable point in space that influences a curve. Control vertices make it very easy to manipulate complex geometry.

Creating a Racecourse

A racecourse for a game is a specialized type of terrain model. It needs to look like the player is traveling through a world that goes on forever, while at the same time using as little geometry as possible. In the following example you will build an oval outdoor course. You will be using Maya for this project.

1. In Maya there are two types of curves. For this example you will be working with an EP curve. EP stands for *edit point*—the point that separates two segments of a curve. The EP Curve tool is located in the Create menu, as shown in Figure 7.1.

2. Go to the Top view. When you select the EP Curve tool, the cursor will change. To use the tool all you have to do is click with the left mouse button in the Panel. Go to the Top Down view and click the mouse three times in a line, as shown in Figure 7.2.

3. Continue placing edit points to form the shape of the track, as shown in Figure 7.3. When you are almost finished with the shape, press Enter on the keyboard to finish the curve. Leave a little space between the two ends of the curve.

4. Now you need to connect the two ends of the curve. Right-click on the curve and select Control Vertex from the Marking menu.

5. Select one of the ends of the curve using the Move tool.

6. Hold down the V key and move the end of the curve toward the other end. (The V key is a shortcut key for snapping to a vertex.) Now go to Open/Close Curves in the Edit Curves menu to bring up the Open/Close Curves Options box. Set the options, as shown in Figure 7.4 and click Apply to close the curve.

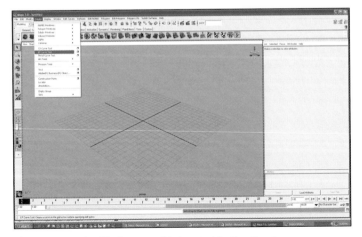

Figure 7.1 The EP Curve tool is located in the Create menu.

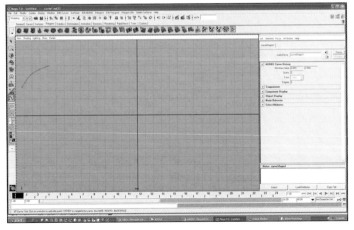

Figure 7.2 Start drawing the curve using the EP Curve tool.

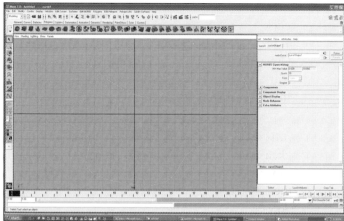

Figure 7.3 The finished EP curve.

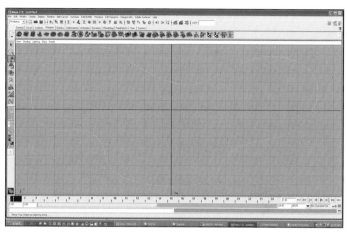

Figure 7.4 Join the two ends of the curve.

7. Now that the ends are joined, take a few minutes and get used to moving control vertices. Notice all the small dots around the curve. Select one and move it using the Move tool. Watch how the curve moves with the control vertex. Move your curve around until it looks like Figure 7.4.

8. Now that you have the desired shape, you need to rebuild the curve so that all your edit points are equal distances from each other. Maya has an automatic function for rebuilding

curves. To bring up the tool, select Rebuild Curve in the Edit Curves menu, as shown in Figure 7.5.

9. The segment of a curve between edit points is called a *span*. Set the number of spans for the curve to 30. Make sure all the check boxes in the Rebuild Curve Options dialog box are set exactly as shown in Figure 7.6, and then click on Apply.

10. The curve you have just built will be the outside of the road. Now you need to build the

inside. Select the curve in Object mode and duplicate it.

11. Use the Scale tool to reduce the size of the duplicated curve, as shown in Figure 7.7. By duplicating the curve, you preserve the CVs so later when you loft the geometry, it will match.

12. The Scale tool will only work for part of the reduction process. To get the curve to follow the original curve like the two sides of a road, you will have to go in and adjust the curve using the control vertices, as shown in Figure 7.8.

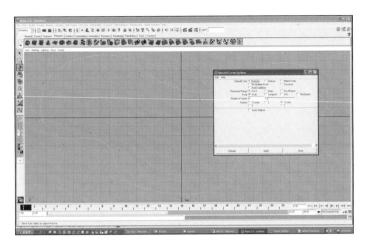

Figure 7.5 The Rebuild Curve menu item.

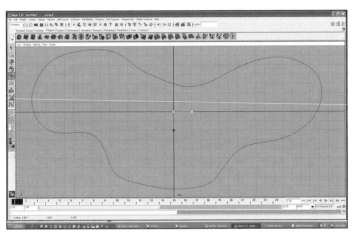

Figure 7.7 Use the Scale tool to reduce the size of the curve.

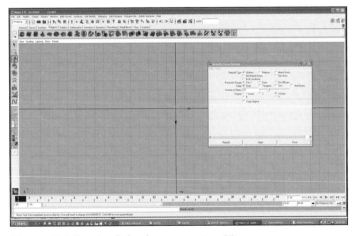

Figure 7.6 Set the dialog box to create a 30-span curve.

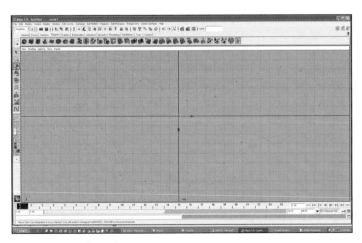

Figure 7.8 Adjust the inner curve.

13. Now that you have the sides of the road, you need to create the area around the road. Duplicate and resize two more curves. Place one outside of the road curves and one inside the road curves. Refer to Figure 7.9 for an example of the four curves. The curves for the banks need to follow the road, but they don't need to be as exact as the curves for the road.

14. You will want the banks of the roadside areas to go up from the road. Select the inside and outside curves and move them up a little, as shown in Figure 7.10.

15. You now have the base shape for the road. It is time to add polygons to the areas between the curves. You add polygons using a process called *lofting*. Select the road curves and then select Loft from the Surfaces menu, as shown in Figure 7.11. This will bring up the Loft Options dialog box.

16. This dialog box is a little complicated because Maya allows for many different options when you are lofting. You can explore the many options later; for now, set the options exactly as shown in Figure 7.12. This

will give you a set of polygons for the road that is two polygons wide by 100 polygons long.

17. You now need to create polygon sets for both of the roadsides. Loft these two areas the same way, but change the Number V option to 2 instead of 3, as shown in Figure 7.13. You want a polygon set that is only one polygon wide so it will be easier to texture the polygon later.

18. Loft both roadside areas. The model should now look like Figure 7.14. Notice that all the polygons line up with each

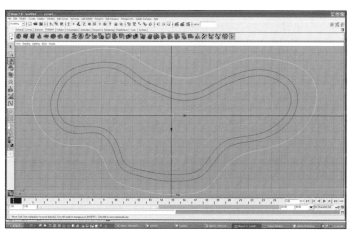

Figure 7.9 Add two more curves for the roadside areas.

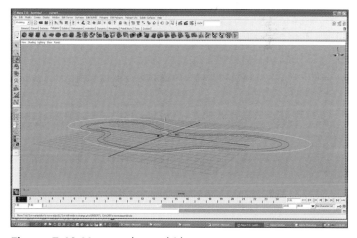

Figure 7.10 Move up the roadside curves.

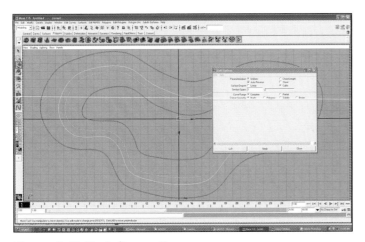

Figure 7.11 The Loft menu item.

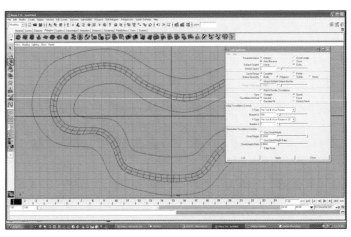

Figure 7.13 Change the Number V option in the dialog box to 2.

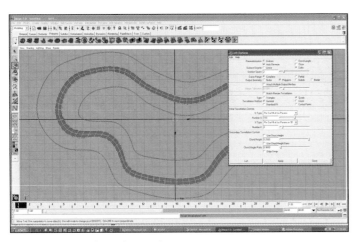

Figure 7.12 Lofting the road.

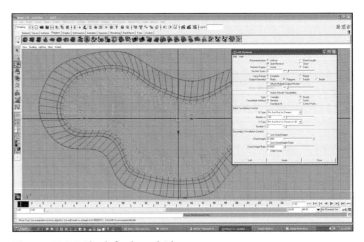

Figure 7.14 The lofted roadsides.

other. This is important to avoid gaps or seams between sets of polygons.

19. Now that you have the polygon sets in place, you need to check the model for potential problems. In Figure 7.15 I have circled two areas where the model needs to be adjusted to eliminate diamond-shaped polygons, which are more difficult to render than square or rectangle polygons and cause unsightly stretching of textures. The problem is compounded if the polygons are large. These diamond-shaped polygons have to be eliminated.

20. The nice part about working with curves in Maya is that as long as the history is not cleared, the polygons will stay attached to the curves. Moving a control vertex on a curve will move the polygon sets with it. All you have to do is adjust the control vertices, as shown in Figure 7.16, to adjust the underlying polygons.

21. Go through the entire model and adjust all the polygons to make them as square as possible. Refer to Figure 7.17 for how the model should look when you are finished.

22. Notice that while you adjusted the polygons, you also adjusted the control vertices to line up with each other from one curve to the next. You will now use that to add a hill to your racecourse. Select the control vertices on a corner of the racecourse, as shown in Figure 7.18.

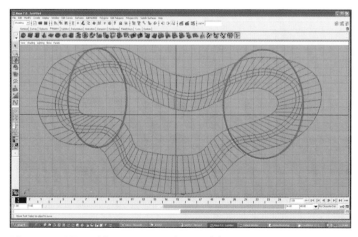

Figure 7.15 Problem areas on the model.

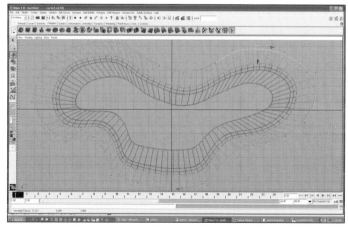

Figure 7.16 Adjust the curves to move the polygons.

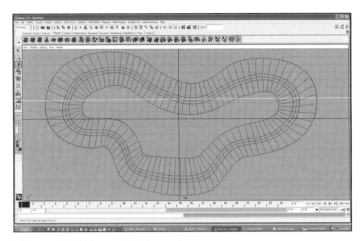

Figure 7.17 The model after adjustments.

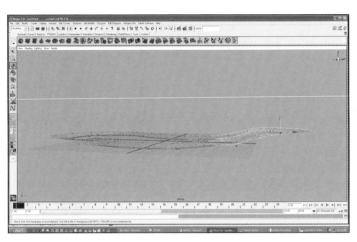

Figure 7.18 Select the control vertices on a corner of the racecourse.

23. Move the selected corner up slightly.

24. Deselect the first and last rows of control vertices along the road and then raise the remaining control vertices a little more, as shown in Figure 7.19. The more you raise each set of vertices, the steeper the grade of the road will be in the final model.

25. Continue to build the hill until you have it to your liking.

Hint

Hills in racing games are deceiving. It only takes a little rise in elevation to make a big difference in the course. Most people consider a six-percent grade a steep road. Unless you are making an off-road rock climbing game, be careful how steep you make the roads in your models.

26. Racecourses are more fun if the outside of a curve is higher than the inside. In real life, these curves help to keep the car from sliding off the track or rolling while traveling at high speeds. If the racing game is using a simulated physics routine for the cars, the same thing will hold true for the game. Select the control vertices on the outside of a corner, as shown in Figure 7.20, and move them up a little. Do not move them too far or the curve will seem unnatural.

27. Go through each curve and raise the outside edge.

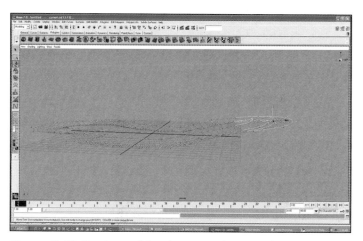

Figure 7.19 Continue raising the successive control vertices to build a hill.

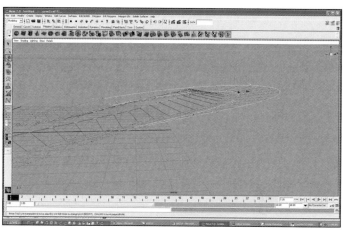

Figure 7.20 Raise the outside of the curve.

28. Now for a little excitement. What's the fun of racing if you can't catch any air? On a straighter section of the road, select a row of control vertices and move them up to form a small hill, as shown in Figure 7.21.

29. The layout of the road is now almost complete. The next thing you need to do is create the tree line. A *tree line* is the vertical area off the road that blocks your view. Most of the time this line is made up of trees, hence the name tree line.

Tree lines are sometimes very complex, but for this game you will make a simple one. Select both the inside and outside curves of the model.

30. Next you will build a line of trees to block the view on the edges of the track. Duplicate the curves and move them up, as shown in Figure 7.22.

31. You also want a fence on either side of the road to keep your racecars from going off the track. Select the curves you used for the road.

32. Duplicate the curves and raise them. Don't raise them too far unless you want a huge fence. Figure 7.23 shows the correct height.

33. In the Loft Options dialog box, set the same values you used for the roadsides to loft between the new and old curves, as shown in Figure 7.24.

34. It is time to start adding some textures to your model. Open Hypershade and create new materials for the textures. All the texture files are on the CD in the directory for this chapter.

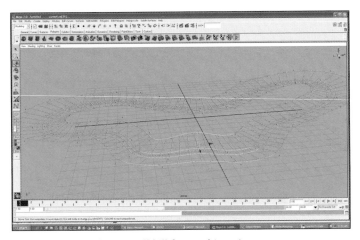

Figure 7.21 Make a small hill for catching air.

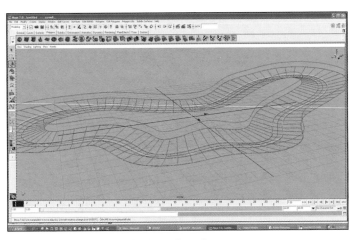

Figure 7.23 Raise the duplicated road curves.

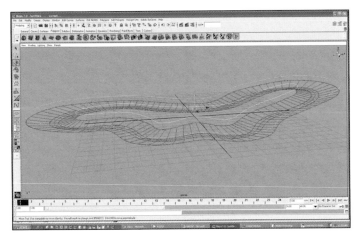

Figure 7.22 Duplicate and move up the new curves.

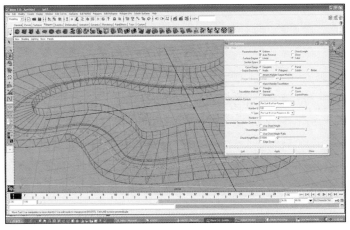

Figure 7.24 Loft polygon sets between the new and old curves.

Load all the .tga files, road.bmp, and side.bmp. Rename the materials to match the textures, as shown in Figure 7.25. The black-and-white mask files go with the .tga files. The mask files are for use with some game engines that require a mask for transparency. I will not be using those files in this example, but they are included on the CD to help you with your projects. You can hide the curves now, if you like, to help when selecting faces.

35. Select the road polygon set.

36. Apply the road material to the selected polygons. Notice that the material looks distorted, as shown in Figure 7.26.

37. Unitize the material (see Figure 7.27). Many of the textures will be rotated incorrectly. You can come back and fix the problem after you finish applying the rest of the materials.

38. Apply the side material to both sides of the road.

39. Unitize the material. It should now look like Figure 7.28. Notice that because you are using a polygon set that is only

one polygon wide, the textures map correctly.

40. Apply the treeline material to the tree line polygons and unitize those materials like you did the others. The model should now look like Figure 7.29.

Hint

The treeline texture is a Targa file with an alpha channel. The alpha channel gives the texture a transparent area because it is set up with a mask. Take a look at the texture file in Corel Photo Paint to see how the alpha channel was made. You can see the channels in the Docker under the Channels tab.

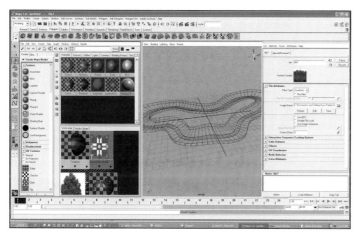

Figure 7.25 Load the texture files into Hypershade.

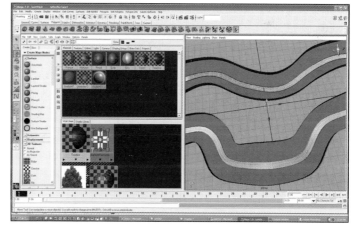

Figure 7.26 Apply the road texture to the model.

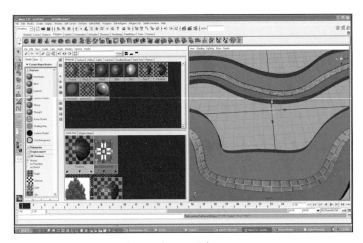

Figure 7.27 Unitize the road materials.

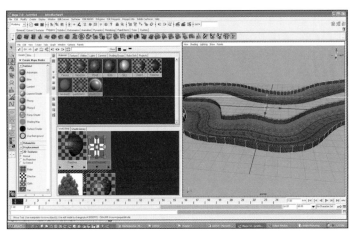

Figure 7.29 The model with the tree line textures added.

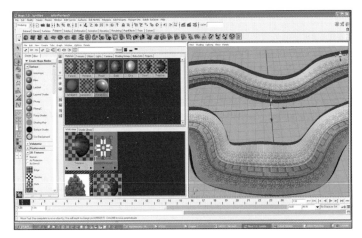

Figure 7.28 Apply the side material to the roadsides.

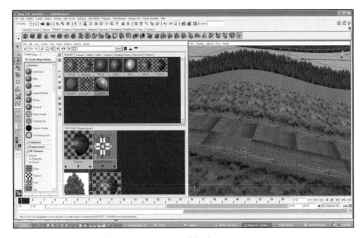

Figure 7.30 The fence material added.

41. Now apply the fence material to the fence polygon sets and unitize them, as shown in Figure 7.30.

42. Now you have to deal with the road textures. Go to the Top view and select the road polygons, as shown in Figure 7.31.

43. Convert the selection to UVs by selecting Selection > Convert to UVs from the Edit Polygons menu.

44. Rotate the UVs 90 degrees. You can access the Rotate UVs dialog box by selecting Textures > Rotate UVs from the Edit Poly-

gons menu. The rotated UVs should look like Figure 7.32.

45. You fixed a little more than half of the texture problems of the road. You need to select the remaining problem textures individually. Change the Selection mode to Face and select the problem textures, as shown in Figure 7.33.

46. Convert the selected faces to UVs.

47. Rotate the selected UVs 270 degrees. You can either change the number in the Rotate UVs dialog box or simply hit the Apply button three times with

the default 90 degrees option selected. The road should now look like Figure 7.34.

You now have a functioning track with textures. You could stop here, but this track doesn't look very good because there is nothing along the sides of the track to break up the scenery. In most racing games, the artist puts many interesting elements along the course to give the game personality. These elements can include buildings, people, parked cars, signs, and more often than not, trees. For this exercise you will add a number of trees because they are the most common sideline element.

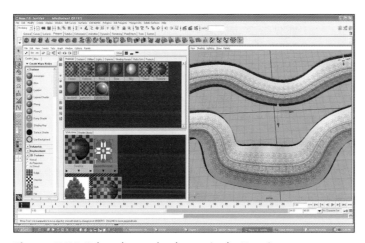

Figure 7.31 Select the road polygons in the Top view.

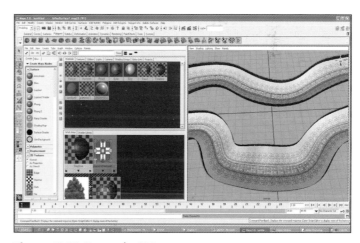

Figure 7.32 Rotate the UVs.

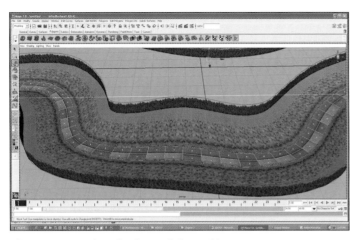

Figure 7.33 Select the faces of the problem textures.

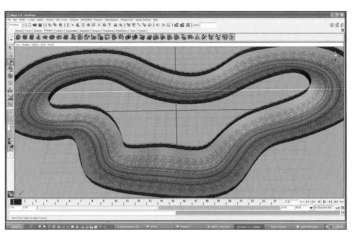

Figure 7.34 The corrected textures on the road.

Adding Scenery Elements to the Racecourse

You are going to build a simple tree to put in the racecourse as a background scenery element. There are three basic approaches to building trees for games—billboards, fans, and geometry.

The most basic approach is to create what is sometimes called a billboard. A *billboard* is a single polygon with a picture of a tree, character, or other background element. The billboard is rotated so that it always faces the cam-era. This system has the advantage of using the least number of polygons (one), so you can add a maximum number of trees to the game. The disadvantage is that the flat nature of the tree is very noticeable.

A tree *fan* is similar to a billboard in that a texture of a tree is applied to a single polygon, but rather than rotating the image to the camera, the polygon is duplicated and rotated once or twice to form a fan. It is kind of like taking a couple cardboard cutouts and intersecting them in the middle. This method has the advantage of not using very many polygons and still giving the tree a 3D look. The problem with this method is that the fans sometimes cast weird shadows that reveal the artificial nature of the tree.

The final method is to build a tree (leaves and all) out of polygons. This method will give the trees in the game the most realistic look possible. The problem with this method is that trees are organic elements, and organic elements usually require many polygons to look right. Imagine how many polygons it would take to build a tree if you only used one polygon for each leaf. It is somewhat impractical for a high-speed racing game.

For this racing game you will use the second method—creating fans and planting the trees along the sides of the racecourse. You should hide the racecourse by pressing Ctrl+H so it will be easier to build the tree model.

1. You start with a single polygon. Create one that is twice as high as it is wide, as shown in Figure 7.35.

2. Move the polygon up one unit so the base is even with the origin point.

3. Apply the tree texture to the polygon, as shown in Figure 7.36. If you were using the billboard method, you would be finished at this point.

4. Duplicate the polygon. As I stated earlier, normals only face in one direction. You need to see this polygon from both sides. You duplicate the polygon for exactly that purpose.

5. With the duplicate polygon selected, reverse the normals, as shown in Figure 7.37.

6. Combine the two polygons into the same object. You will find the Combine function under the Polygons menu.

7. Now duplicate the new object and rotate the duplicate 60 degrees.

8. Repeat Step 7, but this time rotate the new duplicate 120 degrees. The tree should now look like Figure 7.38.

9. Combine the three objects into a single object.

10. Now you need to size the tree so it is the same height as the tree line. Bring back the model of the racecourse by selecting Show > Show Last Hidden from the Display menu, and move the tree so the bottom is

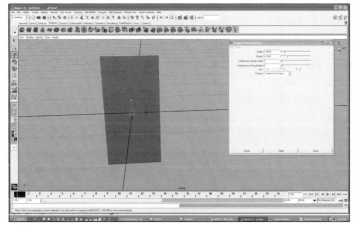

Figure 7.35 Create a single polygon.

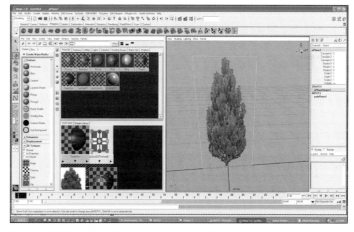

Figure 7.36 Apply the tree texture to the polygon.

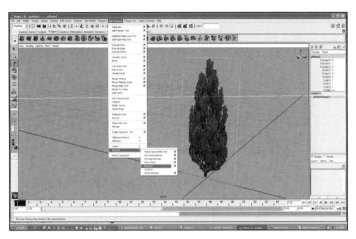

Figure 7.37 Reverse the normals of the duplicate polygon.

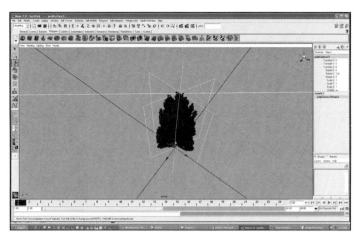

Figure 7.38 The tree fan.

level with the bottom of the tree line.

11. Size the tree so it is the same height as the tree line, as shown in Figure 7.39.

Hint

Maya sometimes has difficulty sorting scenes with multiple transparent textures. You might find that when you are placing objects like the tree you just created, they appear behind the tree line when they should be in front of it. This can sometimes get very confusing. Hang in there—it is only a sorting problem. The guys at Alias are working on it and should have it fixed in their next edition.

12. Next you need to plant some trees. Go to the Top view. Make sure you have Wire Frame Shaded turned on.

13. The critical areas for the tree are on the inside of the curves near the tree line. You need to plant trees coming out of the tree line so the player doesn't see a flat polygon edge as he comes around the corner. Place the tree so that it intersects the tree line, as shown in Figure 7.40.

14. Place several trees along the tree line to break up the edge that

will be seen by the player. Create each new tree by duplicating the first tree. Refer to Figure 7.41 for spacing.

15. Continue to duplicate and plant trees throughout the course. Pay attention to the inside curves. When you are finished, your model should look similar to Figure 7.42.

16. Now go to the Perspective view. As shown in Figure 7.43, you will notice that many of the trees are either floating above the ground or sunk below the ground. It is easiest to see this in the Flat Shaded mode.

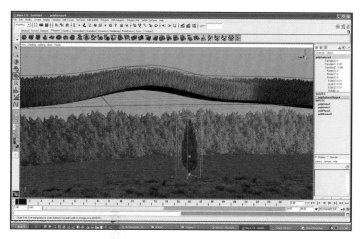

Figure 7.39 Size the tree to fit the model.

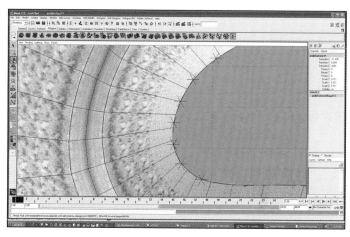

Figure 7.41 Space the trees along the edge of the model.

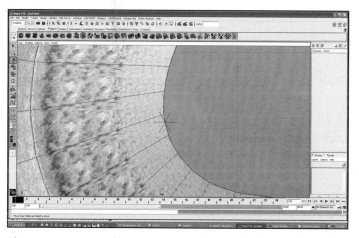

Figure 7.40 Move the tree to the edge of the model.

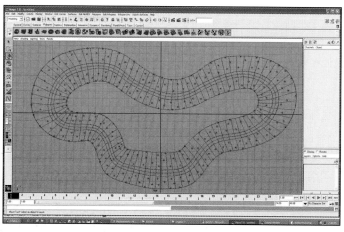

Figure 7.42 Plant several trees in the scene.

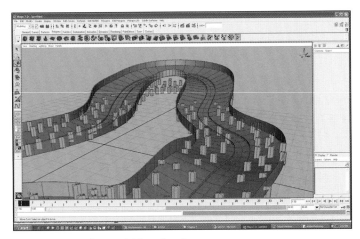

Figure 7.43 The model has floating trees.

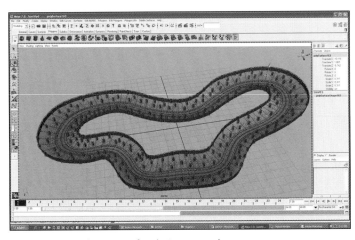

Figure 7.45 The trees after being moved.

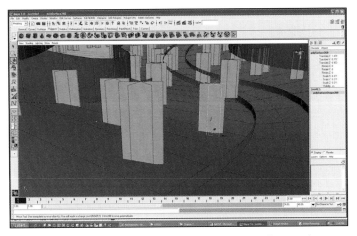

Figure 7.44 Move the trees to intersect the ground correctly.

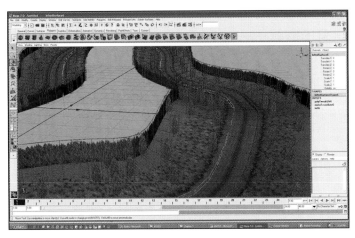

Figure 7.46 Reverse the normals of the duplicate fences.

17. Select each tree and move it so that it intersects the ground correctly, as shown in Figure 7.44.

18. When you are finished, go to Smooth Shaded mode. Your model should now look similar to Figure 7.45.

19. Remember how you duplicated and reversed the normals on the tree polygon? You need to do the same thing with the polygons forming the fence. Otherwise, the fence will disappear if it is seen from the back side. Select the fence polygon sets and duplicate the polygons.

20. Reverse the normals of the duplicate fences, as shown in Figure 7.46.

21. While you're at it, you need to check the direction of the normals for the rest of the track. Turn on Backface Culling.

22. Reverse the normals of any polygon set that is facing the wrong direction.

23. Save the current model.

Level of Detail

The current model you have is okay, but it might not look good on close scrutiny. It is what you would call a *base* or *low-resolution* model. In many racing games, several versions of a course model are used. These different models represent *levels of detail*, or LOD, as they are sometimes referred to in the industry. The way it works is that one model is substituted for another depending on an object's distance from the player. For example, a more detailed high-resolution model is used near the player for maximum detail. Farther away from the player, a low-resolution model is used because the detail is lost in the distance.

The higher-resolution model has more polygons and larger textures than the lower-resolution model. I won't go into a lot of detail about LOD in this book, but I'll give you a quick look at how to create a higher-resolution model from the base low-resolution model.

1. Select the faces of the polygon set that make up the road.

2. Change the Selection mode to Face and select all the faces of the road set, as shown in Figure 7.47.

3. Select Subdivide in the Edit Polygons menu to access the Subdivide dialog box.

4. Set the subdivisions to 1 and click on Apply.

5. Repeat the process to subdivide the other polygon sets in the model. When you are finished, the model should look similar to Figure 7.48.

6. The next step for creating a high-resolution model is to adjust individual vertices to add more interesting terrain features. The adjustments should be small so that the high-resolution model does not change dramatically from the base model.

7. After you finish the geometry adjustments, the last step is to replace the low-resolution textures with higher-resolution textures. You can change the textures by simply loading the new texture files into the material in Hypershade.

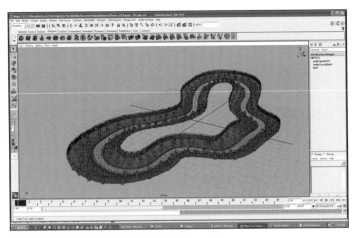

Figure 7.47 Select the faces of the road.

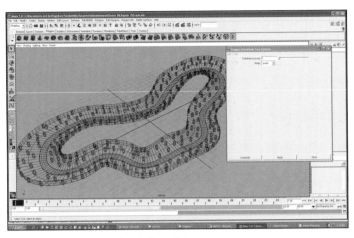

Figure 7.48 The subdivided model.

Once you are done with the higher-resolution model, save it as a separate file. During the game both files will be used. The higher-resolution model will be used for close terrain and the low resolution model for distant terrain.

Prelighting the Racecourse

As you learned in the previous chapter, the higher the model's resolution, the better prelighting will work. Now that you have a higher-resolution version of the model, you can set up the

lighting. If you want more detail in the lighting you can subdivide the model further. Just remember that game engines have polygon limits, so be careful how many times you subdivide.

1. Create a directional light. Set the intensity to 5 and make the light a little yellow.

2. Adjust the position of the light so it shines on the course from an angle, as shown in Figure 7.49. Use the Show Manipulator tool to move the light. This tool gives you a Move tool for the light and one for the target.

3. Select the light and the entire model, as shown in Figure 7.50.

4. Prelight the model with the same setting you used to prelight the room in Chapter 6. Figure 7.51 shows the model after prelighting.

You will note that the prelighting is a little harsh, with very dark shadows. You can adjust the color of the shadow in the Light Attribute editor before prelighting. You will also note that the shadows don't come all the way to the treeline. This is because the treeline is only one polygon thick and the back

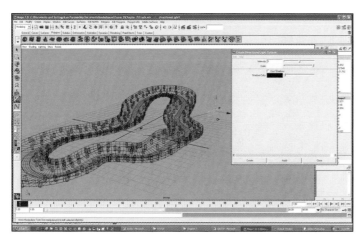

Figure 7.49 Put a directional light in the scene.

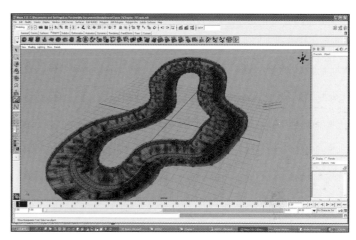

Figure 7.51 The model after prelighting.

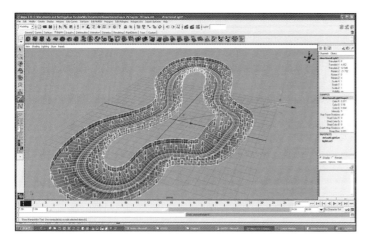

Figure 7.50 Select all scene elements.

is receiving light from the light source. You will have to color the errors in lighting using the Apply Color feature as explained in the last chapter.

Building Skyboxes

A *skybox* is a model used for the sky and distant terrain features. It is a separate model from the racecourse, and it is rendered differently from the racecourse model. The game engine renders the skybox last, after everything else is finished rendering. This keeps the distant terrain features in the back, behind the rest of the course. Because it is rendered last, you don't need to build the skybox large enough to cover the entire course. In fact, most skyboxes are relatively small compared to the world geometry.

You will build a simple skybox for the racecourse. Hide the current scene so it will be easier to work on the skybox.

1. Create a polygon cylinder, as shown in Figure 7.52.

2. Delete the top and bottom faces.

3. Apply the horizon material using the Cylindrical Mapping tool, as shown in Figure 7.53.

4. Create a polygon sphere slightly larger than the cylinder, as shown in Figure 7.54.

5. Go to the Side view.

6. Delete the lower five rows of faces from the sphere.

7. Apply the sky material using the Cylindrical Mapping tool, as shown in Figure 7.55.

8. Turn on Backface Culling to see the inside of the skybox. You will need to reverse the normals on the sphere and cylinder. You will also have to soften the edges. It should look like Figure 7.56.

The skybox is now finished. Figure 7.57 shows how it will work for the horizon of the game.

For this example you used a clear blue sky and a mountain horizon. You can experiment with different sky textures and horizons to get different looks. Some games have very complex systems for developing skyboxes, including cloud-generation programs and the movement of the sun across the sky.

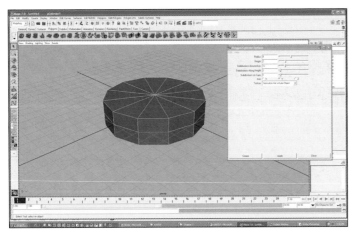

Figure 7.52 Create a cylinder.

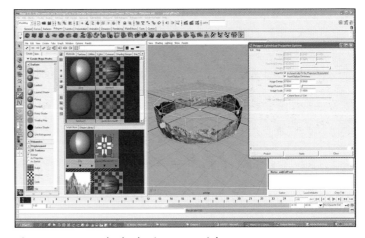

Figure 7.53 Apply the horizon material.

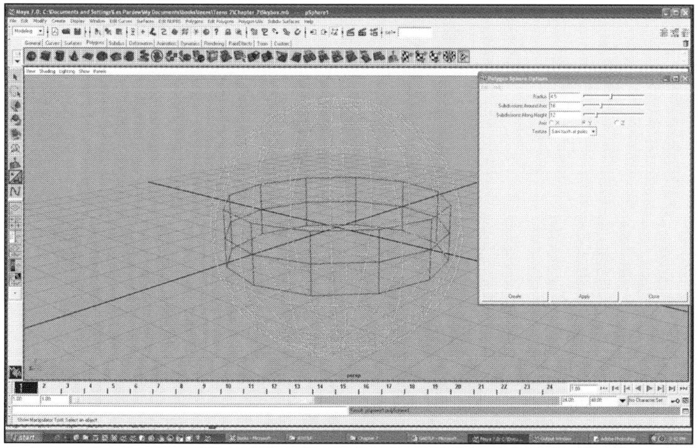

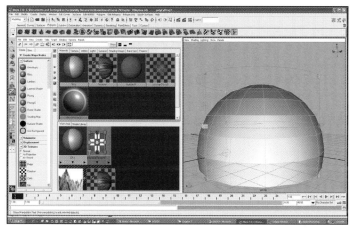

Figure 7.54 Create a polygon sphere.

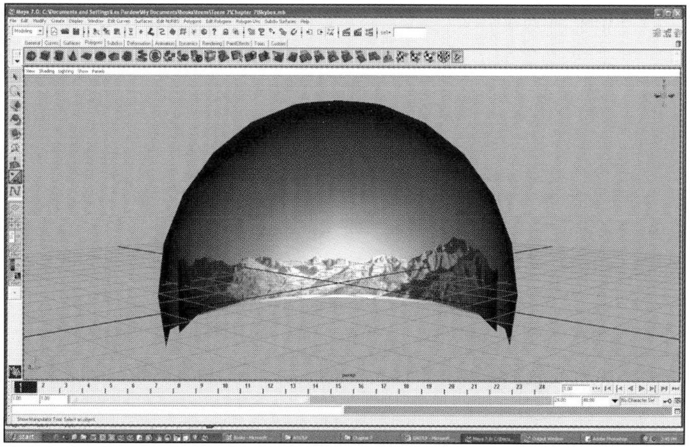

Figure 7.56 The completed skybox.

Figure 7.55 Apply the sky material to the sphere.

Figure 7.57 The skybox horizon.

Summary

Congratulations! You have just finished building a racecourse. Figure 7.58 shows a mock-up of how the racecourse will look in a game.

In this chapter I covered some very basic NURBS modeling techniques.

- ▪ EP curves
- ▪ Control vertices
- ▪ Rebuilding curves
- ▪ Lofting

As you can see, NURBS modeling is a very powerful way to create models. Continue to experiment with NURBS to see other ways in which they might be helpful in your modeling efforts.

I also covered techniques for building specialized terrain models, such as racecourses, as well as level of detail and building skyboxes. Many of the techniques you learned are used in other types of games, too, such as adventure games and first-person shooters. Try to build some other environments using the same techniques.

Figure 7.58 View of the finished racecourse.

CHAPTER 8

BUILDING GAME OBJECTS

Objects in games are non-character game elements that are separate from the environment geometry. An *object* is something that can be moved or manipulated in the game. When you build a set, items such as walls, columns, floors, mountains, and so on do not move and are built into the set geometry. Items such as swords or guns are things that a player can pick up. Because they can be moved, these items are defined as *game objects*. Although characters could be defined as game objects, they are typically more complex than objects and therefore have their own designation as characters.

The trend in games is to have more and more objects. Like in real life, in a game you can interact with your environment. In real life, you can pick up a rock and throw it. You can break windows if you want. You can get in a car and drive. Players want to do the same things in a game environment.

When they are setting up a game environment, the development team needs to designate the items that are part of the environment and those that are separate objects. Objects take more programming and processor time than scene elements. As an artist, you have to be constantly aware of the limitations of the game engine. Usually the development team will give you some guidelines on the number and scale of objects possible in the game.

Types of Objects

A game object can be almost anything. Some objects are very simple, such as a rock or a piece of paper. Other objects are complex, such as cars or helicopters. The types of objects in a game depend on the type of game. For example, a racing game might have cars or some other vehicles. An adventure game might have clue items, such as notes or keys. A first-person shooter might have weapons or ammunition lying around. Most objects will fall into the following categories:

- Pick-ups (objects the player collects)
- Power-ups (objects that give the player an advantage in speed, strength, and so on)
- Movable items (objects such as doors, chests, furniture, and so on)
- Destructible items (objects such as barrels, windows, walls, and so on)
- Controllable items (objects such as cars, trucks, tanks, and so on)
- Animated items (objects such as water fountains, torches, fires, and so on)

Naming Conventions

Each of these object types is used differently in game development. Most games have a naming convention for designating the role the object will

play in the game. For example, a door might have a file name of drsl04, where the "dr" means door, the "sl" refers to the type of door (in this case sliding), and the "04" means that it is the fourth door created for the game. It is often wise to set up the naming conventions at the beginning of a project so the art files are well organized.

Building a Game Object

In the project for this chapter, you will build an ATV (*All-Terrain Vehicle*). You will build the ATV so it is ready for animation, with all the moving parts as separate pieces. Bring up Maya so you can get started.

1. You will be using a template to help you build the ATV. Create a single-polygon plane, as shown in Figure 8.1.
2. Duplicate the plane and rotate it 90 degrees around the X axis so it is perpendicular with the first plane.
3. Now duplicate the plane again and rotate it 90 degrees around the Y axis, as shown in Figure 8.2.
4. Create a new material and load the ATV texture from the Chapter 8 directory on the CD.

5. Project a planar map on the first polygon and apply the new material to the plane, as shown in Figure 8.3.

Hint

The ATV texture is called a blanket texture. A *blanket texture* is a texture in which most (if not all) of the textures used on an object are on one piece of art. The advantage of a blanket texture is that there is only one file for the game to keep track of. It is also easier for the artist to edit the texture's UVs. It is common for some objects and almost all characters to use blanket textures.

6. Now you need to move and rescale the textures so they line up with each other in your template. You will use the Planar Mapping tool to accomplish this.
7. The Planar Mapping tool has several manipulators. The light-blue boxes on the corners are for Scale Objects Equally. You can use these manipulators to keep the ATV scale correct. Select one of the corner manipulators and expand the texture image until the Top view of the ATV is about the width of the polygon, as shown in Figure 8.4.

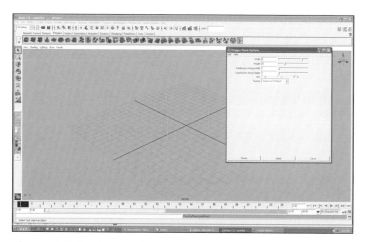

Figure 8.1 Create a single polygon plane.

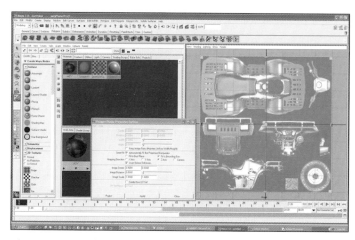

Figure 8.3 Apply the texture to the plane.

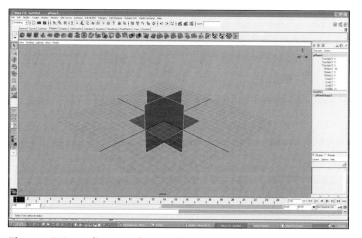

Figure 8.2 Duplicate and rotate the plane.

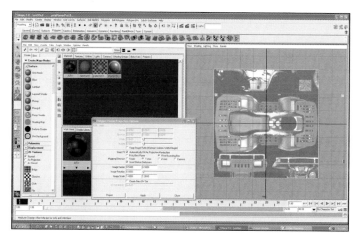

Figure 8.4 Scale and center the Top view image.

8. Now go to the Front view and scale the side image of the ATV the same way you did the Top view. It should look like Figure 8.5.

9. Go to the remaining plane from the Side view and line up the Front view image with the other two images. You will need to go back and forth between the Side and Perspective views to get it right. Refer to Figure 8.6 for an example of how it should look.

10. Your template is now finished and ready to be used in modeling the ATV. Activate the X-Ray View mode. Start with the body. Create a polygon cube, as shown in Figure 8.7.

11. Scale the cube using the Scale tool so that it approximates the scale of the body, as shown in Figure 8.8.

12. Use the Scale tool to shape the contour of the vertices, as shown in Figure 8.9.

13. Continue to scale each row of vertices until the cube conforms to the contour of the body as seen from the Top view. The cube should now look like Figure 8.10.

14. Go to the Front view and shape the contours of the cube from that direction, as shown in Figure 8.11. Don't get confused by the fact that you are looking at the side of the ATV in the Front view. I usually put the most complex view in the Front view.

15. Now you need to shape the body of the ATV from the Side view. Notice that the Side view template does not help you here because the radiator obscures the body. Just follow the example in Figure 8.12.

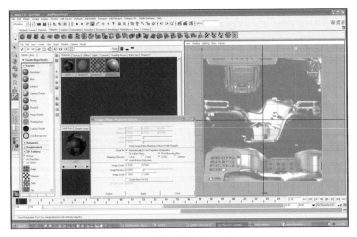

Figure 8.5 Scale and move the Side view image.

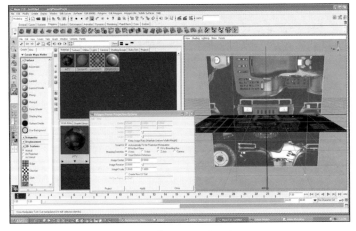

Figure 8.6 Scale and move the Front view image.

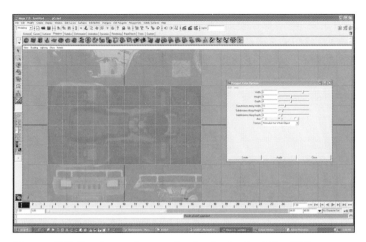

Figure 8.7 Create a polygon cube for the body of the ATV.

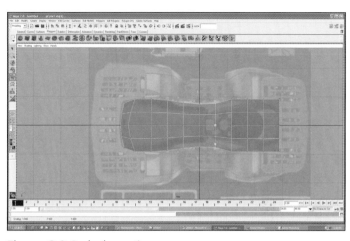

Figure 8.9 Scale the vertices.

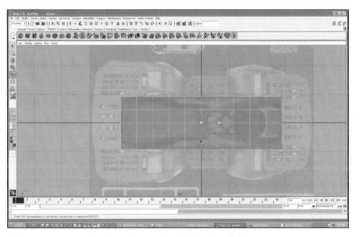

Figure 8.8 Scale the cube to fit the body of the ATV.

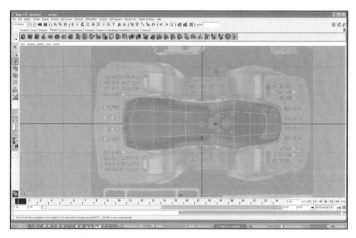

Figure 8.10 The shaped sides of the ATV.

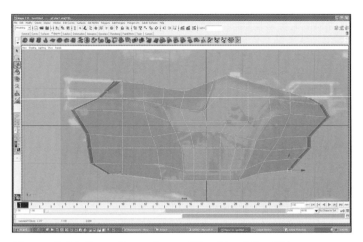

Figure 8.11 Shape the contours of the side of the ATV.

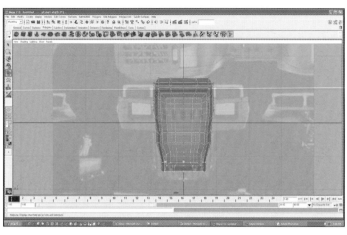

Figure 8.12 Shape the body from the Side view.

16. Shaping in the three orthographic views will only do part of the work. You must do the rest in the Perspective view. You need to round many of the corners, especially around the seat and gas tank. Do this by adjusting the vertices.

17. Now you need to extend the body in the front and back to where the axles are. Use Figure 8.13 as a guide to how the body should be shaped.

18. Now you will work on the fenders. Create another cube, as shown in Figure 8.14.

19. Adjust the vertices of the cube so it follows the contour of the fender, as shown in Figure 8.15.

20. In the Top view, adjust the vertices to follow the shape of the fenders, as shown in Figure 8.16.

21. Touch up the shape of the fenders in the Perspective view.

22. Create a new polygon cube, as shown in Figure 8.17.

23. Move and fit the new cube to the tray behind the seat, as shown in Figure 8.18.

24. Shape the tray from the top, as shown in Figure 8.19.

25. Duplicate the tray and move the duplicate to the front tray of the ATV.

26. Adjust the front tray to fit the template, as shown in Figure 8.20.

27. The front tray is smaller than the rear tray, so make sure you shape it from the Top view as well.

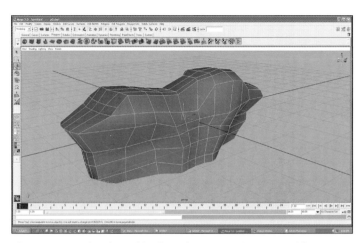

Figure 8.13 The shaped body in the Perspective view with templates hidden.

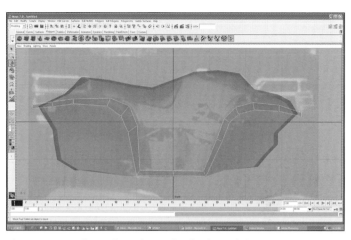

Figure 8.15 Shape the cube to the fenders of the ATV.

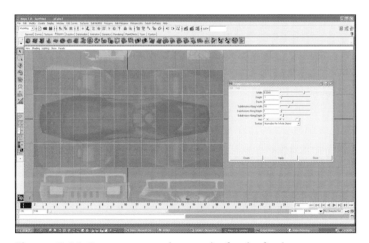

Figure 8.14 Create a new polygon cube for the fender.

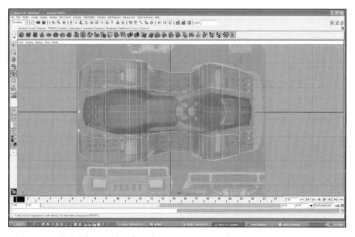

Figure 8.16 Shape the fenders in the Top view.

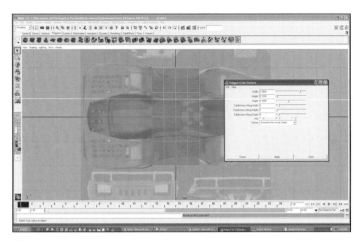

Figure 8.17 Create a new polygon cube for the tray.

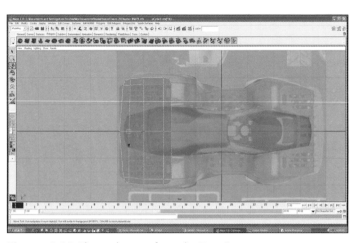

Figure 8.19 Shape the tray from the Top view.

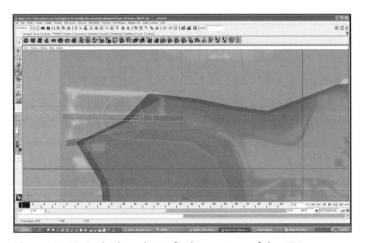

Figure 8.18 Scale the cube to fit the rear tray of the ATV.

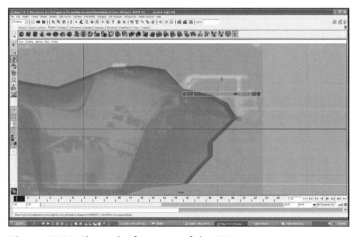

Figure 8.20 Shape the front tray of the ATV.

28. Now you need to make the rail bars for the trays. Create a new polygon cube, as shown in Figure 8.21.

29. Move the new cube to the rails on the back of the ATV.

30. Adjust the vertices so the geometry conforms to the shape of the back rail, as shown in Figure 8.22.

31. Select the faces of the two ends of the rail.

32. Extrude the faces to form the side rails, as shown in Figure 8.23.

33. Extrude the rails two more times, rotating and moving them to form the anchor of the rails, as shown in Figure 8.24.

34. Duplicate the faces of the last extrusion and move them to the back of the rail for the back supports, as shown in Figure 8.25.

35. Scale and move the support rails into the corner of the railing, as shown in Figure 8.26.

36. Duplicate the finished rail and move it to the front tray.

37. Rotate and scale the rail to fit the front tray.

38. Create a new polygon cube for the front grille, as shown in Figure 8.27.

39. Shape the new cube to fit the grille of the ATV, as shown in Figure 8.28.

40. Now create another box for the radiator, as shown in Figure 8.29.

41. Shape the box to fit the radiator. This will be easy from the front, but there is no reference from the side. Use Figure 8.30 as a guide for how it should look and 8.31 for how it should look from the front of the ATV.

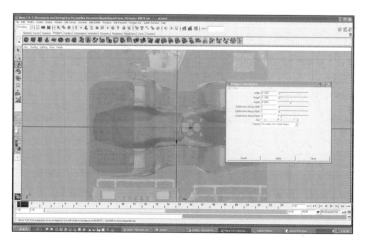

Figure 8.21 Create a new polygon cube for the rail bars.

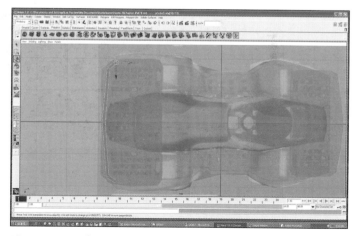

Figure 8.22 Shape the cube to the template of the back rail.

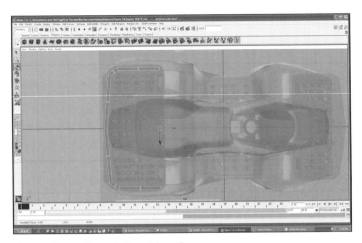

Figure 8.23 Extrude the side rails.

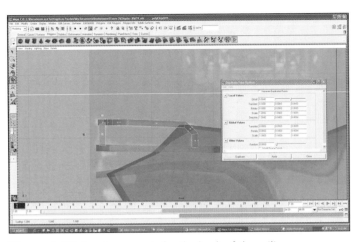

Figure 8.25 Create supports for the back of the railing.

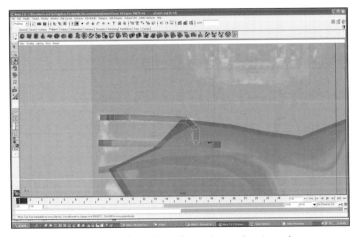

Figure 8.24 Extrude the rails to form the anchor into the tray.

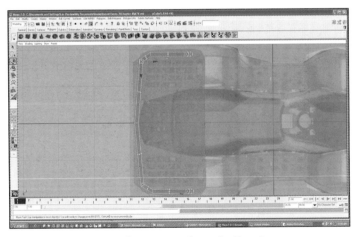

Figure 8.26 Position the supports from the Top view.

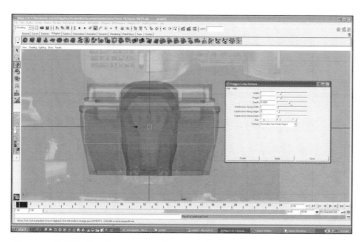

Figure 8.27 Create a new polygon cube.

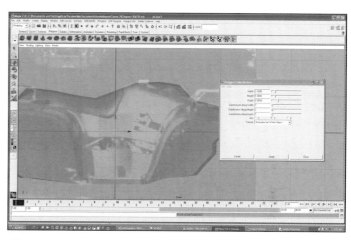

Figure 8.29 Create another new polygon cube.

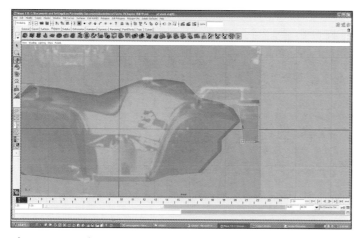

Figure 8.28 Shape the cube to fit the front grille of the ATV.

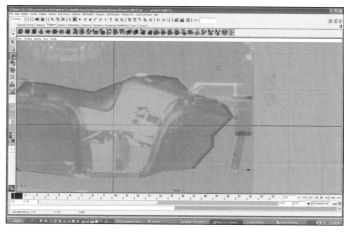

Figure 8.30 Shape the cube for the side of the radiator.

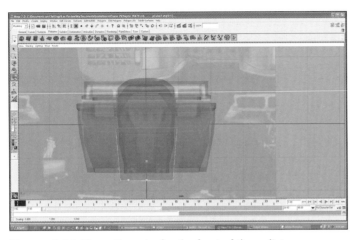

Figure 8.31 Shape the cube for the front of the radiator.

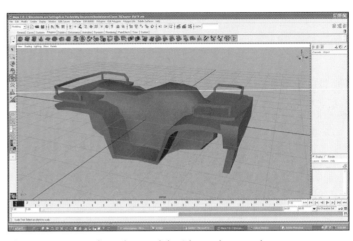

Figure 8.32 Look at the model without the template.

42. You are almost finished with the geometry for the ATV body. Hide or delete the template and deselect X-Ray view. Your model should look similar to Figure 8.32.

43. Notice that the fenders are very square. Move and scale the vertices of the fender to pull them in just a bit, as shown in Figure 8.33.

44. Now select all the objects you have created so far and combine them into a single object, as shown in Figure 8.34. Hide the templates.

45. In the Front view, select all the faces that are facing directly toward or directly away from the view, as in Figure 8.35. You will need to look at several views to make sure you get all of them.

46. Use the Planar Mapping tool to project the ATV blanket material in the Z direction, as shown in Figure 8.36.

47. Move and scale the material until the texture is placed correctly, as shown in Figure 8.37.

48. Now select the faces on the top of the model. This may take some time and a lot of rotating the model to make sure you have all of the faces selected (see Figure 8.38).

49. Project and fit the material so the Top view image fits correctly to the model, as shown in Figure 8.39.

50. Select the faces on the front of the ATV and project the Front view image onto them, as shown in Figure 8.40.

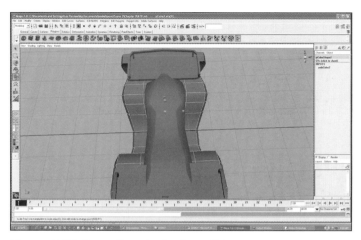

Figure 8.33 Shape the cube for the radiator.

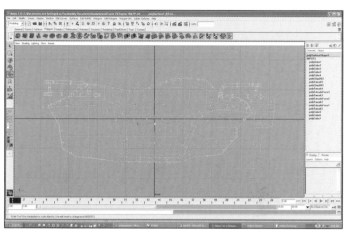

Figure 8.35 Select the faces that will make up the sides of the ATV.

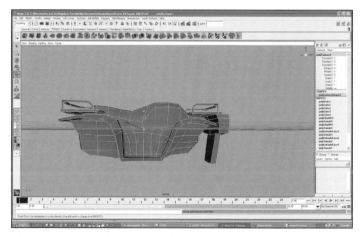

Figure 8.34 Combine all the objects into a single object.

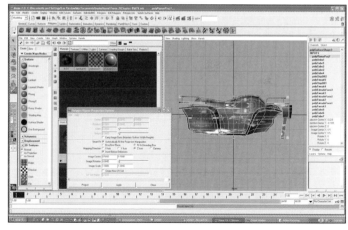

Figure 8.36 Project the ATV blanket material onto the selected faces.

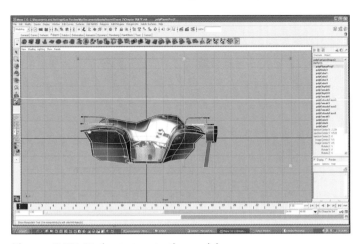

Figure 8.37 Fit the texture to the model.

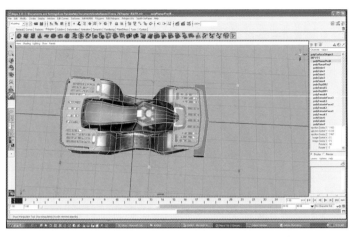

Figure 8.39 Project the Top view image onto the model.

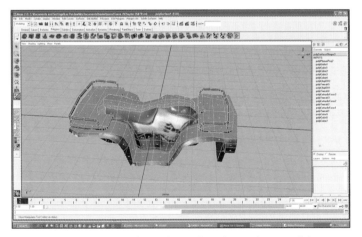

Figure 8.38 Select the faces that will make up the top of the ATV.

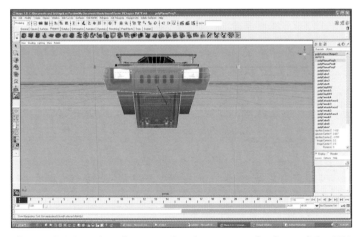

Figure 8.40 Project the Front view image onto the front of the ATV.

51. Now select the faces on the back of the body, below the fenders, and project the taillight image, as shown in Figure 8.41.

52. You will need two more materials, but you will be using colors instead of texture files. Bring up Hypershade and create a new material. Name the new material Black.

53. Instead of clicking on the Checkerboard icon to the right of the color slider, click on the gray solid square on the left side to bring up the Color palette.

54. Make a new Lambert material. This color needs to be a matte black, as in Figure 8.42; that is why you selected a Lambert material.

55. Move the color slider so the color square is completely black.

56. Create a new Blinn material.

57. For railing you will want a cool, light-gray color, so move the color selection toward blue and increase the value to lighten the color.

58. Set the Specular Roll Off and Eccentricity options as shown in Figure 8.43.

59. The unmapped faces other than the railing will receive the matte black material. Click on the ATV blanket material.

60. In Hypershade choose the Select Objects With Material from the Edit menu (see Figure 8.44). This feature will automatically select all mapped faces.

61. Hold down the Shift key and drag a selection box around the model to select all unselected faces.

62. Now unselect the railing faces and apply the black texture to the remaining selected faces, as shown in Figure 8.45.

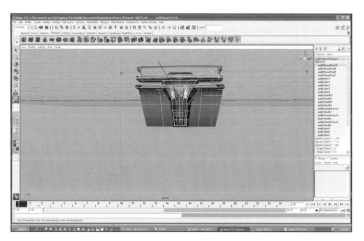

Figure 8.41 Project the taillight image onto the back of the ATV.

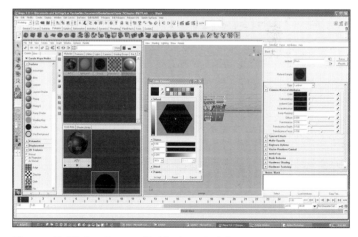

Figure 8.42 Create a matte black material.

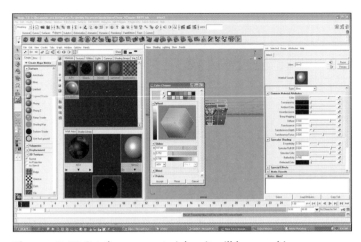

Figure 8.43 Set the new material so it will have a shiny appearance.

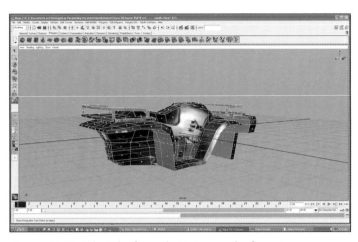

Figure 8.45 Select the faces that intersect the front tray.

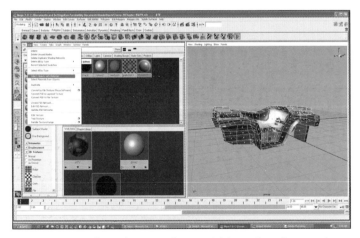

Figure 8.44 Select Objects With Material from the Edit menu in Hypershade.

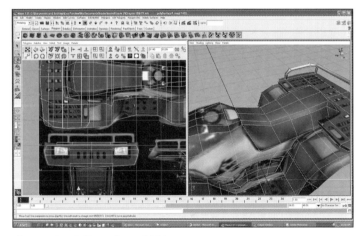

Figure 8.46 The adjusted UVs.

63. Select the rails and apply the gray material to them.

64. Soften the edges of the rails.

65. If you rotate the ATV, you will notice that there are some seams between projections. For example, the side images don't line up with the top images. You can use the UV Editor to adjust the UVs. Bring up the Two-Panel Side-by-Side view.

66. Change the left panel to the Panel > UV Editor in the Panels menu.

67. Change the selection type to UVs in the UV Editor.

68. Now you can use the Move tool to adjust the UVs so they match up with each other. Look at Figure 8.46 to see how I moved the UVs.

You now have the main body elements of the ATV. You still need to complete a lot of texture cleanup for the model, though. Go over the model in detail to fix any areas that have seams or don't look right.

Moving Parts

The ATV is meant to be an animated object. You must create separately the parts of the model that move so they can be animated. These parts include the handlebars, the rear struts, and the tires. You can start by creating the tires.

1. Create a cylinder with the attributes shown in Figure 8.47.

2. Select the inside center vertices and scale them in to form the shape of the tire rims. Also scale out the vertices along the center of the tire. Look at Figure 8.48 for reference.

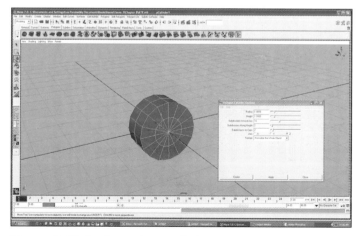

Figure 8.47 Create a polygon cylinder.

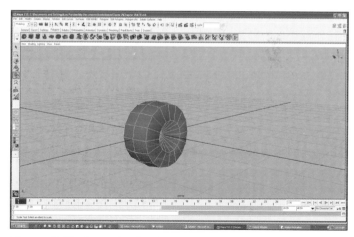

Figure 8.48 Shape the tire rims.

3. The texture for the side of the tire is located on the ATV blanket. Use the Planar Mapping tool to apply the texture, as shown in Figure 8.49.

4. Now we need to do the tire tread. From the Front view, select the four centermost faces and use the Planar Mapping tool to apply the ATV blanket material.

5. In the UV Editor, scale the faces to the tire tread area of the blanket, as shown in Figure 8.50.

6. Convert the Selection mode in the UV Editor to UVs.

7. Adjust the UVs to fit the shape of the texture, as shown in Figure 8.51.

8. Now rotate the tire 45 percent so that the next set of four faces is centered. Select these faces and project the texture to them.

9. Scale the UVs and snap them to the UVs already on the tire tread, as shown in Figure 8.52.

10. Continue repeating Steps 8 and 9 until the tire is complete (see Figure 8.53).

11. Move the tires into the wheel wells of the ATV, as shown in Figure 8.54. Duplicate the tire

as needed. Notice that the tires are small. I enlarged the front tires by 115 percent and the rear tires by 125 percent.

12. Now you will build the struts. Create a polygon cylinder, as shown in Figure 8.55.

13. Scale and move the vertices of the cylinder, as shown in Figure 8.56.

14. Now duplicate the faces of the cylinder and use it for the vertical strut. Rotate the duplicate and scale it, as shown in Figure 8.57.

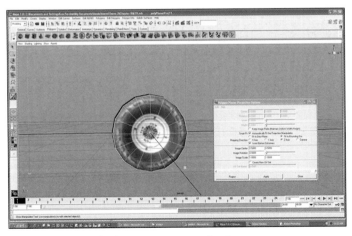

Figure 8.49 Apply the ATV texture to the tire.

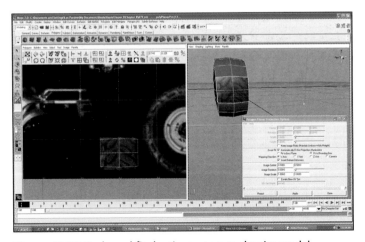

Figure 8.50 Scale and fit the tire texture to the tire model.

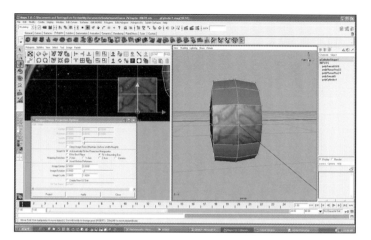

Figure 8.51 Move the UVs to fit the texture area.

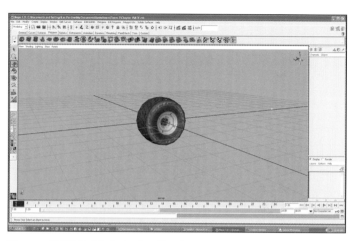

Figure 8.53 Finish texturing the tire.

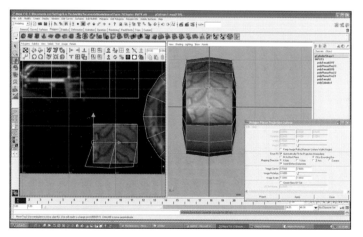

Figure 8.52 Move the UVs to fit the texture area.

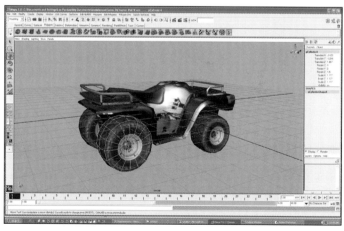

Figure 8.54 Place the tires around the ATV.

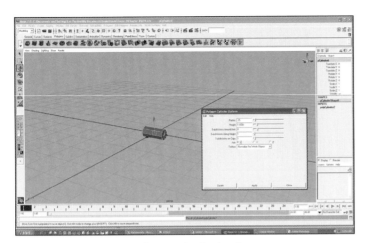

Figure 8.55 Create a polygon cylinder for the struts.

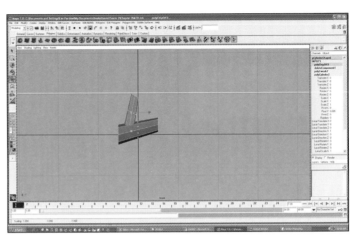

Figure 8.57 Create a vertical strut.

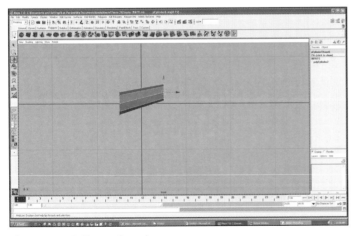

Figure 8.56 Shape the axle.

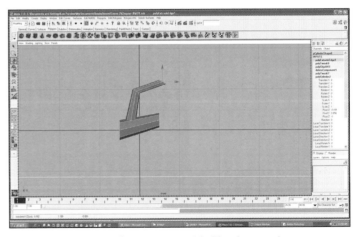

Figure 8.58 Create the struts as guided by the template.

15. Extrude the top of the duplicated cylinder's edges to form an additional horizontal strut, as shown in Figure 8.58.

16. Use the Planar Mapping tool to apply the ATV blanket to the struts.

17. In the UV Editor scale and fit the UVs to the struts on the blanket, as shown in Figure 8.59.

18. Place the finished model so it intersects with the wheel and the ATV, as shown in Figure 8.60.

19. Duplicate the struts and rotate them 180 degrees in the Y axis.

Move them over to the other wheel well, as shown in Figure 8.61.

20. Now for the handlebars. Hide all of the current models. Create a polygonal cube, as shown in Figure 8.62.

21. Snap the outside vertices on the top of the cube to the inside vertices. Figure 8.63 shows this process in action.

22. Repeat Step 21 for the bottom vertices as well.

23. Shape the cube to match the shape of the base of the handlebars. Refer to Figure 8.64 for an

example of how the model should look.

24. Create a small, single-polygon-per-side cube for the handlebars (see Figure 8.65).

25. Shape and place the cube, as shown in Figure 8.66.

26. Place the inside of the handlebars on the centerline, as shown in Figure 8.67.

27. Use the Mirror Geometry tool found in the Polygon menu to mirror the handlebar to the other side of the model, as shown in Figure 8.68.

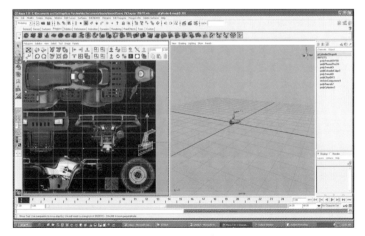

Figure 8.59 Apply the strut and axle texture to the model.

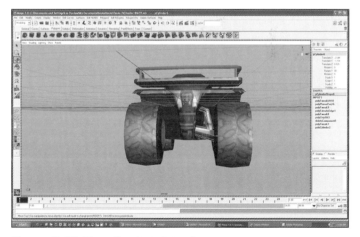

Figure 8.60 Move the struts into place.

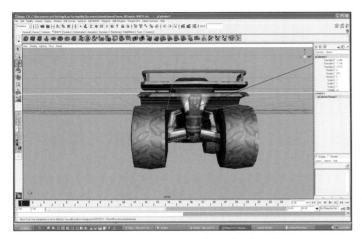

Figure 8.61 Place the struts in the other wheel well.

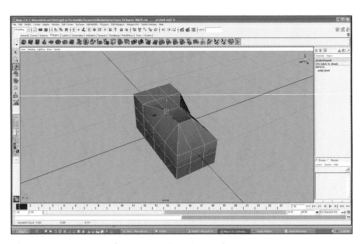

Figure 8.63 Snap the top vertices inward.

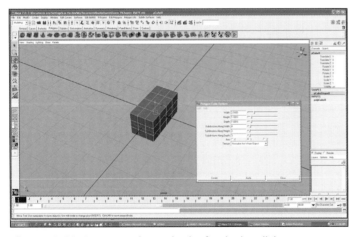

Figure 8.62 Create a polygonal cube for the handlebars.

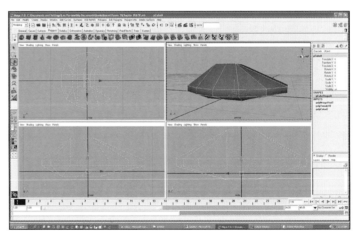

Figure 8.64 Shape the vertices to create the handlebar base.

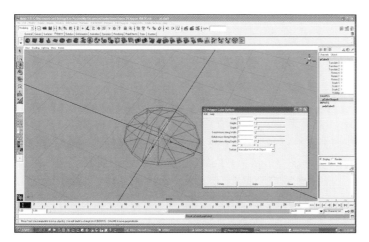

Figure 8.65 Create a new cube for the handlebars.

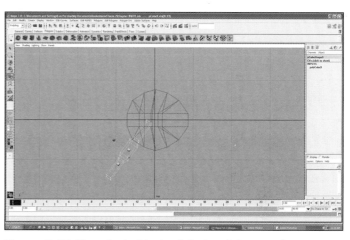

Figure 8.67 Place the inside tip of the handlebars on the centerline.

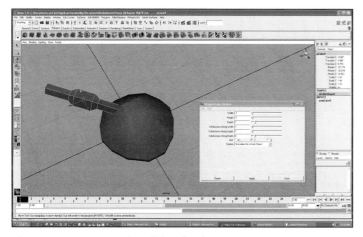

Figure 8.66 Create a handlebar for the ATV.

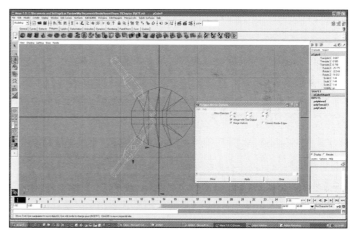

Figure 8.68 Mirror the handlebars.

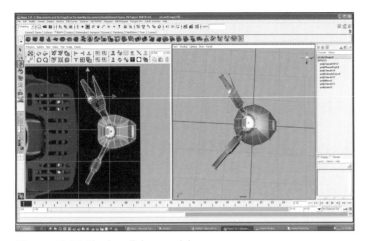

Figure 8.69 The handlebar model.

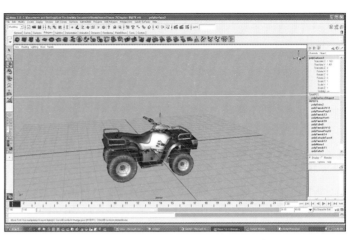

Figure 8.71 Move the handlebar unit to the top of the ATV.

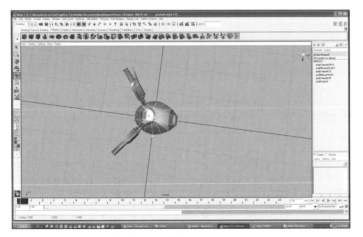

Figure 8.70 Reshape the handlebar unit.

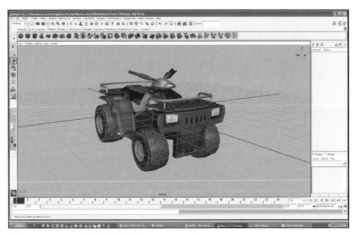

Figure 8.72 The finished ATV model.

28. Use the Extrude Faces tool to create a handbrake on the left handlebar.

29. Set up the texture using the Planar Mapping tool. Adjust the mapping in the UV editor. The model should now look like Figure 8.69.

30. Notice that the handlebar unit is too wide. Figure 8.70 shows how I narrowed it to better fit the actual shape.

31. Now move the handlebars into place, and you are done. The model should look similar to Figure 8.71.

Well that's it. The model is finished and ready to set up for animation. The tires, struts, and handlebars are all separate models and can be moved in the game to look like a real ATV in motion. Figure 8.72 shows the finished ATV. Your model should look similar to the model depicted.

Summary

In this chapter, I explained many important aspects of objects in games, including:

- Game objects versus environments
- Types of game objects
- Building game objects

This chapter also showed how objects are different from environment models. I indicated the reasons why you need to make objects separately. I also covered the different types of objects used in games. You then created a model of a game object. In this case, it was an ATV model.

Try to think of a scene from a game that you want to create. Make a list of all the objects that your game will need, and then practice making objects for your game.

CHAPTER 9

MODELING A HEAD

Now we are moving on to something a little more challenging, but if you have made it this far, you should be fine. What would games be without characters? This chapter will introduce creating characters for games. We will take it slow at first and only cover creating the head here. The next chapter will cover creating the body, and the one after that will cover animation.

Characters are the main focal point of most games. Whether they are the main character controlled by the player or an enemy character or maybe even just a bystander, they are scrutinized more than almost any-

thing on screen. This means that game characters should take more time and effort in their creation than many other elements.

In addition to being important if the character is human, there is even more pressure to do a good job because we are familiar with people. No one really cares if you move a branch on a tree a few feet up or down, but try that with an eye on a human character and everybody will notice.

Beginning the Model

Before you bring up Maya, you need to have an idea of what you want to

model. You should start with a good drawing of your character. On the CD is a drawing of a head from the front and the side. Use these drawings for this first example. Notice that they are exactly proportional to each other. They will be used to create a template

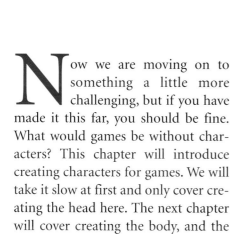

that will be our guide in creating the head. To be an effective template they have to be proportional.

It is always a good idea to create a template for each character you create. The templates help to make complex models easier to model because they form guidelines to place the 3D geometry. They don't solve everything, but they do help.

1. The first step will be to create the template in Maya. Create two planes exactly the same size, 10 units by 10 units square. The planes should only be one polygon each. Create one on the X axis and one on the Z axis. This will set them up so they are perpendicular to each other, crossing in their exact center.

2. Now create two new materials in Hypershade. Load the two drawings, one into each material.

3. Apply the drawing of the front of the head to the polygon plane facing the front view and the drawing of the side of head to the one facing the side view, as shown in Figure 9.1.

4. Create another plane that is subdivided into 8 polygons along the width and 20 along the height, as shown in Figure 9.2. This plane will be the basis for the model for the head. It is a little square right now, but we will fix that soon enough.

5. Go to the side. From here select the vertices and move them to follow the shape of the head, as shown in Figure 9.3.

6. Now go back to the front view and use the Scale tool to get the plane to take on the shape of the head, as shown in Figure 9.4. You will need to turn on X-Ray shading in the Panel's Shading menu to see the drawing.

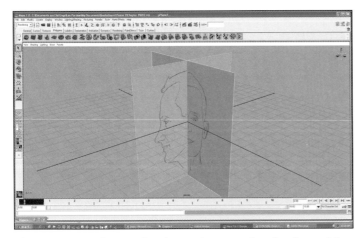

Figure 9.1 Set the two drawings to be a template for the model.

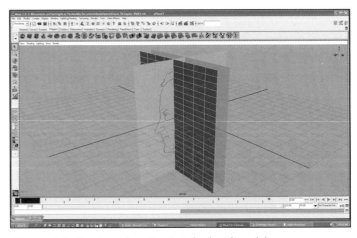

Figure 9.2 Create a plane to start the head model.

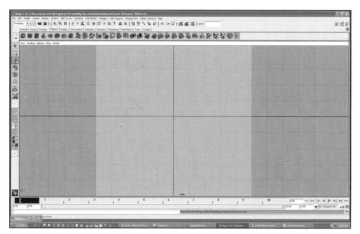

Figure 9.3 Move the vertices of the plane to follow the contour of the face.

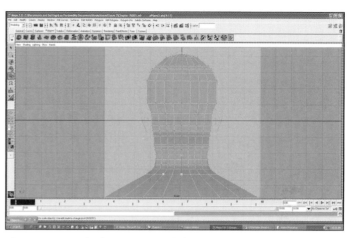

Figure 9.4 Scale the vertices to follow the shape of the head.

7. One easy way to make sure your model is exactly the same from left to right is to use the Mirror function. With that in mind, we will only model half of the face and then mirror the geometry to form the full face. Select the faces of half the plane, as shown in Figure 9.5 and delete them.

8. The next step will be to move the vertices to follow the features and contours of the face. Figure 9.6 shows the vertices

moved around the features of the face.

9. The nose will be a little tricky. Select the vertices to the side of the nose, as shown in Figure 9.7.

10. Move the selected vertices in the side view to fit the contour of the cheek, as shown in Figure 9.8.

11. Select all vertices except the top and bottom along the outside edge of the plane.

12. Use the Scale tool and pull the vertices into a vertical line in the side view, as shown in Figure 9.9.

13. With the selected vertices lined up vertically you can now move them to the center line along the Z axis, as shown in Figure 9.10.

The basic shape of the head is now formed, but the edge along the cheekbone and forehead is too sharp. It will need to be rounded to achieve the correct structure of the head.

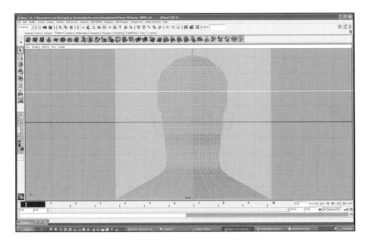

Figure 9.5 Select half of the faces of the plane.

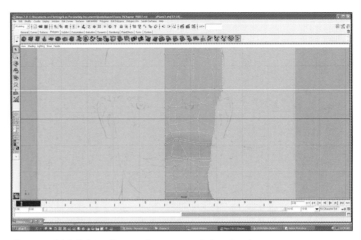

Figure 9.7 Select the vertices around the cheek.

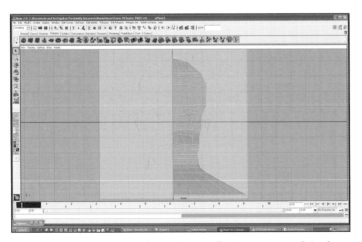

Figure 9.6 Start moving the vertices to fit the contours of the face.

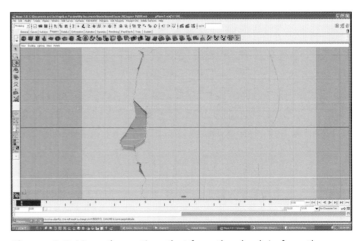

Figure 9.8 Move the vertices that form the cheek in from the contour of the nose.

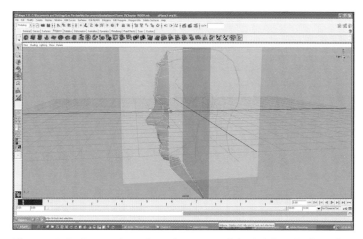

Figure 9.9 Line up the selected vertices of the left hand edge of the face vertically.

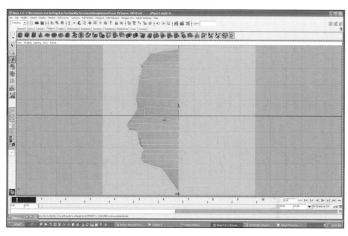

Figure 9.10 Move the vertices to the center line of the Z axis.

Fine-Tuning the Face

To make the face more natural looking, the vertices need to be moved so they fit the natural contour of the human head. Each vertex could be moved manually, but there is an easier way. Maya has a sculpting tool that will ease the vertices to something close to where they need to be. They can then be adjusted manually to fine-tune the model.

1. Activate the Sculpt Polygon tool found in the Edit Polygon menu by selecting the dialog box.

2. Choose the Smooth option. The Smooth tool will gently move vertices to smooth out rough edges.

3. Use the Smooth tool to shape the contours of the face, as shown in Figure 9.11.

4. Now the model is ready for some finer adjustments. Go to the front view and move individual vertices so they fit the features of the face, as shown in Figure 9.12.

5. Fine-tuning the model of the face is an interactive process. In some places, like around the eye, nose, and mouth, you will need to use the Split Polygon tool to create new polygons that more closely fit each feature. In other places, like the cheek area, you will need to merge vertices, as shown in Figure 9.13.

6. Continue to move, split, and merge vertices as needed. Figure 9.14 shows the model a little further in the process.

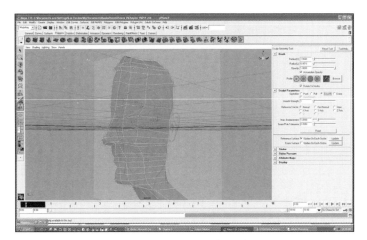

Figure 9.11 Smooth the sharp edges of the face.

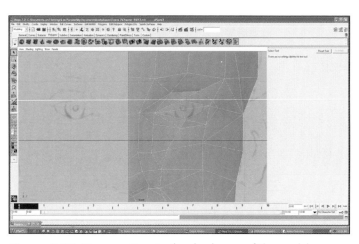

Figure 9.13 Merge vertices in the cheek area of the model.

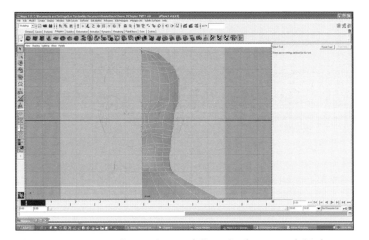

Figure 9.12 Move the vertices to follow the features of the face.

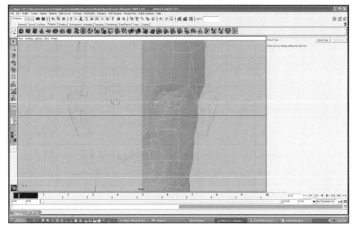

Figure 9.14 The model is conforming to the shape of the head.

Notice the polygons around the eye and mouth form concentric rings radiating out from the features. This is important to not only achieve the right shape but also in helping with facial animation.

7. After creating the polygons needed to create the features, you'll just need to move the vertices in the Z axis to their right positions. Go to the perspective view and adjust the vertices, as shown in Figure 9.15. For this process it is easier to turn off the X-Ray shading options.

8. Use the same procedure to refine the model along the jaw and neck as you did in the face. Figure 9.16 shows how the jaw and neck area are modified.

The face should now look natural. Check it against the template from the front, side, and perspective views. Make any adjustments that seem appropriate.

Interior Elements

Now it is time to build some of the interior elements of the model like the eye and mouth. This will enable the face to fully animate within the game. Let's begin with the eye.

1. Select the faces where the eyeball is and use the Extrude Face function to move the faces into the head forming the upper and lower lids of the eye, as shown in Figure 9.17.

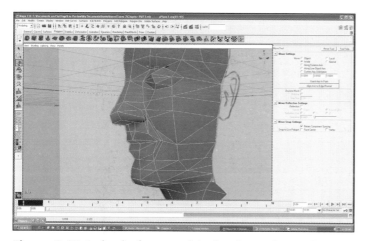

Figure 9.15 Sculpt the features of the face by moving vertices in the Z axis.

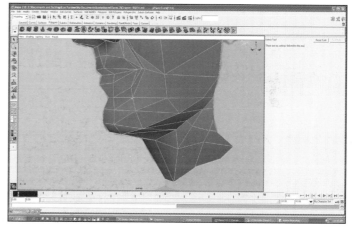

Figure 9.16 Refine the neck area of the model.

2. Delete the selected faces to remove them from the model and create a hole where we will later place the eye.

3. Move in close to the mouth. Right now it only has a polygon edge separating the upper and lower lips. To create the mouth cavity, we will need to split the polygons. Figure 9.18 shows how to do this. Notice that they are very thin.

4. Select the new faces and extrude them inward similar to the eye, as shown in Figure 9.19. Make sure to only move

the extruded faces in the Z axis. This is so the model mirrors correctly later in the process.

5. Switch the selection mode to vertex and move the vertices vertically to open the mouth cavity.

6. Now do one more extrude and move the faces further into the model to form the top, bottom, and back of the mouth cavity. Figure 9.20 shows how the cavity should look in Wire Frame view mode.

7. Select the faces on the inside of the mouth cavity, as shown in

Figure 9.21, and delete them because they will not be needed when the model is mirrored.

8. Now it is time to give this guy some teeth. Create a torus, as shown in Figure 9.20. Use the options shown in Figure 9.22.

9. From the top view, select all of the outside vertices and scale them inward, as shown in Figure 9.23.

10. Position the torus in the mouth cavity so that it occupies the position for the lower teeth, as shown in Figure 9.24.

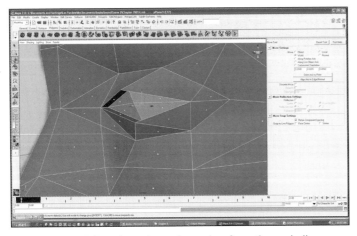

Figure 9.17 Select the polygon faces that form the eyeball.

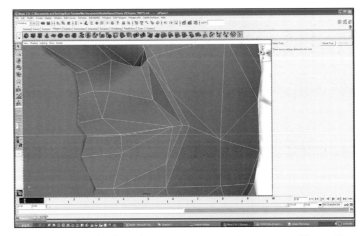

Figure 9.18 Split the polygons to separate the upper and lower lips.

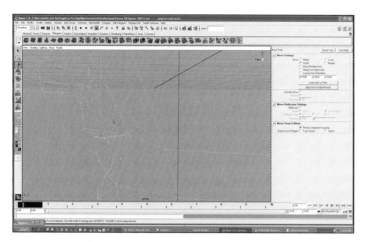

Figure 9.19 Extrude the faces along the Z axis.

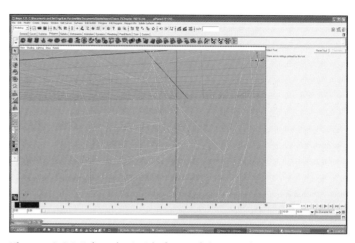

Figure 9.21 Select the inside faces of the mouth cavity.

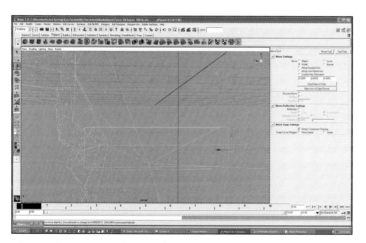

Figure 9.20 Create the mouth cavity.

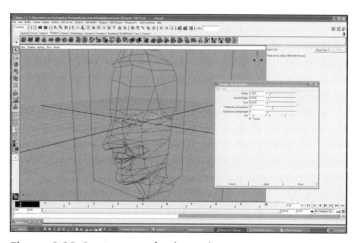

Figure 9.22 Create a torus for the teeth.

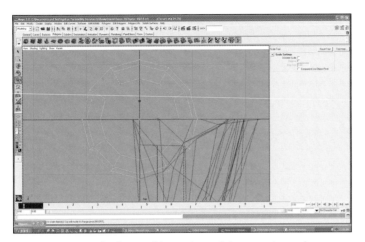

Figure 9.23 Scale the outside vertices of the torus inward.

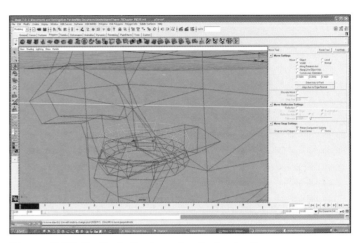

Figure 9.25 Duplicate the torus for the top teeth.

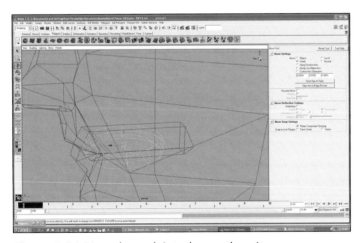

Figure 9.24 Move the teeth into the mouth cavity.

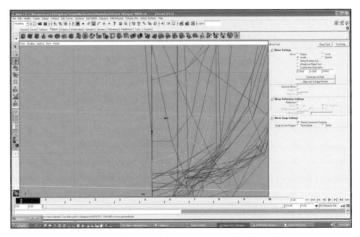

Figure 9.26 Delete the extra faces not needed for the teeth.

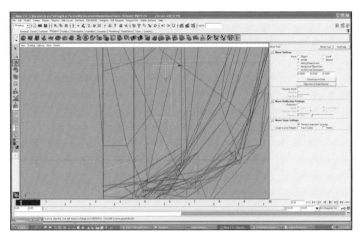 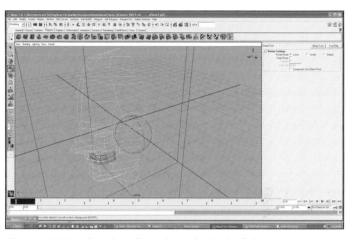

Figure 9.27 Move the edges of the back of the teeth toward the back of the mouth cavity.

Figure 9.28 Select the edges along the back of the model.

11. Duplicate the torus and move the duplicate up for the top teeth. The top and bottom teeth need to be separate so they can animate independently from each other. Figure 9.25 shows how they should look.

12. Only a quarter of the torus is really needed for the teeth so the rest of it can be deleted. Select 3/4 of the faces from the top view, as shown in Figure 9.26, and delete them.

13. Pull the back of the teeth back into the mouth cavity, as shown in Figure 9.27.

We will come back and create the eye and the tongue later. For now let's move on to forming the back of the head.

Creating the Back of the Head

For the back of the head we will be rotating the back edge of the model around the central pivot point. To make this work you will need to make sure the vertices along the inside of the face line up along the 0 X axis. You may have noticed in Figure 9.23 that one of the vertices of the head is out

of place. I had to snap it to 0 in the X axis before I could go on to this next step. If you have any stray vertices, you should do the same now.

1. First, select the edges for the back of the model, as shown in Figure 9.28.

2. To complete this next step, you will have to change the pivot of the selected edges. With the edges selected, press the Insert key while viewing from the Top view. Pressing the Insert key allows you to freely place the pivot point of the selected

object or component. Hold the X key down and move the pivot point to the X 0 and Z 0 position, as shown in Figure 9.29.

3. Press the Insert key again to lock the pivot point.

4. Extrude the selected edges and rotate them around the pivot point to form a section of the back of the head.

5. Repeat steps 2-4 rotating the extruded edges. You will need to do this about four more times to bring the edges even with the X 0 axis. Figure 9.30

shows how the model should look.

6. There will be several vertices at the pivot point of the extruded edges. These vertices need to be merged. Figure 9.31 shows the vertices selected. Merge these vertices.

7. Now to ensure that all of the vertices on the back of the head are lined up exactly on the X 0 axis, select the individual vertices and use the X key to snap the vertices to the X 0 axis, as shown in Figure 9.32. When

snapping a vertex in one direction, don't move it by clicking on the center of the Move tool. Click only on the arrow in the direction you want to move the vertex. Check your work in the Perspective view to make sure you didn't make a mistake.

8. Select all of the new vertices created for the back of the head in the side view.

9. Move the pivot point to the point of the selected vertices to 0 in the Z axis.

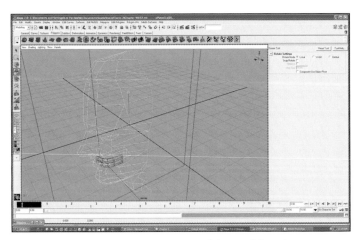

Figure 9.29 Change the pivot point of the model to the 0 point on the X and Z axes.

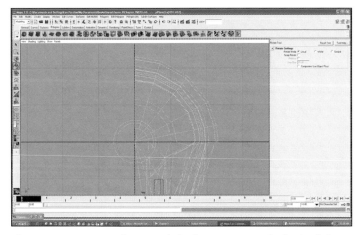

Figure 9.30 Rotate the extruded edges to create the back of the head model.

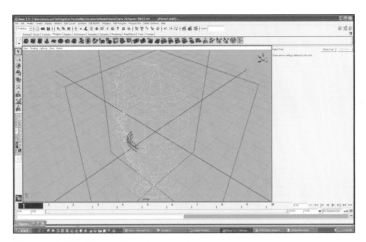

Figure 9.31 Merge the pivot vertices.

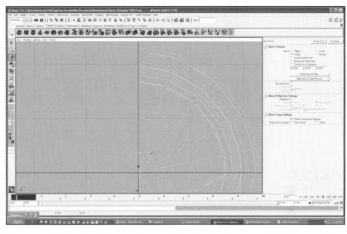

Figure 9.32 Line the vertices of the final extrude with 0 in the X axis.

10. Scale the selected vertices until they come close to the template, as shown in Figure 9.33.

11. Move the vertices of the head so they line up more precisely with the back of the head. The model should now look like Figure 9.34.

12. Select the faces at the bottom back of the neck, as shown in Figure 9.35, and delete them.

The model should now be very close to the final shape of the head. Examine it carefully to make sure it looks correct.

Creating the Ear

Right now the model doesn't have ears. Modeling a completely accurate ear is a very complex process that will take many more polygons than is normally available in a video game. Most video game models have simplified ears.

1. Split the polygons around the ear to follow the shape of the back of the ear, as shown in Figure 9.36. Use the template as a guide.

2. Continue to split polygons to follow the shapes of the inside of the ear.

3. Select the faces of the ear, as shown in Figure 9.37.

4. Extrude the ear faces twice, as shown in Figure 9.38.

5. Now select the faces within the ear, as shown in Figure 9.39.

6. Extrude the selected faces inward, as shown in Figure 9.40.

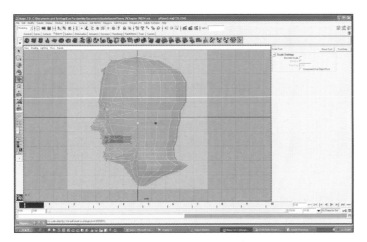

Figure 9.33 Scale the vertices of the back of the head to match the template.

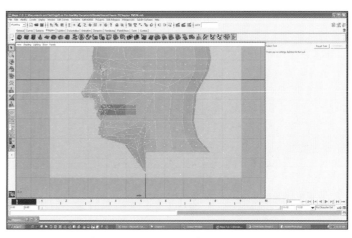

Figure 9.35 Delete the unnecessary faces in the neck.

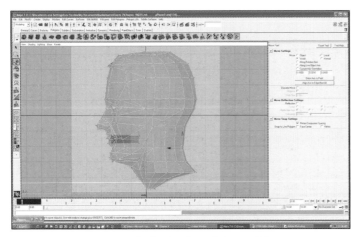

Figure 9.34 Fine-tune the back edge of the model.

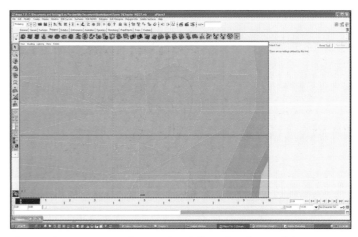

Figure 9.36 Create polygons that follow the shape of the ear.

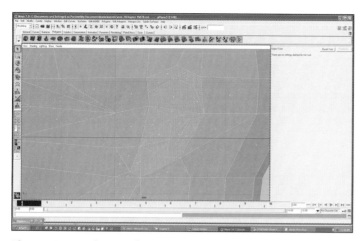

Figure 9.37 Select ear faces.

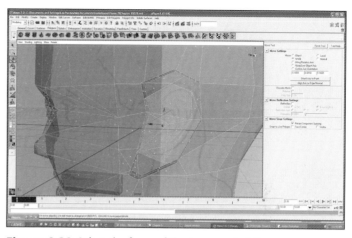

Figure 9.39 Select the faces of the inner part of the ear.

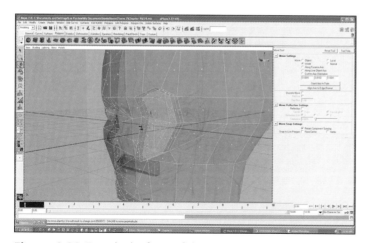

Figure 9.38 Extrude the faces of the ear.

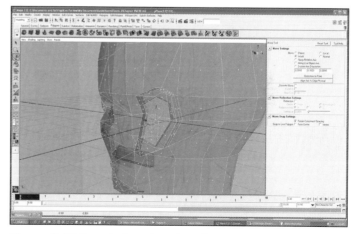

Figure 9.40 Extrude the selected ear faces in to create the outer ridge of the ear.

7. Merge the vertices of the front of the ear together, as shown in Figure 9.41, to create the correct transition from the head to the ear.

8. The vertices at the bottom of the outer ridge of the ear where it joins to the ear lobe also need to be merged, as shown in Figure 9.42.

9. Now select the faces of the inner ear and extrude them inward, as shown in Figure 9.43.

10. You now have a simplified ear. Move the vertices to shape the ear as well as possible. Use Figure 9.44 as an example of how it should look.

11. Select the vertices next to the head around the back of the ear and scale them in, as shown in Figure 9.45.

12. The ear should now look pretty close to a simplified ear. Make any adjustments needed. Use the template as a guide. Figure 9.46 shows the finished ear.

Finishing the Head Model

The head geometry is almost finished. The model should be looking like a 3D version of the original template. Now all that needs to be done is some work around the neck, as shown in Figure 9.47.

Check the model one final time to ensure it looks correct. It should now look similar to Figure 9.48.

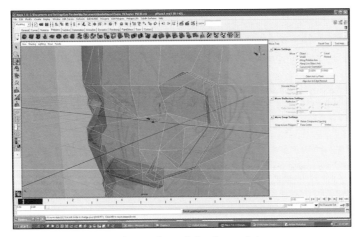

Figure 9.41 Merge the vertices of the front of the ear.

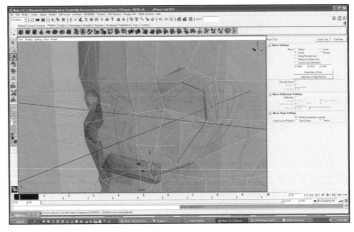

Figure 9.42 Merge the vertices at the bottom of the ear ridge.

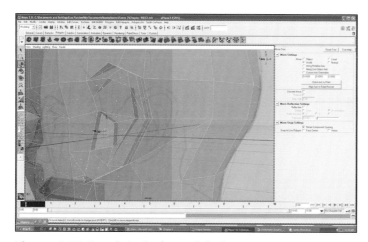

Figure 9.43 Extrude in the faces of the inner ear.

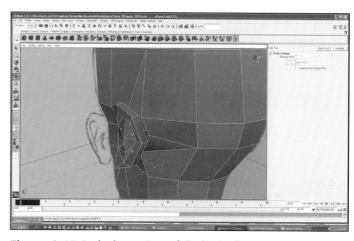

Figure 9.45 Scale the vertices of the back of the ear.

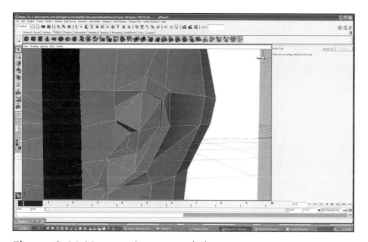

Figure 9.44 Move vertices as needed.

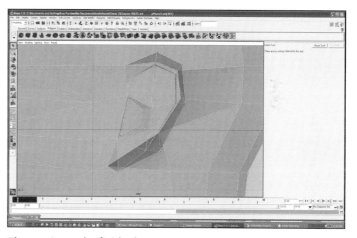

Figure 9.46 The finished ear.

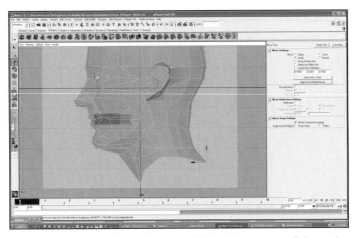

Figure 9.47 Move the polygons to follow the contour of the neck.

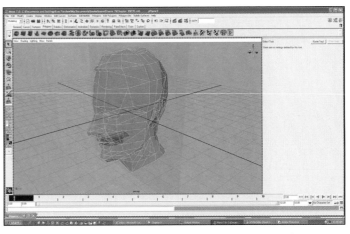

Figure 9.48 Check the geometry of your model against this picture.

The last elements that yet need to be built are the eyeball and the tongue. We will start with the eyeball.

1. An eyeball is basically a sphere. Create a sphere that has eight subdivisions around the axis and four along the height. Set the radius to .5. Refer to Figure 9.49.

2. Scale the sphere in the Z axis, as shown in Figure 9.50.

3. Place the sphere in the eye socket and adjust the vertices of the head as needed to close all gaps between the eyeball and the head. The eye should look like Figure 9.51.

4. Only the front of the eyeball is needed so the faces forming the back of the sphere can be deleted. Figure 9.52 shows those faces selected.

5. Create another sphere, as shown in Figure 9.53, to create the tongue.

6. Scale the sphere to form the shape of the tongue, as shown in Figure 9.54.

7. Delete the back faces of the sphere and move the remaining vertices through the back of the mouth cavity, as shown in Figure 9.55.

8. Delete the unneeded faces of the tongue, as shown in Figure 9.56, so the model will mirror correctly.

9. Next, combine all the objects into a single object by selecting all and using the Combine function, as shown in Figure 9.57.

10. Now the head can be mirrored. Use the Mirror function, as shown in Figure 9.58.

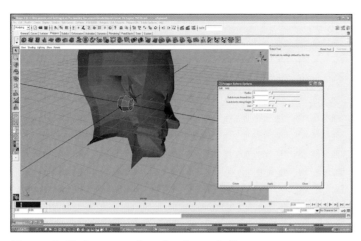

Figure 9.49 Create a sphere for the eyeball.

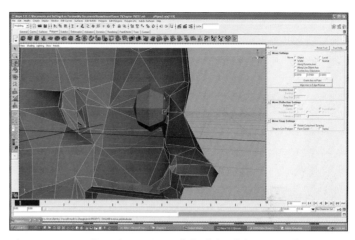

Figure 9.51 Adjust the vertices of the lids of the eye to fit the eyeball.

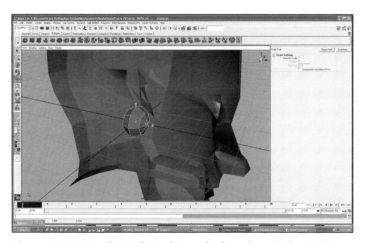

Figure 9.50 Use the Scale tool to scale the sphere in the Z axis.

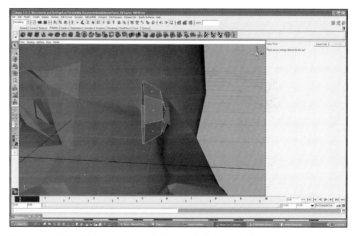

Figure 9.52 Delete the back faces of the eyeball.

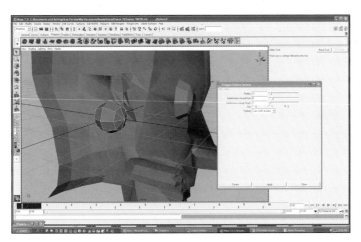

Figure 9.53 Create another sphere for the tongue.

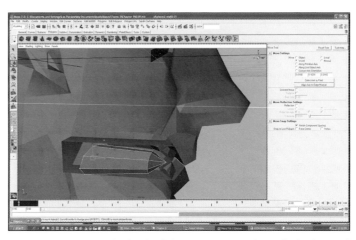

Figure 9.55 Have the back of the tongue pass through the back of the mouth cavity.

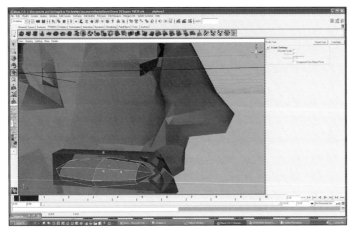

Figure 9.54 Use the Scale tool to form the basic shape of the tongue.

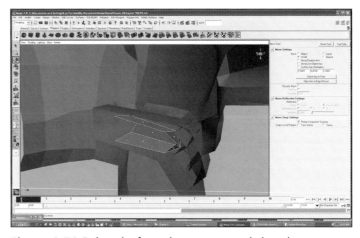

Figure 9.56 Delete the faces that are not needed on the tongue.

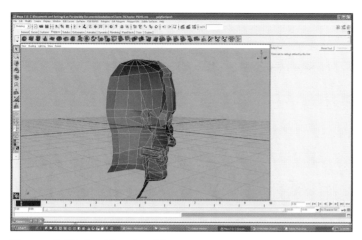

Figure 9.57 Combine the objects.

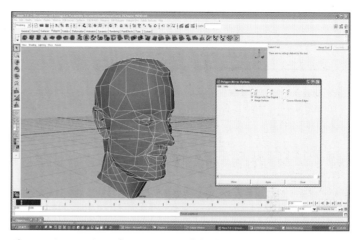

Figure 9.58 Mirror the geometry of the head across the X axis.

11. The head looks pretty good, but it doesn't look very smooth. Use the Soften/Harden Edge function to smooth the edges of the face. It is found in the Edit Polygon menu under Normals. Set the smoothness to 90, as shown in Figure 9.59.

There. You have just created a model of a human head for a game. It wasn't so hard, now was it? In the next chapter, you will learn how to create the body and apply a texture to it to create a finished character for a game.

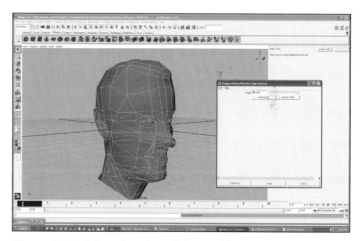

Figure 9.59 Soften the edges of the model.

Summary

In this chapter you

- Learned how to create a human head using a template drawing.
- Started with a simple polygon plane and from it made a complete head with detailed features built so that the head can animate correctly.
- Created eyes and a mouth complete with teeth and a tongue.
- Learned how to mirror your model.

CHAPTER 10

MODELING AND TEXTURING A CHARACTER

In this chapter you will learn how to texture the model of the head you built in the last chapter. From there you will go on to build the rest of the character and texture him. That is a lot to cover in one chapter, so we had better get started.

Texturing the Head

A texture map is an important part of building a character model for games. The textures add detail to the characters that is not possible with just geometry alone.

To create a good set of textures requires good 2D art as well as good mapping on the model. Let's first start with the mapping process and then go on to creating the texture.

Setting Up the UVs

Textures for games are limited by the amount of memory available for texture maps. Some game systems have more memory than others, but for the most part even the most powerful systems have limits on the amount of memory available for each character. Because of the limitations, it is always wise to make the best use of the texture space available.

In the last chapter you learned that you can mirror a model to save having to model both sides of a symmetrical model. The same thing is true for mapping.

1. Load the model of the head you created in the last chapter.

2. Select half the faces of the head from the front view as shown in Figure 10.1 Delete that half of the face.

3. We will need a base texture to set up the texture mapping for the model. The texture doesn't have to have any detail; it just

needs to be the correct size for the final map. In a paint program like Photoshop, create a black 512×512 pixel texture, as shown in Figure 10.2.

4. Load the new texture into Hypershade and label it "skin."

5. Apply the new texture to the model.

6. Maya has a mapping feature that automatically projects a material from multiple angles. This feature is called automatic mapping and it is located in the Texture submenu of the Edit Polygon menu as shown in Figure 10.3. Use this feature to set up the initial mapping of the head.

7. Change Hypershade in the left-hand panel to the UV Editor. Select the model to bring up the mapping of the texture. It should look like Figure 10.4.

Hint

The UV editor has several tools for manipulating UVs. These tools include UV flipping and rotation in the upper-right icon area of the tool. Just to the right of these tools are tools used to separate and join UV sets together. Roll the mouse over each tool to bring up the little text label for each. You will be using these tools to put this puzzle together.

8. The UV editor shows how the UVs for the model are laid out in 2D space. The editor can be used to adjust the UVs of a model to prepare for creating the texture. In a way it is like putting together a giant puzzle. Right-click on one of the edge lines in the UV editor and change the selection mode to UV.

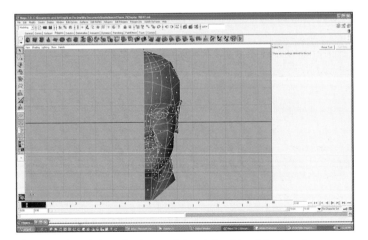

Figure 10.1 Select the faces of the right side of the head.

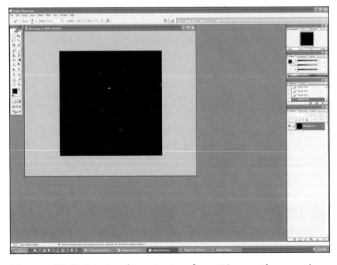

Figure 10.2 Create a base texture for setting up the mapping.

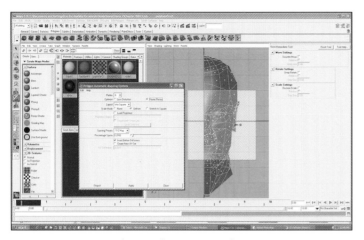

Figure 10.3 Set up the initial mapping with automatic mapping.

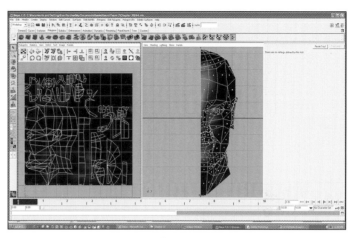

Figure 10.4 Bring texture in the UV Editor.

9. Select the UVs of some of the larger facial sections and use the Move tool to drag them to the side, as shown in Figure 10.5.

Hint

In the UV editor the UVs are split along edges. Where these splits occur the edge is shared. If you change the selection mode from UV to Edge and click on an edge as shown in Figure 10.6, the shared edge will also be highlighted. This feature is a great help in piecing the UV puzzle together.

10. A good UV map is a lot like the maps of the Earth in geography books where they flatten out the 3D globe into a flat 2D plane. Like the geography map, the UV map will have to have some distortions to get it into a 2D plane. Figure 10.7 shows the puzzle put together by arranging the UVs. The edges are welded together using the Move and Sew function found in the Polygon menu in the UV editor or you can also use the icon found in the shelf of the editor.

11. The remaining UVs not used for the face will be for the eye, teeth, and tongue. Figure 10.8 shows how they are arranged and pieced together.

12. The black area in the UV editor is the optimum area for textures. It is black because the material is black right now. Move and arrange the UVs to fit in the upper left-hand quarter of the black area. Save the rest of the area for the character's body. Figure 10.9 shows how the UVs for the face should be arranged.

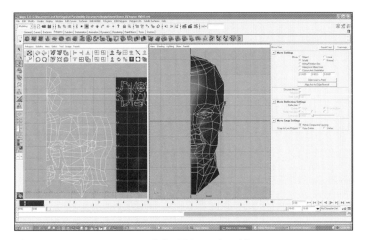

Figure 10.5 Move some of the UVs to the side.

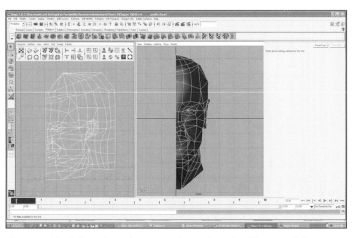

Figure 10.7 Sew the edges together using the Move and Sew function.

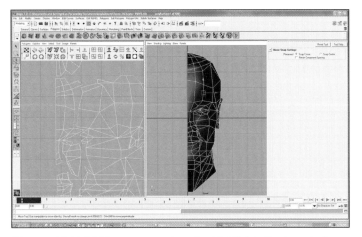

Figure 10.6 Clicking on one edge also highlights its shared edge.

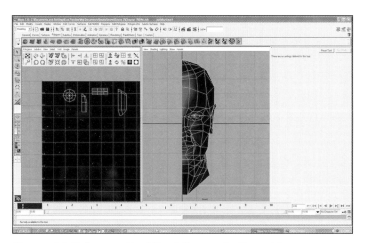

Figure 10.8 Arrange the UVs of the eye, teeth, and tongue.

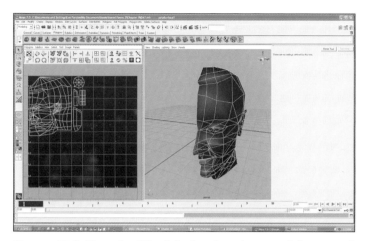

Figure 10.9 Move the UVs of the face into the upper-left corner of the texture area.

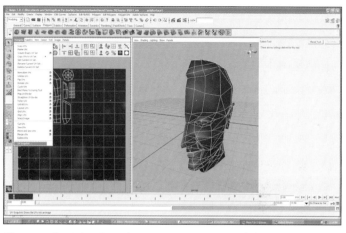

Figure 10.10 UV Snapshot saves a 2D image of the UV layout.

Creating the Texture

Now that the UVs are organized, you are ready to start creating the texture for your character. There are a couple of ways to paint textures for characters, both of which will be explained in this chapter. First we will explore using a 2D paint program for creating textures and then we will explore some of the texturing tools found in Maya.

There are many advantages to using a dedicated 2D paint program when creating textures for characters, not the least being that most artists are familiar with these programs and already know how to use them. For this exercise we will be using Corel Painter to create the textures for the head. Before we can work on the texture in the paint program, we need to save off an image of the UV layout.

1. Make sure the face is selected in Object mode. In the UV editor in Maya go to the Polygon menu and select UV Snapshot, as shown in Figure 10.10.

2. You can use the Browse function to set up where you want to save the file. Set the size to 512×512, as shown in Figure 10.11.

3. Save the file by clicking on OK.

4. Open Corel Painter and load the saved file. It should look like Figure 10.12.

5. Use the layout of the UVs to paint the character's head. Figure 10.13 shows the texture after painting.

6. When you feel good about your texture, save it and go back to the model in Maya.

7. Go to Hypershade and select the original black texture created at the beginning of this exercise.

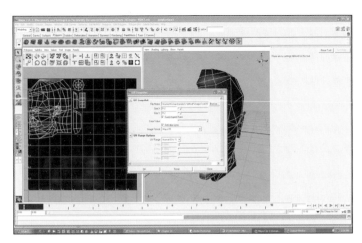

Figure 10.11 Set the UV size to 512 × 512.

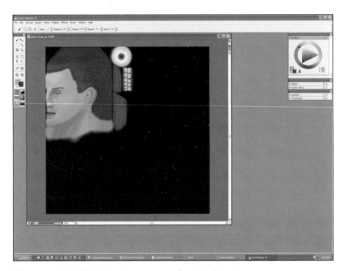

Figure 10.13 Paint the texture for the head.

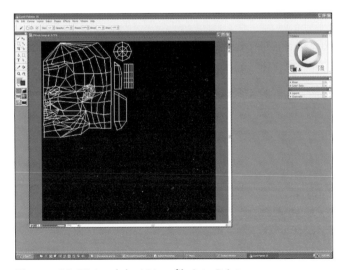

Figure 10.12 Load the UVout file into Painter.

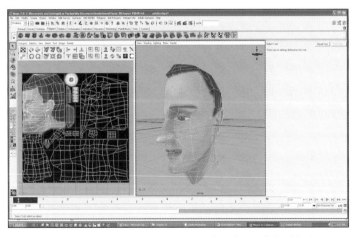

Figure 10.14 Load the new texture in the place of the black texture.

8. Open the Attribute editor and in the place of the black texture load the new texture that you just created. Notice that it matches the face. The texture should look like Figure 10.14.

9. Mirror the geometry once more to create the other side of the face.

10. Notice that there is a sharp edge down the middle of the character's face. This is because of the mirror process. Figure 10.15 shows the sharp edge.

11. Go to the front view and select the center edges, as shown in Figure 10.16.

12. Soften the edges using the Soften/Harden function under Polygon/Normals. Set the softness to 90.

Figure 10.17 shows the finished head.

Now the head is finished and you can go on to create the rest of the body.

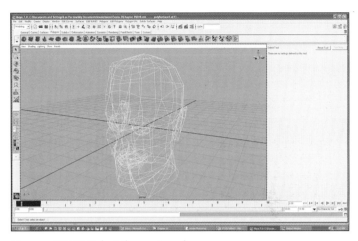

Figure 10.16 Select the center edges.

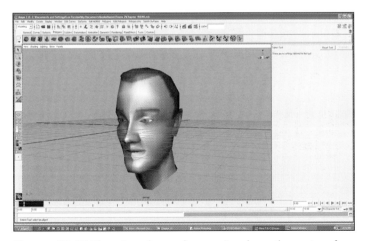

Figure 10.15 There is a sharp edge running down the center of the face.

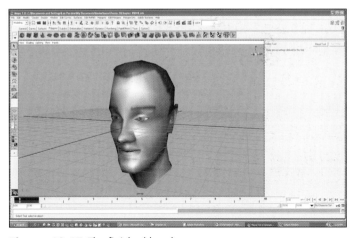

Figure 10.17 The finished head.

Building the Body

In this section you will finish building your character. You have the head, so now you need to build the rest of the body. You will also set up the textures and apply them to your character. For this example, your character is a powerful superhero that we will call Polyman.

Like the design of the head, the design of the human body is very complex and intimidating to beginning artists. However, it does not need to be as difficult a task as you might imagine. The key to building good characters is starting with a good drawing as a template. The drawing will define the character, so spend some time on your drawings. Mistakes in the drawing will transfer to the model. Figure 10.18 shows a simple line drawing of your Polyman character.

Notice that you have front, back, and side views of the character. You also have a top view of your character's arm. You need to set up your character's template a little differently from the other templates in this book. In this template, you need to have a front and a back view.

1. Create a single-plane polygon, as shown in Figure 10.19.

2. Translate the polygon .025 in the Z axis.

3. Now create another polygon the same scale as the first one.

4. Reverse the normal so it is facing the opposite direction of the first polygon.

5. Move the new polygon −.025 in the Z axis.

6. Create a third polygon the same scale as the first two.

7. Rotate the polygon 90 degrees on the Y axis. Your template set up should now look like Figure 10.20.

8. Now the polygons are set up for the textures. Create three new materials and apply them to the template. Use the character drawings found on the CD for Chapter 10. Apply the materials as shown in Figure 10.21.

9. Rotate the planes so that the front picture is facing forward and the back picture is facing backward, as shown in Figure 10.22.

10. Now you need to position the template for the arm. Move the arm plane up to about the center of the arm.

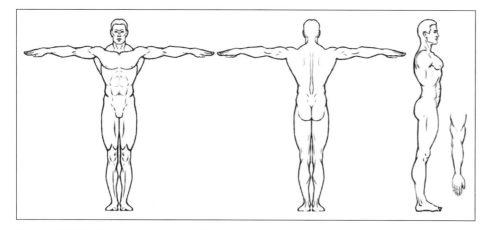

Figure 10.18 Make sure you start with a good drawing.

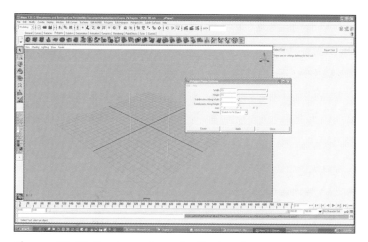

Figure 10.19 Create a polygon for the template.

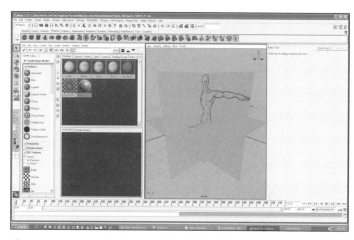

Figure 10.21 Apply the template textures to the template.

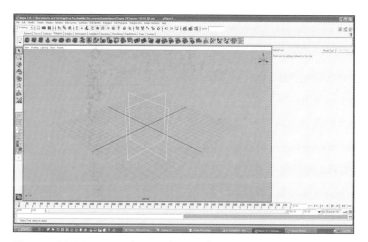

Figure 10.20 Create these polygons for the template.

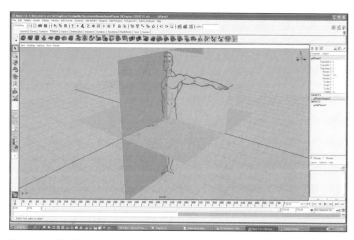

Figure 10.22 Rotate the planes around the Y axis so they are facing the right direction.

11. Rotate the arm so that it corresponds to the arm in the front and back views as shown in Figure 10.23.

Now that the template is in position, you can start to model your character. You will start with a simple polygon cube. From that box you will build the torso. Before you start, change the shading option to X-Ray to make it easier to see the templates through the geometry of the model.

1. Create a polygon cube of the dimensions shown in Figure 10.24.

2. From the side view, use the Move tool to line up the vertices with the major features of the character's body as shown in Figure 10.25.

3. Do the same thing for the back of the cube. The result should look similar to Figure 10.26.

4. We only want to work on part of the model at a time. Select the template for the front view and the front half of the cube as shown in Figure 10.27 and use Show/Isolate from the View Selected menu to isolate that part of the model.

5. Use the Scale tool to adjust the scale of the cube to fit the body, as shown in Figure 10.28.

6. Now isolate the back template and the back half of the cube. Scale the rows of polygons to fit the template from that direction. Use Figure 10.29 as a reference. Notice that the front of the torso is different from the back around the hip area.

7. You will see that the cube is starting to take the shape of a human torso. Like with the head, you don't need to build all of the body; you only need

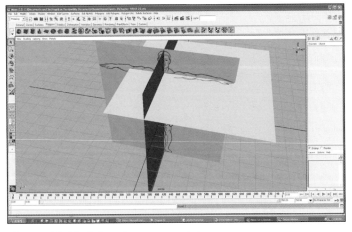

Figure 10.23 Adjust the arm template.

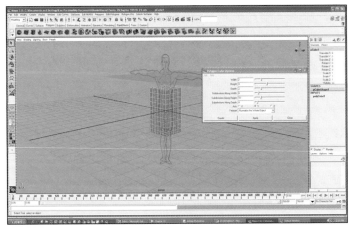

Figure 10.24 Create a cube for the torso.

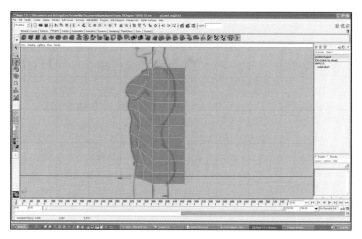

Figure 10.25 Move the vertices to follow the contour of the body.

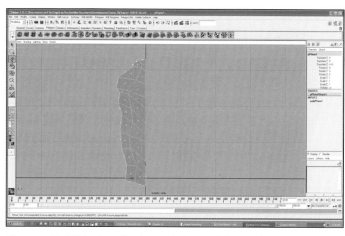

Figure 10.27 Isolate the front of the model to make it easier to work with.

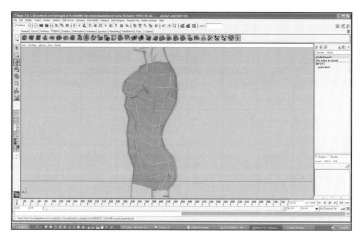

Figure 10.26 Move the vertices to line up with the back of the template.

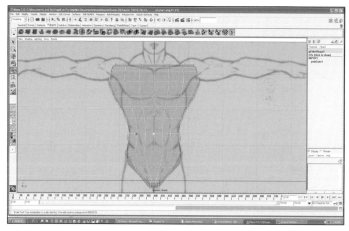

Figure 10.28 Scale the rows of vertices to fit the template.

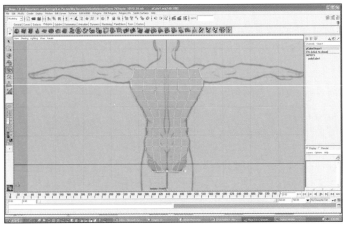

Figure 10.29 Scale the rows of vertices for the back.

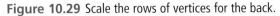

Figure 10.30 Delete the unneeded polygons.

to build half. You can mirror the model later. Delete the unneeded polygons, as shown in Figure 10.30.

8. Now you need to work on the edges of the cube. Select the vertices of the vertical corners of the cube and snap them to the first row of vertices on the sides of the cube, as shown in Figure 10.31.

9. Go through both corners, snapping vertices.

10. Once you have finished snapping the corners, select all the vertices of the model. Merge the

snapped vertices by selecting Merge Vertices from the Edit Polygons menu. Your model should now look like Figure 10.32.

11. Now use the Move tool to fine-tune your torso model. However, you only want to do it one side at a time. You need to get rid of the extra polygons so they will not get in the way. Select the front-facing polygons, as shown in Figure 10.33, and then select View Selected from the View menu. You also need to select the front-facing

template; otherwise, it will disappear, too.

12. Some of the vertices in the crotch area will need to be merged to follow the form. Figure 10.34 shows how they should look.

13. Split the polygons where needed the same way you did for the face in Chapter 9, so they give you the geometry you need to create the detail of the torso. When you're done, uncheck View Selected to bring back the hidden geometry of the back.

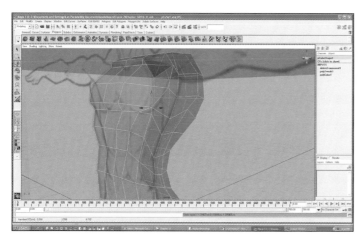

Figure 10.31 Snap the vertices of the corners to the first row on the sides of the cube.

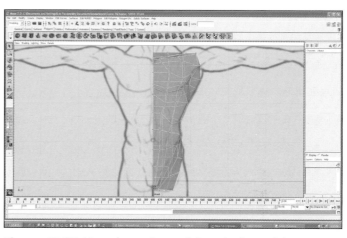

Figure 10.33 Move the vertices to follow the form of the torso.

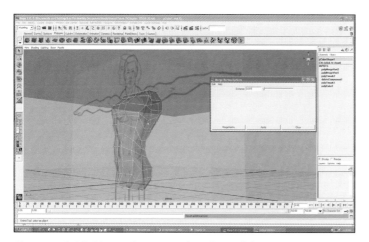

Figure 10.32 Merge the snapped vertices of the corners.

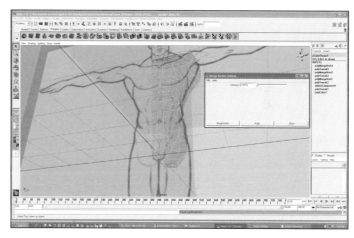

Figure 10.34 Merge some of the vertices in the crotch area.

14. Now isolate the polygons of the back and the back-facing template. Adjust the vertices to fit the back of your character, as shown in Figure 10.35.

15. Now go along the side of the torso and move the vertices to fit the contour, splitting polygons where needed. The model should now look similar to Figure 10.36.

16. Now you need to extrude the arm. Select the faces of the shoulder where the arm joins the body, as shown in Figure 10.37.

17. Extrude the faces then scale them in the X axis so they line up vertically, as shown in Figure 10.38.

18. Extrude the faces and scale them, as shown in Figure 10.39.

19. Continue extruding the faces to the wrist of the arm, as shown in Figure 10.40. Size the faces as you go.

20. Adjust the vertices from the top view to fit the template, as shown in Figure 10.41.

21. Next you need to create the legs of your character. You will be extruding the leg from the torso geometry. Select the faces, as shown in Figure 10.42. You will use these faces to extrude the leg.

22. Extrude the faces and move them down following the template from the front view. Use the Scale tool to adjust the faces, as shown in Figure 10.43. Scale the vertices in the Y axis so they flatten a little horizontally. This will create a better-animating hip area.

23. Extrude the faces again. This time, scale the faces so they flatten out perpendicular to the leg, as shown in Figure 10.44.

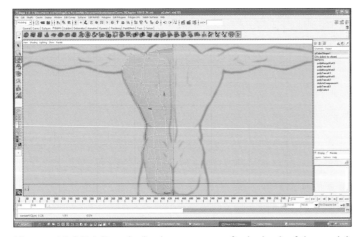

Figure 10.35 Adjust the back geometry to fit the back of the model.

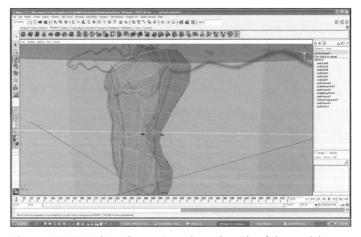

Figure 10.36 Adjust the vertices along the side of the model.

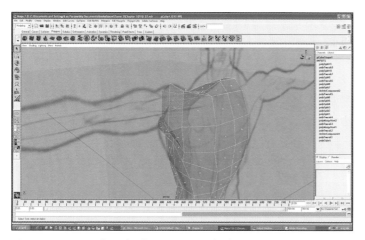

Figure 10.37 Select the faces to extrude the arm.

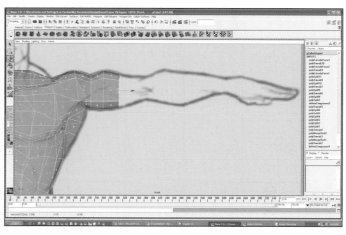

Figure 10.39 Start extruding the faces for the arm.

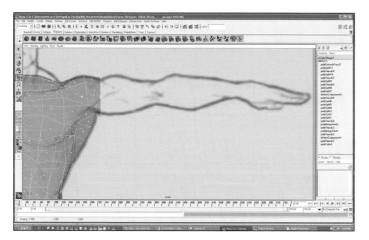

Figure 10.38 Line up the extruded faces vertically.

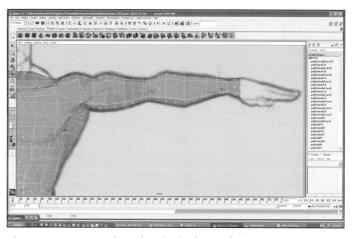

Figure 10.40 Extrude and scale the faces of the arm.

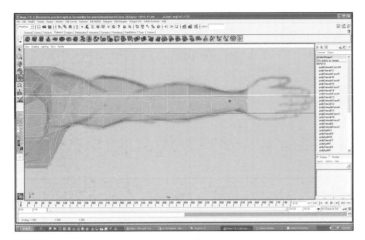

Figure 10.41 Adjust the vertices of the arm.

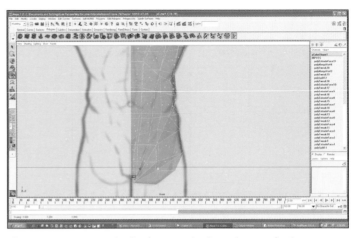

Figure 10.43 Extrude the faces and adjust them to fit the template.

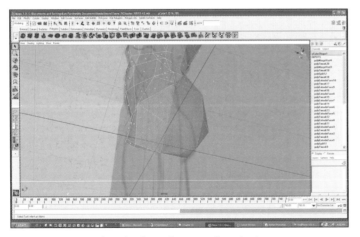

Figure 10.42 Select the faces for extruding the leg.

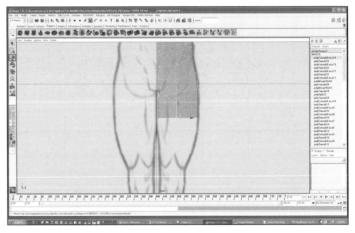

Figure 10.44 Extrude and adjust the faces of the leg to fit the template.

24. Continue extruding the faces until you reach the ankle, scaling them as you go (see Figure 10.45). When you are finished, delete the extruded faces on the end.

25. Change the selection mode to Vertices and from the side view, adjust the rows of vertices to fit the template, as shown in Figure 10.46.

26. Now shape the leg to better match human anatomy. Use Figure 10.47 as a guide.

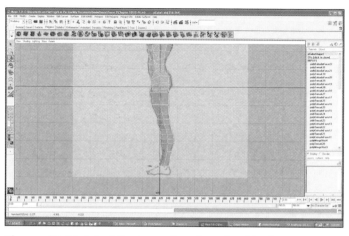

Figure 10.46 Adjust the leg vertices from the side view.

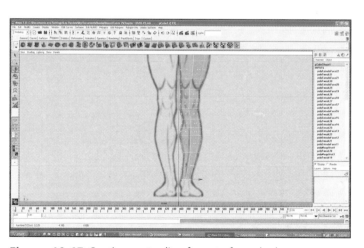

Figure 10.45 Continue extruding faces to form the leg.

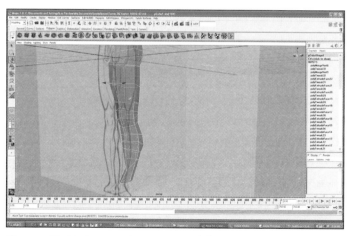

Figure 10.47 Arrange the vertices to follow the contours of the leg.

Building Hands and Feet

You now have the beginnings of the body of your superhero. You are missing only the extremities and the head you created earlier. In this next section you will create the hands and feet.

1. Now you will create the foot. Again, start with a polygon cube. Create a new cube, as shown in Figure 10.48.

2. Move the cube into position at the end of the leg as shown in Figure 10.49.

3. Move the vertices of the cube to match the shape of the foot from the side view, as shown in Figure 10.50.

4. Shape the foot to correspond to the template in the front view.

5. Hide the rest of the body so it will be easier to work on the foot. Your model should look similar to Figure 10.51.

6. You don't need so many polygons down the middle of the model (except for the toes). Snap the inside rows of vertices together, as shown in Figure 10.52.

7. Before we go on to creating the toes, you need to change one of your tool options in the Polygon menu. You need to turn off Keep Faces Together as shown in Figure 10.53.

8. Now you are ready to extrude the toes. Select the face of the toes, as shown in Figure 10.54.

9. Move the extruded faces out from the foot. Scale each toe in, as shown in Figure 10.55.

10. Extrude and scale the faces again to form the toes, as shown in Figure 10.56.

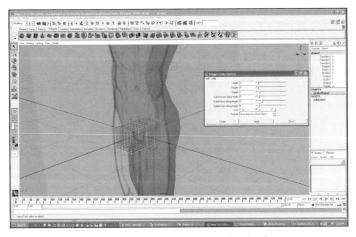

Figure 10.48 Create a new polygon cube for the foot.

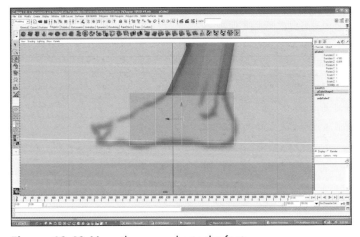

Figure 10.49 Move the new cube to the foot.

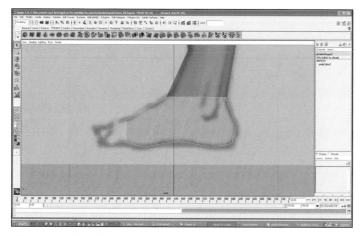

Figure 10.50 Adjust the vertices of the foot.

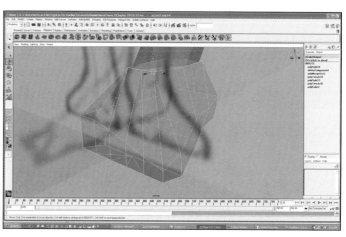

Figure 10.52 Snap the inside vertices together.

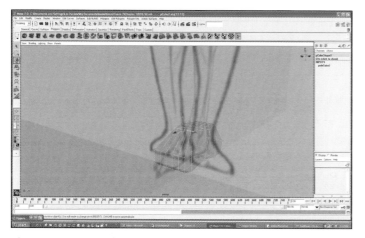

Figure 10.51 The foot model.

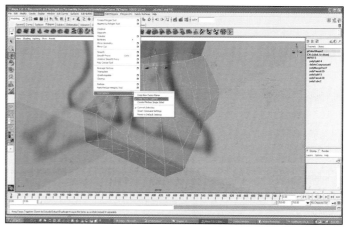

Figure 10.53 Turn off the Keep Faces Together tool option.

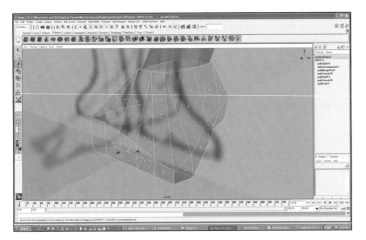

Figure 10.54 The faces of the toe are selected.

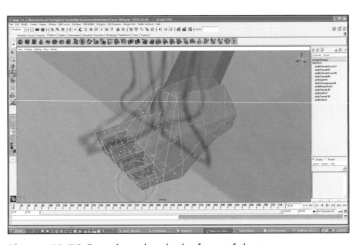

Figure 10.56 Extrude and scale the faces of the toes.

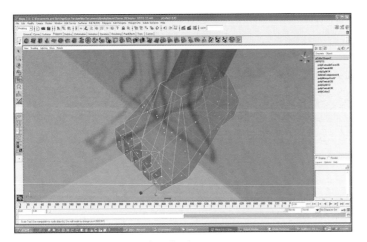

Figure 10.55 Extrude and scale the toes.

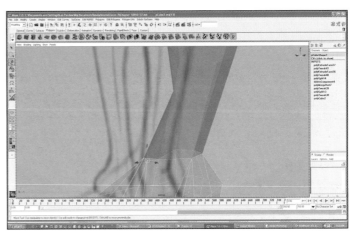

Figure 10.57 Attach the foot to the leg.

11. Now bring back the body model and attach the foot to the leg by first combining the objects and then merging the vertices. Snap the extra vertices together, as shown in Figure 10.57.

12. Give the foot one more pass, adjusting vertices to fit the contours of a human foot. The results should look similar to Figure 10.58.

With the foot modeled, the only thing left to finish on the character is the hand. Instead of building the hand from a separate piece of geometry like the foot, you will be extruding it from the arm. Before you can do that, however, you need to rearrange the vertices of the wrist so that they line up with each other vertically to resemble those shown in Figure 10.59.

1. Select the two faces that make up the wrist and extrude them to follow the contour of the hand as seen from the top view. The extrusions should follow those shown in Figure 10.60.

2. Move the vertices of the hand to better follow its contours, as shown in Figure 10.61.

3. Now go to the front view and adjust the vertices to match the contour of the hand from that direction, as shown in Figure 10.62.

4. The faces at the end of the hand will need to be split so you can extrude the fingers. Split the faces as shown in Figure 10.63.

5. Select the face that corresponds to the index finger and extrude it following the template as shown in Figure 10.64. You will need to scale the finger after each extrude.

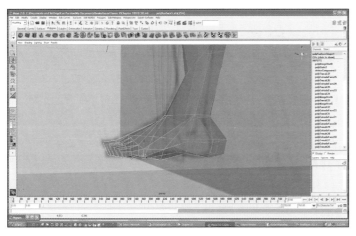

Figure 10.58 Do any fine-tuning necessary for the foot.

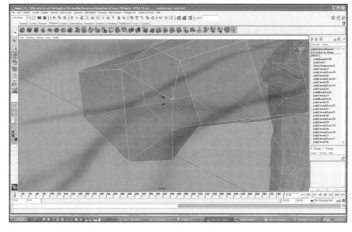

Figure 10.59 Rearrange the vertices of the wrist.

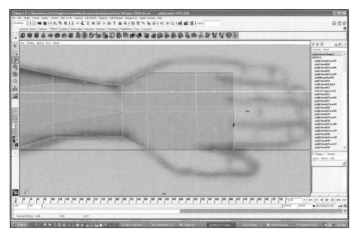

Figure 10.60 Extrude the faces to follow the shape of the hand.

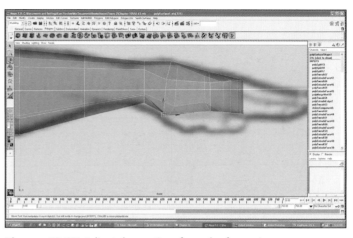

Figure 10.62 Adjust the vertices from the front view.

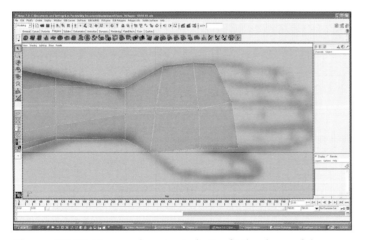

Figure 10.61 Move each vertex to better fit the shape of the hand.

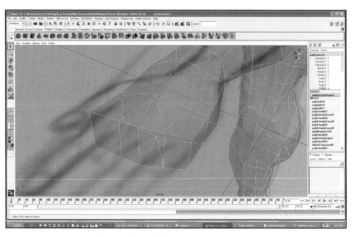

Figure 10.63 Split the faces for each finger.

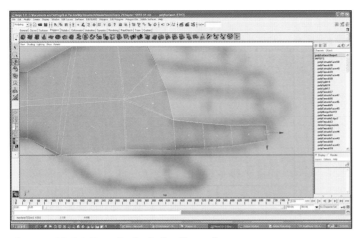

Figure 10.64 Extrude the index finger first.

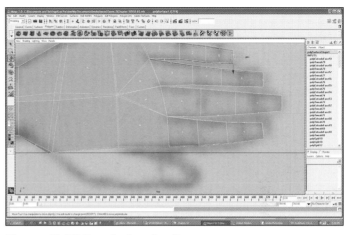

Figure 10.65 Extrude the other fingers.

6. Repeat the extrude process for each finger, as shown in Figure 10.65.

7. Next, extrude the thumb, as shown in Figure 10.66. Rotate the scale of the face as needed to follow the template.

8. Now adjust the vertices of the finger and the hand vertically to follow the contours of the hand. When you are done the hand should look similar to Figure 10.67.

9. Hide the templates so you can better view the model from a

3D perspective. Adjust any vertices that seem odd or awkward. Your model should now look similar to Figure 10.68.

10. Mirror the model, as shown in Figure 10.69.

Adding the Head

You now have a pretty good model of your character, Polyman. He is lacking a head, so you had better fix that. Import the head model you created earlier into the scene, as shown in Figure 10.70. Import is in the File menu.

Notice that the head is too large. You need to scale the head to the body and then attach it to the body.

1. Turn on the X-Ray view mode.

2. Scale and move the head to match the template, as shown in Figure 10.71.

3. Now scale the model to fit the template from the front view, as shown in Figure 10.72.

4. Move the vertices of the lower neck up to meet the model of the head, as shown in Figure 10.73.

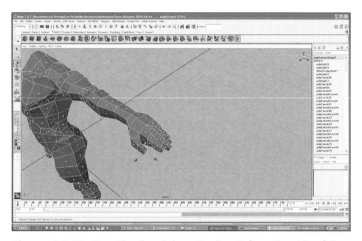

Figure 10.66 Form the thumb by extruding it from the side of the hand.

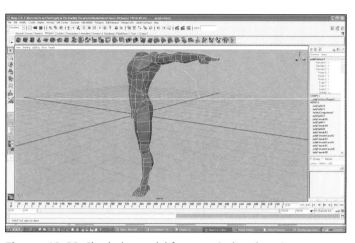

Figure 10.68 Check the model for any misplaced vertices.

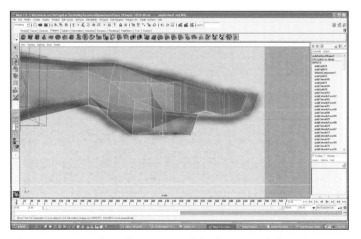

Figure 10.67 Adjust the vertices of the fingers to follow the template.

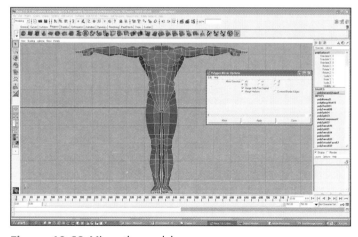

Figure 10.69 Mirror the model.

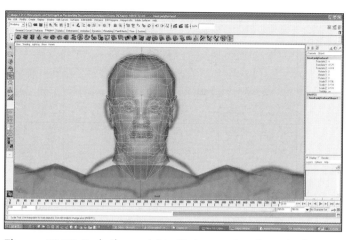

Figure 10.70 Import the head model into the scene.

Figure 10.72 Scale the model to fit the template from the front.

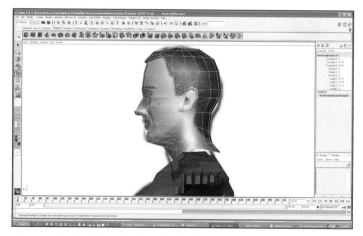

Figure 10.71 Scale the head to fit the template.

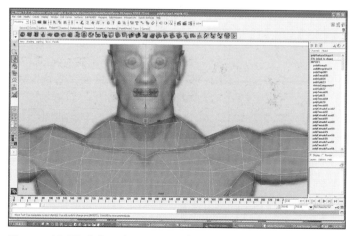

Figure 10.73 Adjust the vertices of the body to match those of the head.

5. This next step will be a little complicated, so I will take it slow. You need to combine the two models and attach the head to the body. The problem is that there are a lot more vertices in the head model than in the body at the point where the two attach to each other. Starting at the back and working your way around to the front of the model, begin snapping the vertices of the head model to the vertices of the body model, as shown in Figure 10.74. There will be more vertices on the head than the body so only snap those vertices that correspond to body. You will attach the other vertices later.

6. As you work your way around the back of the model, you will notice that there are problems with the way the two models match up. You need to split a couple of the polygons on the shoulders so they will match the head model.

7. You will also need to split the polygons for the front of the shoulders to match with the polygons on the head. You must split the shoulder polygons diagonally to follow the geometry of the head model. Use Figure 10.75 as a guide.

8. Now split the polygons again so they match with the vertices of the head, as shown in Figure 10.76.

9. Now snap the vertices of the head model to the body model, as shown in Figure 10.77.

10. The polygons of the body that are now covered by the head model are no longer needed

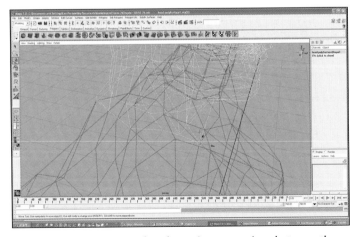

Figure 10.74 Snap together the major connections between the head and the body.

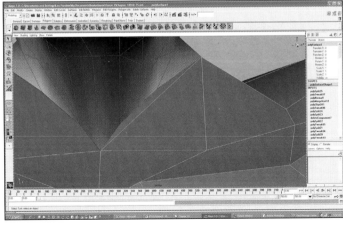

Figure 10.75 Split the polygons on the neck of the body model.

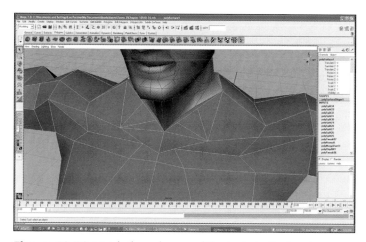

Figure 10.76 Match the polygons of the body to the head.

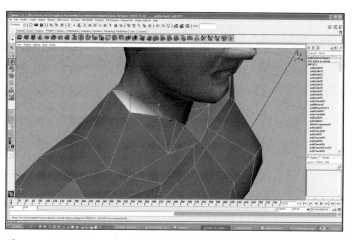

Figure 10.77 Snap the vertices of the head model to the body model.

and should be deleted. Move your view inside the character model in perspective view and delete these polygons.

11. Combine the two models and merge the vertices so you have one complete model, as shown in Figure 10.78.

UV Mapping a Character

You now have a character model. The polygon count of the model is approximately 2,500 polygon triangles, which is about right for many of the games on the more popular game systems today. Some games with multiple characters require characters with lower polygon counts, while others might let you have greater polygon counts. The number will depend on the game and the game engine.

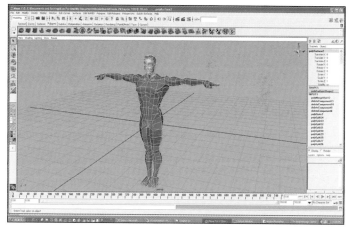

Figure 10.78 The finished character model with the head.

Your model is finished, but you need to do one more thing before you are done. You need to add textures to the body to make him into Polyman. Because our character will be symmetrical, we only need to texture half of the body. Delete the character's right side, as shown in Figure 10.79.

Creating the UV Map

Now you are ready to start setting up the UVs for the character. You will do this similar to how you pieced them together for the head earlier.

1. First apply the material to the model so all UVs are using the one texture blanket you created earlier, as shown in Figure 10.80.

2. Select all of the faces that comprise the body of the model.

3. With the faces selected, apply automatic mapping to arrange the UVs.

4. Now bring up the UV editor. The mapped UVs should look similar to Figure 10.81.

5. Change the selection mode in the UV editor to UVs and select all of the UVs for the body of the character.

6. Move the UVs to the side where you can work on them without interfering with the UVs of the character's head.

7. Start piecing the UVs together similarly to how you put the UV puzzle together for the head. Figure 10.82 shows how the UVs for the leg can be

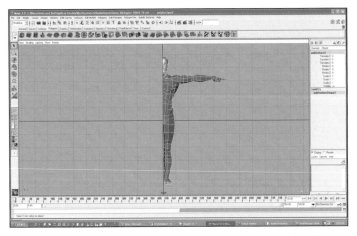

Figure 10.79 Delete the polygons on the character's right side.

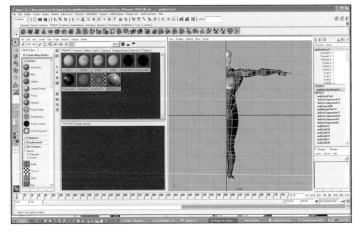

Figure 10.80 Apply the texture blanket to the model.

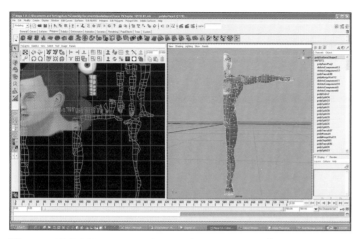

Figure 10.81 Use automatic mapping to arrange the UVs.

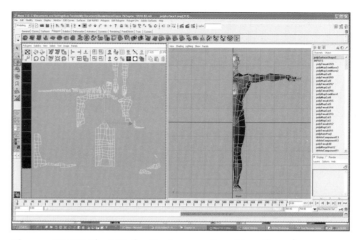

Figure 10.82 The UVs for the leg are pieced together.

pieced together. The body can be split into five major areas: the torso, leg, arm, hand, and foot.

8. Continue to put the UV puzzle together. When you have all the pieces of the puzzle put together, arrange them on the texture blanket. Your UV arrangement should look similar to Figure 10.83.

If you have made it this far, take heart. You are almost done. You only need to create the texture for the character to finish the model building.

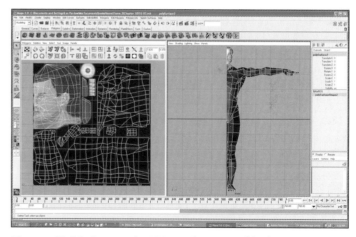

Figure 10.83 Arrange the UVs on the texture blanket.

Painting in 3D

When you created the texture for the head, you used a 2D paint program. For the body you will learn how to paint on your model using Maya's 3D paint feature. If you have ever built a plastic model and then used an air-brush to paint the model, you will find 3D painting to be very similar.

1. The first step for painting your model will be to mirror the geometry to give the character both a right and left side. See Figure 10.84.

2. Now set the menu mode to Rendering.

3. Bring up the 3D paint tool. It is under the Texture menu, as shown in Figure 10.85.

4. The 3D paint tool has a variety of spray modes and features. Figure 10.86 shows the tools in action applying paint to the surface of the torso. Click on color to bring up the Color palette. Change the color to a deep red as shown in the figure.

5. Start painting the model. Have fun. Add highlights to indicate muscles, as shown in Figure 10.87.

6. Continue painting the character until you have all the body

painted in red. He now has a red body suit. He should look similar to Figure 10.88.

7. When you create a 3D texture, Maya creates a directory in your current project directory called 3D textures and saves your work there. Go to that directory and bring up the texture in a 2D paint program like Photoshop.

8. You can now take the 3D texture and add any detail you want in the 2D paint program. In Figure 10.89 blue boots and gloves are added with gold trim. Also a blue and gold circle is painted on the character's chest.

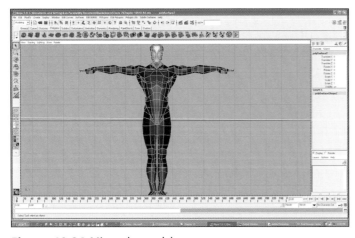

Figure 10.84 Mirror the model geometry.

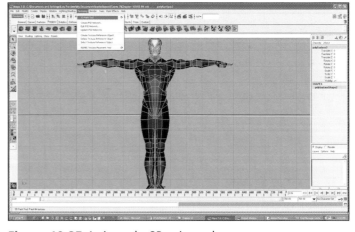

Figure 10.85 Activate the 3D paint tool.

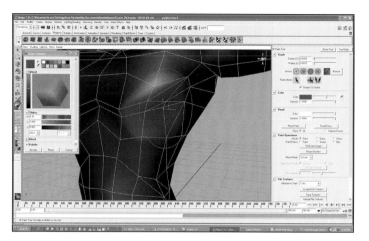

Figure 10.86 Start painting on the model.

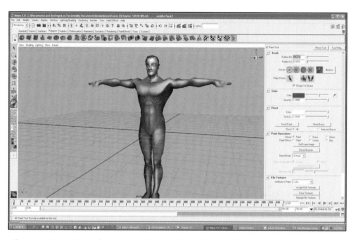

Figure 10.88 Polyman in his red full-body suit.

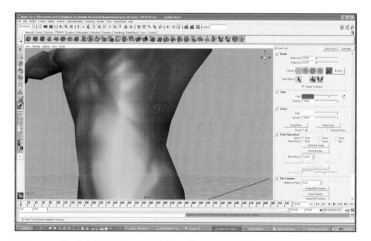

Figure 10.87 Paint the muscles of your superhero.

Figure 10.89 The 3D texture can also be painted in a 2D paint program.

There, you have finished the super hero character, Polyman. You should be proud of your effort. He should look similar to Figure 10.90.

In the next chapter, you will learn how to animate Polyman. Until then, enjoy the work you have just finished.

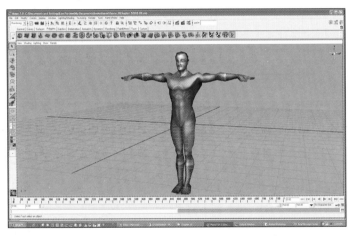

Figure 10.90 You are finished with the super hero character.

Summary

This was a complex chapter, so if you were able to follow all the examples, congratulations. You have just created your first game character. If this chapter was a little confusing or your model didn't turn out quite the way it should have, try going through the steps again.

You learned quite a few concepts in this chapter:

- Setting up UV sets
- Painting a texture using a 2D paint program
- Building the character's body from a basic cube
- Extruding arms and legs
- Building the character's foot and hand
- Importing the head
- Attaching and merging separate objects
- Painting in 3D

Now that you have completed your first character, try building a character of your own design. Perhaps create a villain character for Polyman to fight in your game.

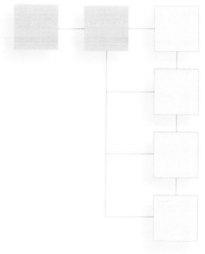

CHAPTER 11

3D ANIMATION

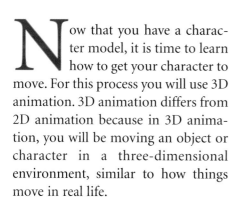

N ow that you have a character model, it is time to learn
how to get your character to
move. For this process you will use 3D
animation. 3D animation differs from
2D animation because in 3D animation, you will be moving an object or
character in a three-dimensional
environment, similar to how things
move in real life.

Before 3D graphics became popular
in games, all animation had to be
drawn one frame at a time in 2D.
With the advent of 3D graphics, a
whole new world opened for animators. Now they could create animation
in a 3D environment and view the
animation from any angle.
Animations became separate elements from the art, making it possible
to do one animation and apply it to
multiple characters.

How 3D Animation
Works in Games

Unlike 2D animation that is stored as
picture files in a game, 3D graphics
are stored as motion files. Motion files
can contain data on almost every
attribute of a 3D model, including
translation, rotation, size, color, and
many others. For this chapter you will
focus your attention on just a few
attributes because not all game
engines support the full range of
attribute animations.

First take a look at how animation is
controlled in Maya. From there, you
will work on understanding how to
get things to move around and react
in a 3D environment. Figure 11.1
shows the animation controls in
Maya.

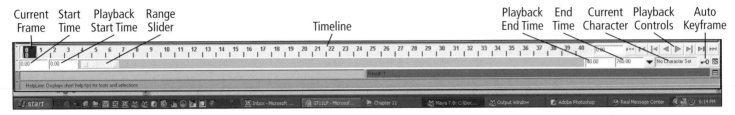

Figure 11.1 Maya's animation controls.

- **Current Frame.** Indicates the current animation frame that is shown in the view screen.
- **Timeline.** Shows in a visual sequence the available frames in an animation. The Current Frame indicator slides along the Timeline.
- **Start Time.** Indicates the beginning frame of an animation. Note that the start time does not need to be 1; it can be any number.
- **Playback Start Time.** Indicates the start time of a playback sequence.
- **Range Slider.** Shows the playback range of an animation within the total number of frames.

- **Current Time.** Indicates the current frame of animation.
- **Playback Controls.** Used to view animations or navigate through an animation. These controls are similar to the controls on a DVD player.
- **Playback End Time.** Indicates the last frame of the playback range.
- **End Time.** Indicates the last frame of the animation.
- **Current Character.** Shows what the current character is.
- **Auto Keyframe.** Indicates whether the Automatic Keyframe feature is turned on or off.

Ball Animation

Now that you know a little about the controls, take a look at how they work. You will start with a simple ball animation. In the top-left corner of the Maya display is a small drop-down box that contains the word Modeling. Click on the down arrow and scroll to the word Animation. This will bring up the animation menu set.

1. Create a polygon sphere, as shown in Figure 11.2.
2. You will animate the ball from the Front view. Go to the Front view.

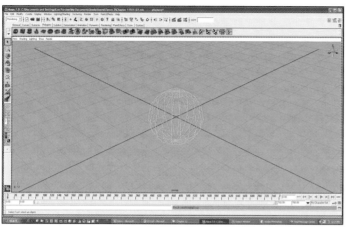

Figure 11.2 Create a polygon sphere.

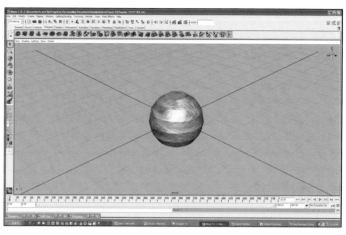

Figure 11.3 Give the sphere a texture.

3. The animation will be of a bouncing ball. Create a new material and load the texture1.bmp file found on the CD for Chapter 11.

4. Apply the new material to the sphere, as shown in Figure 11.3.

5. Move the sphere up and to the left in the view window. You will be creating an animation of a ball bouncing. The ball will fall from the upper left of the screen and bounce to the right.

6. Set a keyframe by choosing Set Key from the Animate menu, as shown in Figure 11.4.

7. Move the current frame to 6 on the Timeline.

8. Move the sphere to the position shown in Figure 11.5. We will use the thicker black line of the grid to represent the ground. This will be the first place that the ball hits the ground.

9. Now have the ball bounce several more times as it crosses the screen. Make the top of each bounce 6 frames from each impact of the ground. Also make each bounce lower than the next. Set a key for each position change you make.

10. Once you have finished, slide the time slider back and forth to see the motion of the ball. Adjust the path if needed by moving the time slider to the keyframe and moving the ball to a better position. Then reset the keyframe.

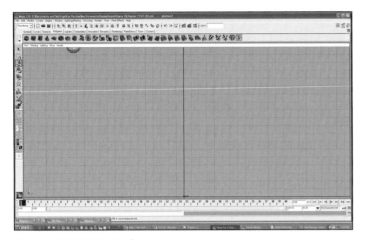

Figure 11.4 Set a keyframe.

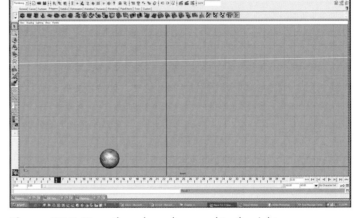

Figure 11.5 Move the sphere down and to the right.

Adding Dynamic Action

You have just created an animation of a bouncing ball, but the ball doesn't seem very animated does it? That is because there is no sense of impact when the ball hits the ground and there is no feeling of dynamics to the ball while it is in flight. In this section you will learn how squash and stretch helps bring life to a simple animation.

Squash and stretch is an old animation term referring to the exaggeration of impact and bounce in animated objects. We will start first by stretching the ball.

1. Start with a ball in the first keyframe. Select the ball.

2. Use the Scale tool to stretch the ball vertically and reduce it horizontally.

3. Now use the Rotate tool to rotate the ball so the stretch lines up with the path of the ball, as shown in Figure 11.6.

4. Adjust keyframe 5 to the same shape as keyframe 1 and set the keyframe.

5. Now flatten the ball at frame 6, as shown in Figure 11.7. Reset the keyframe.

6. Now play the animation. See how much more dynamic the first bounce looks than the other bounces of the ball?

7. Try adding squash and stretch to the rest of the animation. When you are finished, play the animation to see how it looks.

So far you have seen how to move an object. You also have seen how an object's shape can change in an animation. In the last example, you learned how to set keyframes and how to reset them after adjustments to an animation. Practice animating simple shapes until you become comfortable with the animation controls.

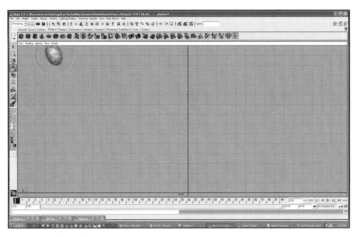

Figure 11.6 Stretch and rotate the ball.

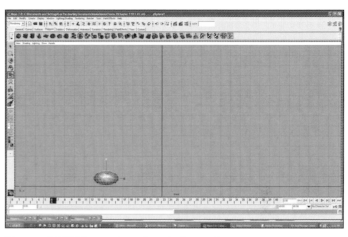

Figure 11.7 Flatten the sphere in frame 6.

Character Animation

Character animation is one of the most complex things an artist will come across when preparing art for games. The complexities can be overwhelming. In this chapter I have attempted to simplify the process so it will be easier to understand. I will be touching only the surface of all the controls and options for animating characters. Wherever possible, I will indicate where additional features are used, but it will be impossible to explain everything about 3D character animation in one chapter.

I want to start with your character that you built in the last two chapters,

so go ahead and load Polyman. Characters are many times more complex than spheres. Simple shape changes are not good enough to get characters to move correctly. To solve this problem, Maya and most other good animation programs have developed a system of joints and bones. These joints and bones work the same way that the bones and joints in your body work. In fact, studying your own skeletal structure is a good way to learn how to set up joints and bones in your characters.

Before you start, you will need to change the joint display size to fit your model. Maya has four default

sizes and a custom size. For this project, go into custom size and change the joint size to 0.1.

1. Go to the Side view and select the Joint tool in the Skeleton menu. Never place a joint while in Perspective view. Always use an Orthogonal view for placing joints.

2. Using the tool, click inside the hip area. Notice that a green sphere indicates the joint. The Joint tool works best in an Orthographic view. This is because when you are in an orthogonal view, the joints are

placed at 0 in the depth plane for whatever axis is perpendicular to your view.

3. Each time you make another click with the Joint tool, Maya will place a new joint in that position and connect the joints with a bone. Create several joints to make up the spine, neck, and head of the character, as shown in Figure 11.8. Press Enter to finish this first section of the skeleton.

4. Now go to the Front view and place joints in the shoulder and arm, as indicated in Figure 11.9.

5. Now we will connect the joints for the arm to the spine. With the arm joints selected, click on the joints of the spine shown in Figure 11.10.

6. With the two joint sets selected, press the P key. The P key parents the first selected joint set to the last selected joint set. Notice that the bones are shaped like cones, with the larger ends pointing toward one joint and the smaller ends pointing toward the other. The larger end indicates which joint

is the control joint over the bone. The control joint is called the *parent*. You will want the joint on the spine to be the parent joint and the joints of the shoulder and arm to be the child joints. Figure 11.11 shows the two joints connected.

7. Go to the Top view and use the Move tool to place the joints of the shoulders and arm, as shown in Figure 11.12.

8. Now you need to create the joints of the leg. Go to the Side view and center the screen over the character's leg.

9. Center the first joint of the leg in the hip area.

10. Place other joints for the knee, ankle, and foot of the character, as shown in Figure 11.13.

11. Go to the Front view and select the hip joint. Move the joint into the character's left leg.

12. Adjust the other joints to follow the model, as shown in Figure 11.14.

13. Make the bottom spine joint the parent of the joints of the leg.

14. Now you need to create joints for the hand. Go to the Top view and center the view over the character's left hand. Create joints as shown in Figure 11.15. You will not be making a separate joint for each finger. This is to keep the number of joints down. Many games have very strict limits on the number of joints for each character.

15. Go to the Front view. Notice that the joints of the hand are placed on the center point of the Y axis, as shown in Figure 11.16.

16. Move the joints up and place them in the hand, as shown in Figure 11.17.

17. Bring up the Mirror Joint tool from the Skeleton menu, as shown in Figure 11.18.

18. Like Mirror Polygon, the Mirror Joint tool mirrors across an axis. Set the tool to mirror across the YZ axes and make sure the Merge check box is checked.

19. Select the left arm joint just up from the spine. Click on Apply and the joints should mirror, as shown in Figure 11.19.

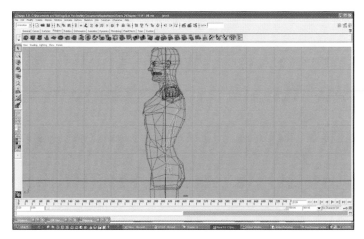

Figure 11.8 Place joints in the spine, neck, and head of the character.

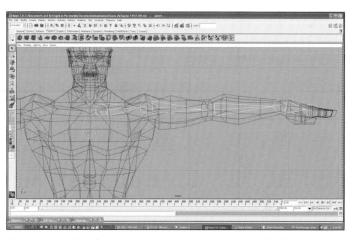

Figure 11.10 Select the spine joint to connect it with the arm.

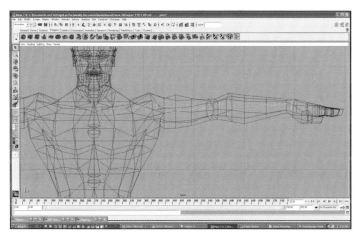

Figure 11.9 Create joints for the left shoulder and arm.

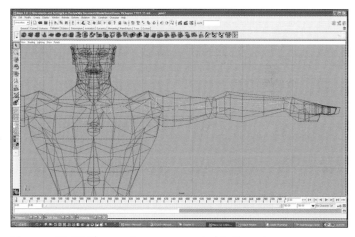

Figure 11.11 The arm is now connected to the spine.

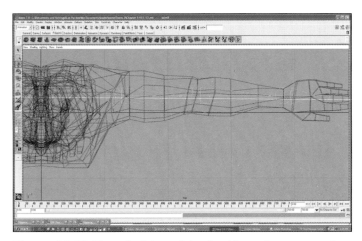

Figure 11.12 Move the joints of the shoulder and arm to match the model.

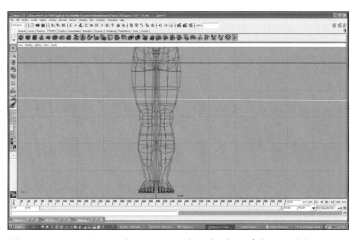

Figure 11.14 Center the joints within the leg of the model.

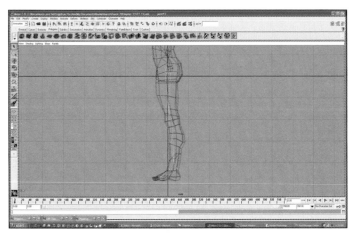

Figure 11.13 Create joints for the leg.

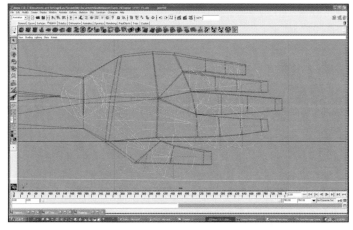

Figure 11.15 Create the joints for the hand.

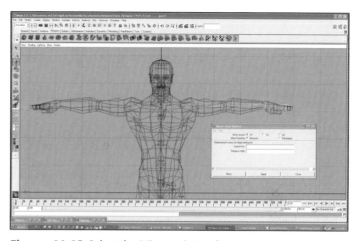

Figure 11.16 The joints of the hand need to be placed in the hand.

Figure 11.18 Select the Mirror Joint tool.

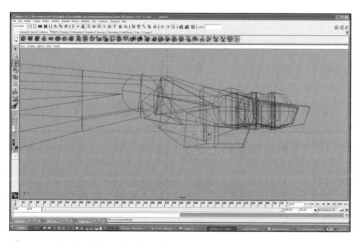

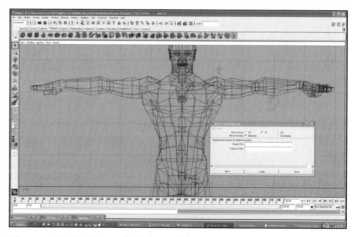

Figure 11.17 Place the hand joints in the hand.

Figure 11.19 Mirror the joints of the arm.

20. Now mirror the joints of the leg in the same way that you did the arm. You now have a complete skeleton for your model. It should look similar to Figure 11.20.

21. The joints of the skeleton need to be labeled to avoid confusion later. Bring up the Outliner from the Window menu and rename each joint. Use Figure 11.21 as a guide on how the joints should be labeled.

Skinning the Model

The next step in the process of preparing your model for animation is to attach the skeleton to the model. This process is called skinning. There are two types of skinning in Maya: rigid binding and smooth binding. For this lesson we will use smooth binding because most of the game engines support smooth binding, and it works much better for character animation.

1. First select the wire mesh of the model.

2. Now select the pelvis joint of the skeleton. Your screen should look like Figure 11.22.

3. Bring up the Smooth Bind dialog box and set the options as shown in Figure 11.23. Press Apply to skin the model.

4. The model is skinned, but it still needs some fine-tuning. The skinning process does most of the work, but if you try rotating the shoulder of the character, you will notice that there are some problems, especially under the arms. Press Ctrl+Z to bring the character back to the original pose.

5. You need to fix the skinning problems. You can do this in a number of ways, but the easiest is to paint the Skin Weights. When Maya skins the model, it assigns weights to each vertex.

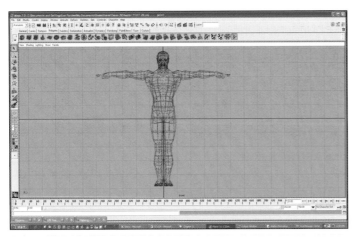

Figure 11.20 Mirror the leg joints.

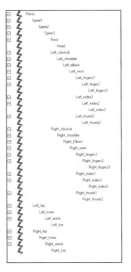

Figure 11.21 Label the joints in Outliner.

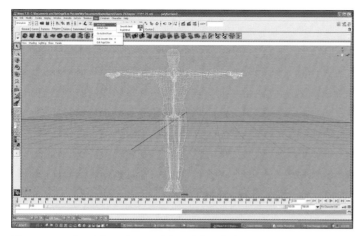

Figure 11.22 Select the model and the skeleton.

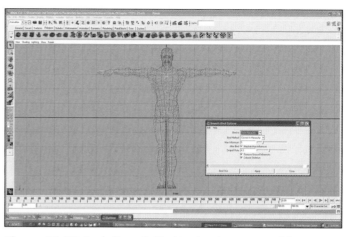

Figure 11.23 Apply Smooth Bind to the character model.

The weights are influences that a joint has over the vertex. If the weight is high for a given joint, when that joint rotates the vertex will move with the rotation. Select the wire frame mesh of your model and press the 5 key to change the shading option.

6. Bring up the Paint Skin Weights tool found in the Skin/Edit Smooth Skin menu, as shown in Figure 11.24.

7. The tool has several features to help you when painting weights. Notice that there are options for increasing the size of your Brush. There are also a variety of brushes that you can choose from. Notice also that there is a list of joints. Aren't you glad that you labeled your model's joints? Set the options as shown in Figure 11.25.

8. Start with the pelvis and apply weights to the pelvic area as shown in Figure 11.26. White on the model indicates a heav-

ier weighting and black represents a lower weighting.

9. As you paint, jump out of the tool from time to time to check how your weighting affects the model, as shown in Figure 11.27.

10. Work your way up the spine and to the head. When you get to the head, instead of painting all the vertices, go to the Side view and bring up the Component editor found under General Editors in the Window menu.

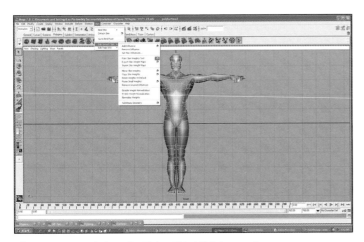

Figure 11.24 Select the Paint Skin Weights tool.

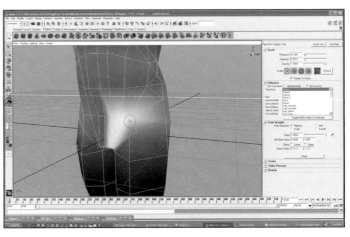

Figure 11.26 Start painting in the pelvic area.

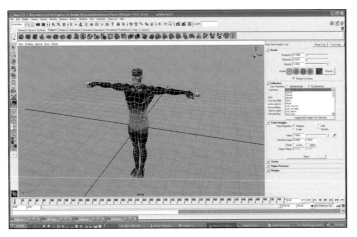

Figure 11.25 Set the options for painting skin weights.

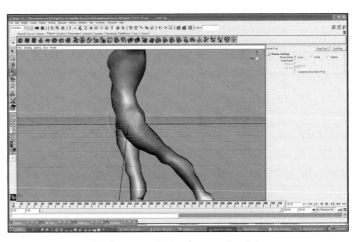

Figure 11.27 Check your painting by rotating joints.

11. Change the shading mode to wire frame and the selection mode to vertex.

12. Select all the vertices of the head, as shown in Figure 11.28.

13. In the Component editor, click on the Smooth Skin tab, then in the grid below, click on head. The column below head should now be black.

14. Now move the slider at the bottom of the Component editor all the way to the right. This will fully weight all the vertices of the head to the head joint, as shown in Figure 11.29.

15. Similar to other mirroring features in Maya, there is a Mirror Skin Weights feature in the Edit Smooth Weights menu, as

shown in Figure 11.30. You only need to paint the weights for the left half of the model. Once you have painted the weights on that half and they look correct, mirror the weights.

16. You can check the mirroring in the Paint Skin Weights tool. Figure 11.31 shows the weights mirrored across the body, with one of the spine joints selected.

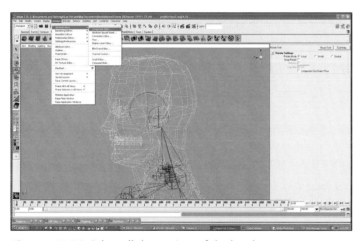

Figure 11.28 Select all the vertices of the head.

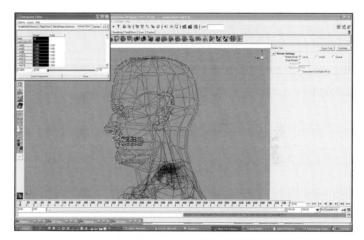

Figure 11.29 Use the Component editor to fully weight the vertices of the head.

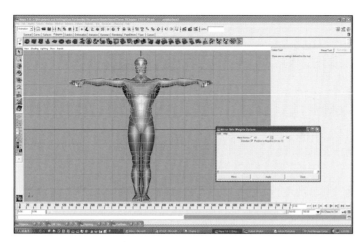

Figure 11.30 Maya has a Mirror Skin Weights .

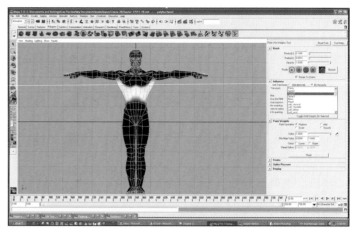

Figure 11.31 Check the mirrored weights in the Paint Skin Weights tool.

Adding Solvers

Maya has several ways to help make animating easier. One of these ways is to use Inverse Kinematics solvers. You will learn how to add these solvers to your model in this section.

1. Go to the Side view and select the knee joint of the left leg. Rotate the joint in the Z axis 10 degrees, as shown in Figure 11.32. This is to indicate to Maya what direction you want the knee to rotate.

2. Change to the Front view and select the left hip joint.

3. Now go to the Skeleton menu and select Set Proffered Angle, as shown in Figure 11.33, so Maya knows in what direction you want the joint to bend.

4. Go to the Skeleton menu again and select the IK Handle tool, as shown in Figure 11.34.

5. First click on the left hip joint and then on the left ankle joint.

Maya will place an IK solver on the left leg, as shown in Figure 11.35.

6. You will notice a small L-shaped handle near the ankle of the left leg. This is the IK handle. Use the Move tool to move the handle. See how the leg moves (see Figure 11.36). When you are done, press Ctrl + Z to return the foot back to where it started.

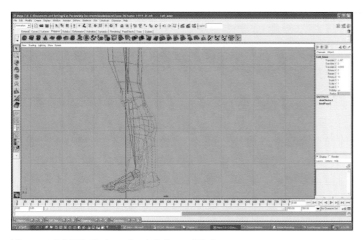

Figure 11.32 Rotate the left knee 10 degrees.

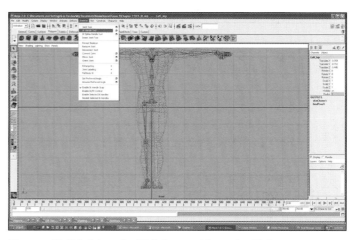

Figure 11.34 Select the IK Solver tool from the Skeleton menu.

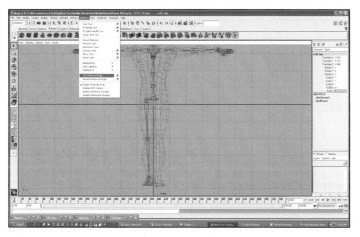

Figure 11.33 Set the Preferred Angle of the knee joint.

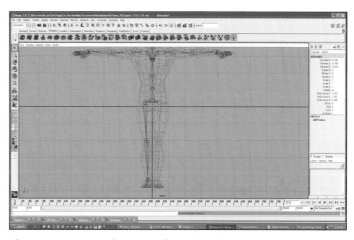

Figure 11.35 Use the IK Handle tool to place an IK solver on the left leg.

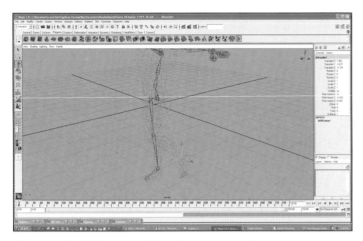

Figure 11.36 Move the IK handle to see how the Inverse Kinematics work.

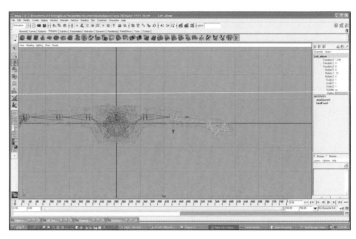

Figure 11.37 Rotate the left elbow −10 in the Y axis.

7. Select the left knee joint and rotate it back to 0 in the Z axis.

8. In the Top view, rotate the elbow joint −10 degrees in the Y axis, as shown in Figure 11.37.

9. Select the left shoulder joint and set the preferred angle.

10. Attach an IK solver to the left arm, as shown in Figure 11.38

11. Now use the same process to create IK solvers for the right leg and right arm.

12. Bring up the Hypergraph and select the pelvis joint.

13. Create a new group by selecting Group from the Edit menu, as shown in Figure 11.39. Label the new group IK Group.

14. Select the four IK solvers in Hypergraph and then select the IK Group. Parent the IK solvers to the Group. This grouping will make it so that moving the pelvis will not move the feet and hands. We can use the IK Group when we want to move the entire model. Hypergraph should now look like Figure 11.40.

You now have a model rigged with joints and solvers ready to animate. I know it was a long process, but believe me, this is much easier than trying to animate vertices like we did with the ball. Your finished rigged model should look similar to Figure 11.41.

Save this version of your model. This will be your base model from which you can create several animations.

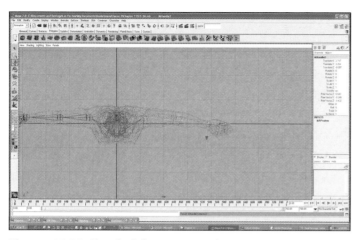

Figure 11.38 Give the left arm an IK solver.

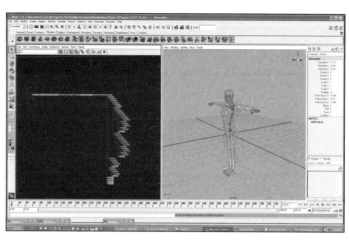

Figure 11.40 Parent the IK solvers to the IK Group.

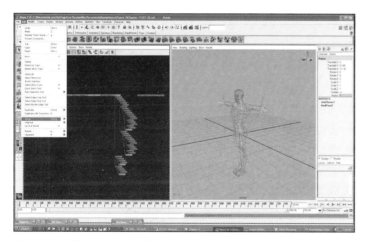

Figure 11.39 Create an IK Group.

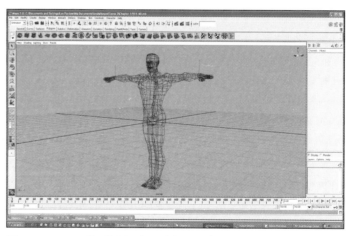

Figure 11.41 The finished model is ready to animate.

Animating Polyman

You are now ready to animate your first game character. I hope you are excited. Character animation is an art form in and of itself. Good animators are hard to find and it takes years to learn how to do it correctly. This section will help get you started.

If you haven't already got him up, load Polyman into Maya. Now before you go any further, save him under a different name. You will be learning how to make him run, one of the most common animations in games, so you might want to call the file Polyman-run.

1. Start first by helping Polyman to lean forward so he looks right when he runs. Select the pelvis joint and rotate it -18 degrees in the Z axis, as shown in Figure 11.42.

2. Now rotate the other joints of the spine, neck, and head so that his body leans forward but his head looks straight ahead.

Use Figure 11.43 as an example of how he should look.

3. Now lower the pelvis joint to bring Polyman a little closer to the ground. Notice that the feet and arms remain in place. (See Figure 11.44.)

4. Create a polygon plane to help keep track of where the ground is located. Move the plane down to Polyman's feet, as shown in Figure 11.45.

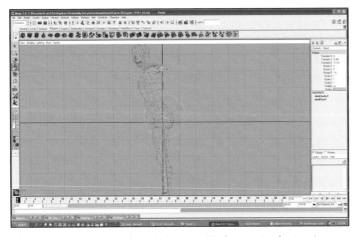

Figure 11.42 Rotate the pelvis joint -18 degrees in the Z axis.

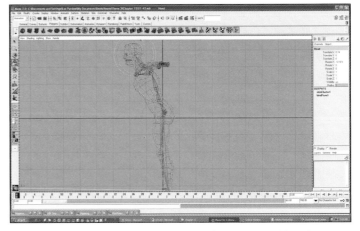

Figure 11.43 Rotate the other joints of the back and head.

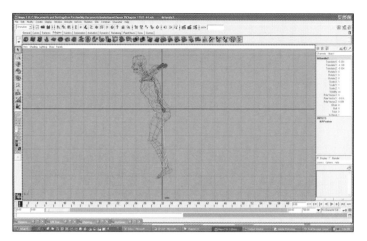

Figure 11.44 Lowering the pelvis causes the model's legs to bend.

Figure 11.45 Give Polyman something to stand on.

5. We will start the run animation at the transition point where the two legs are close together during the run cycle. This will help with the transition between a standing animation and the run animation. First lift the left foot as if it were being brought forward, as shown in Figure 11.46.

6. Next, rotate the right foot to match the surface of the ground, as shown in Figure 11.47. Make sure you rotate the ankle joint and not the IK handle.

7. Now go to the Front view. During this phase of the run, the hips are tilted because one leg is in contact with the ground and the other is in the air. Rotate the pelvis joint so the right hip is higher than the left, as shown in Figure 11.48.

8. The next joint of the spine needs to be rotated as well to bring the back into a vertical position, as shown in Figure 11.49.

9. Use the IK handles in the arms to bring them down to the model's sides. Give each arm a slight bend at the elbow. (See Figure 11.50.)

10. When running, the spine tends to bow from side to side during this phase of the run cycle. The shoulders will naturally tilt in the opposite direction from the hips. Refer to Figure 11.51 for an example. Remember to keep the head vertical.

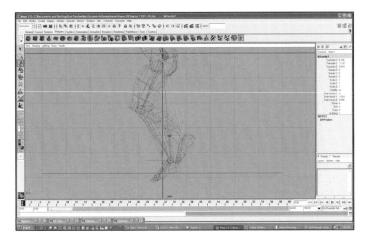

Figure 11.46 Lift the left foot.

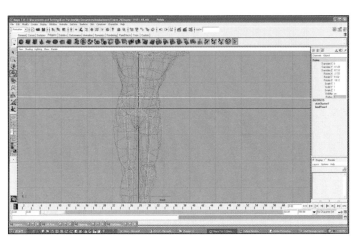

Figure 11.48 Rotate the pelvis.

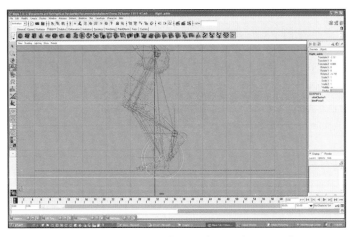

Figure 11.47 Rotate the right foot to follow the ground.

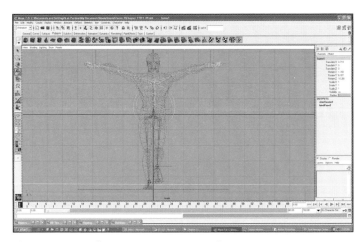

Figure 11.49 The spine remains vertical.

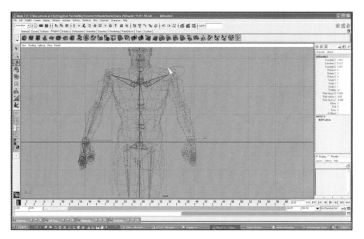

Figure 11.50 Lower the arms.

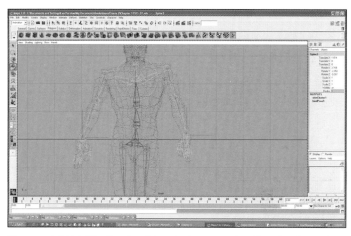

Figure 11.51 Tilt the shoulders in the opposite direction from the hips.

11. Now you need to move the arms into position. During a run cycle, the arms will swing opposite the legs for each side. When the left leg is moving forward, as it is in this frame, the left arm is moving back. Place the left hand slightly forward of the body and the right hand slightly back of the body, as shown in Figure 11.52.

12. Now bend the fingers of each hand into a relaxed fist, as shown in Figure 11.53.

13. The model should now be in the proper position. Rotate the model in the Perspective view and see if he looks natural. Make any changes that are needed.

14. If you haven't already done so, click on the Auto Keyframe toggle to turn on auto keyframing. Auto keyframing will set keyframes automatically for each movement of an animation. We will use this later in the animation sequence.

15. You now need to lock the model into the pose you just created by setting a keyframe. In Maya every node can have its own keyframe. To make sure you set all the possible nodes, bring up the Hypergraph and select all the nodes of the skeletal system, as shown in Figure 11.54.

16. Press the S key to set a keyframe.

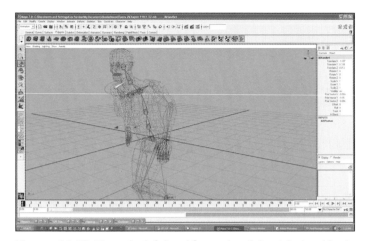

Figure 11.52 Move the left hand forward and the right hand back.

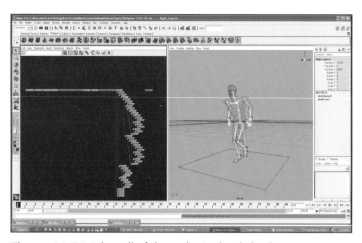

Figure 11.54 Select all of the nodes in the skeletal system.

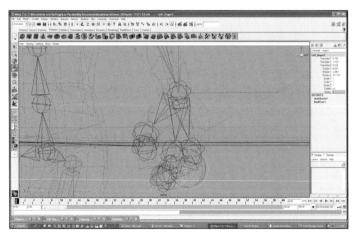

Figure 11.53 Give each hand a relaxed fist.

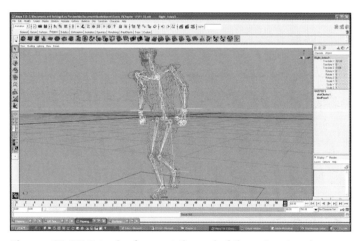

Figure 11.55 Set a keyframe at the end of the animation that matches the first.

17. Running is a cycle animation. This means that it loops and can repeat indefinitely. To create a looping animation, the first and last frame of the animation should be nearly identical. To simplify this process, move the time slider to frame 60 and set a keyframe there, as shown in Figure 11.55.

18. Go to frame 30.

19. Frame 30 should look exactly like frame 1 and 60 except the left and right sides should switch. In other words, if the left leg is moving forward in frame 1, the right should be moving forward in frame 30. Frame 1 and frame 30 should be mirrors of each other. Change all of the joints at frame 30 so they mirror those in frame 1. The result should look like Figure 11.56.

20. Now go to frame 15.

21. In frame 15 the model will be making the widest separation of the legs and the arms. He will also be at the apex of his stride vertically. Move the pelvis up, as shown in Figure 11.57.

22. Separate the legs. Move the right leg back and just touching the ground. Move the left leg forward and up as if the character were just taking off in a leap. (See Figure 11.58.)

23. At this point in a run cycle the hips swing horizontally. Rotate the pelvis, as shown in Figure 11.59.

24. Now go to the spine 1 joint and rotate it to bring the spine back to a parallel position compared to the center line, as shown in Figure 11.60.

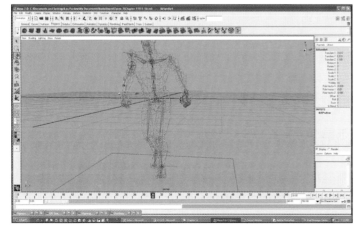

Figure 11.56 Frame 30 should be a mirror image of frame 1.

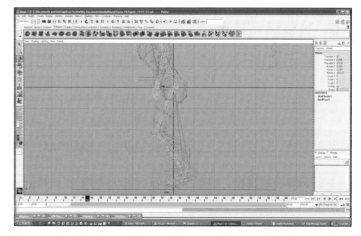

Figure 11.57 The model is at the apex of his stride in frame 15.

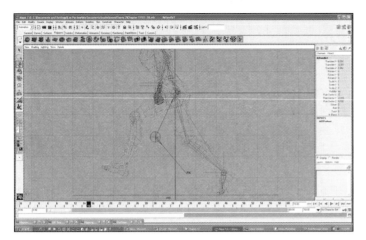

Figure 11.58 Reposition the legs.

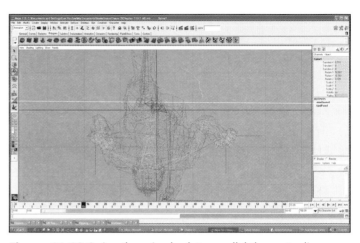

Figure 11.60 Swing the spine back to parallel the center line.

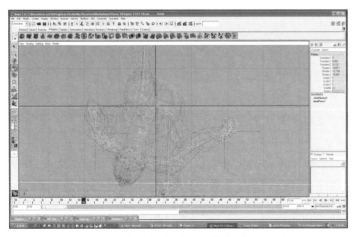

Figure 11.59 Rotate the hips horizontally in the Top view.

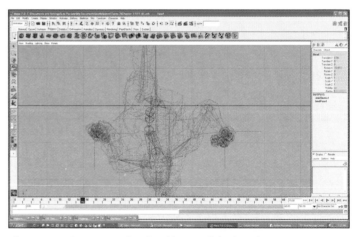

Figure 11.61 Rotate the shoulders and the head.

25. Like in the animation at frame 1, the shoulders should rotate in the opposite direction of the hips. Rotate the shoulders and the head, as shown in Figure 11.61

26. Now swing the arms out opposite the legs of each side, as shown in Figure 11.62. The auto frame feature will keep track of each of your adjustments so you don't need to set keyframes.

27. Frame 45 will be a mirror image of frame 15. Go to frame 45 and adjust the position of your model to be an exact mirror of frame 15. You can use the time slider to go back and forth between frames to check your positioning. The results should look similar to Figure 11.63.

28. Go to frame 20.

29. Frame 20 is the first solid impact of the left foot with the ground. Move the left foot down and line up the foot with the ground, as shown in Figure 11.64. Also lift the right foot up and rotate it back.

30. Frame 50 is a mirror of frame 20. Go to frame 50 and make the necessary adjustments.

31. Play the animation.

Congratulations! You have just created your first character animation. That wasn't so bad, was it? Actually, I left out a lot of control subtleties, but now you know the basics of character animation. Save this file and try animating some other motions. As you learn to animate, read up on some of the more advanced animation controls in Maya.

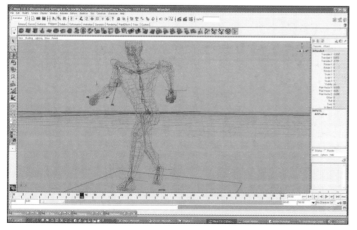

Figure 11.62 Move the arms opposite the legs.

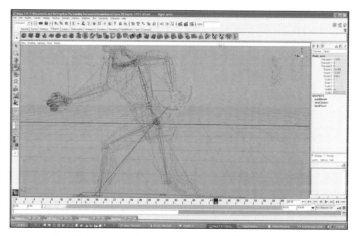

Figure 11.63 Frame 45 is a mirror image of frame 15.

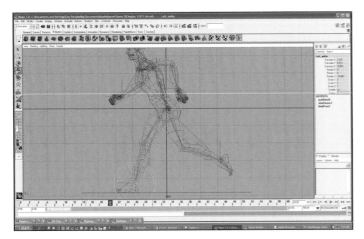

Figure 11.64 The left foot hits the ground at frame 20.

Summary

This was a somewhat complex chapter, but I tried to keep it as basic as I could. Maya is a very deep software program with a rich animation system; I only scratched the surface of its power. In the chapter you learned how to

- Control animation in Maya
- Create skeletons
- Skin characters
- Create IK solvers
- Animate a character run cycle

You are now armed and ready to start experimenting with the animation system. Try setting up your own character model. Create some animations of your model. The more you practice with the animation system, the better you will get. Study the way people move in real life as an example for your animations.

CHAPTER 12

SPECIALIZED GEOMETRY AND SPECIAL EFFECTS

So far in this book you have covered a lot of territory. If you have followed the examples and experimented on your own, you have gained the beginning of what you will need to know to be a game artist. In this last chapter, you need to learn about two more important areas of game art—the creation of specialized geometry and the basics of developing special effects for games.

Creating Specialized Geometry

Many game engines require the creation of polygon models that are never seen in the game. These models are used for setting up boundaries, triggering special events, creating spawning points, and any number of other functions. These models are usually exported separately from the other models and are used primarily by programmers to store information for the engine to use when the game is running. The most common type of specialized geometry for games is a collision map.

Collision Maps

Collision maps derive their name from the early days of game development, when all games were created in 2D. In those days a collision map was a two-color invisible picture in which one color represented where a character could walk and the other color represented where he couldn't. As games have advanced, so have collision maps. Now collision maps not only define the boundaries of character movement, they also can have other information, such as surface qualities or physics.

In theory, game engines could use the model geometry from the game models for collision maps. The problem with the game models is that they often use significantly more polygons than are necessary for a collision map. When you use a collision map with fewer polygons, you are left with a greater number of polygons available for the models you actually see in the game.

Let's build a collision map so you can see how it is done. Bring up Maya and load the room you created in Chapter 5. You will build a collision map for this model.

1. The first thing you must do is turn the room model into a template. Select all the objects in the scene and then choose

Object Display > Template from the Display menu, as shown in Figure 12.1.

2. The room will no longer be in Shaded mode; it will be in Wire Frame mode. Click beside the model and notice that the wire frame turns gray.

3. Try selecting the model. You cannot select a template in Maya in the view screen. This comes in very handy when you are building collision maps because it makes it easier to build new geometry without interference from the older geometry.

4. Create a polygon cylinder, as shown in Figure 12.2. Notice that you are using fewer polygons than the original model.

5. Scale the cylinder so it is just inside the wall of the dome model, as shown in Figure 12.3.

6. From the Front view, move up the cylinder so the bottom is about the same level as the floor.

7. Adjust the top of the cylinder so it is about level with the bottom of the balcony, as shown in Figure 12.4.

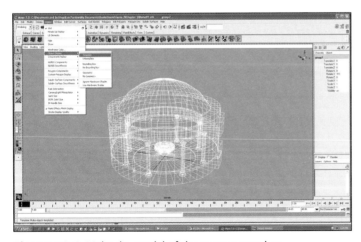

Figure 12.1 Make the model of the room a template.

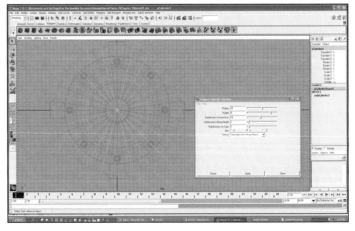

Figure 12.2 Create a polygon cylinder.

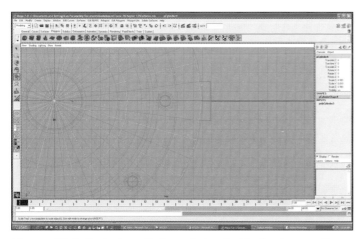

Figure 12.4 Scale the cylinder to fit just inside the dome well.

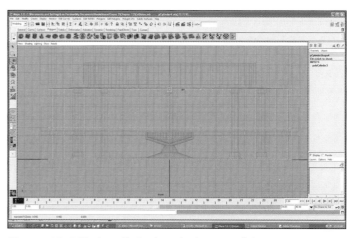

Figure 12.4 Fit the cylinder into the bottom of the room.

8. Select the inside ring of vertices on the bottom of the cylinder and scale them to match the platform on the floor of the room, as shown in Figure 12.5.

9. Extrude the faces on the inside ring of polygons to form the platform, as shown in Figure 12.6.

10. Now select the faces on the inside of the top of the cylinder and scale them to fit just inside the balcony, as shown from the Top view in Figure 12.7.

11. Extrude the faces to follow the rail of the balcony, as shown in Figure 12.8.

12. Extrude the faces again and scale them to fit over the top of the rail.

13. Extrude the faces again to fit down the other side of the rail.

14. Extrude the faces again to follow the floor, as shown in Figure 12.9.

15. Extrude the faces again to follow the wall. Only go as high as the top of the doors.

16. Extrude the faces again to follow the walls to where they meet the ceiling.

17. Continue extruding faces following the shape of the ceiling, as shown in Figure 12.10.

18. Select the top central vertex and pull it up to the top of the dome, as shown in Figure 12.11.

19. Find the ring of vertices in the middle of the wall on the ground floor and move them to the top of the doorways, as shown in Figure 12.12.

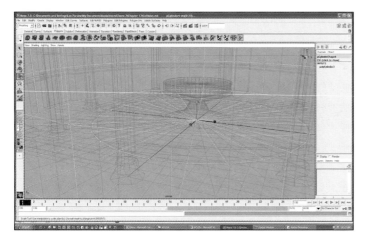

Figure 12.5 Scale the vertices to match the platform.

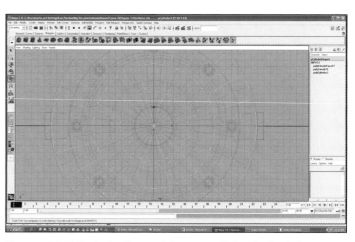

Figure 12.7 Scale the faces of the top to fit inside the balcony.

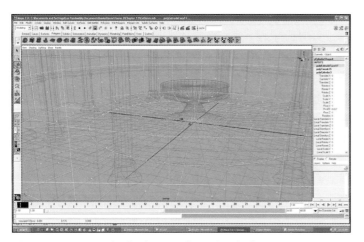

Figure 12.6 Extrude the faces to form the platform.

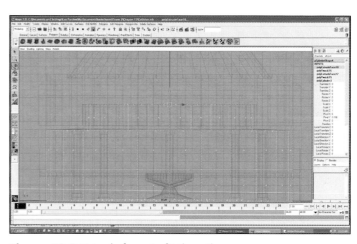

Figure 12.8 Extrude faces to fit the rail.

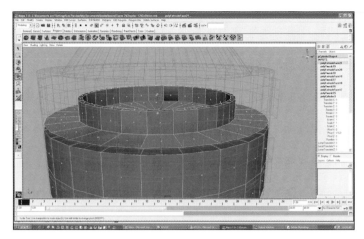

Figure 12.9 Extrude faces to follow the geometry of the balcony.

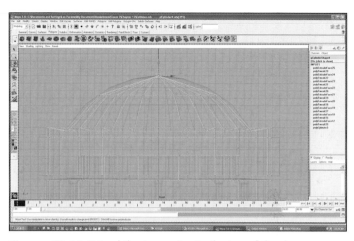

Figure 12.11 Extend the top vertex to the top of the dome.

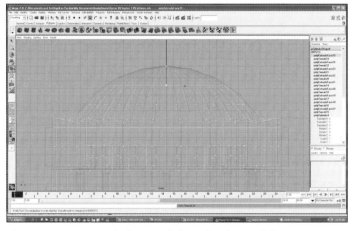

Figure 12.10 Extrude faces to follow the shape of the room.

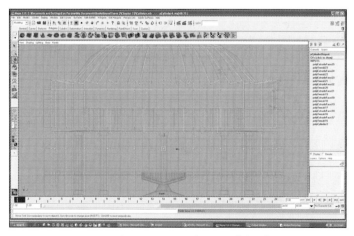

Figure 12.12 Move the vertices to the top of the doorway.

20. Now for the doorways. The collision map needs to be rotated so that it lines up with the doors. Rotate the collision map 7.5 on the Y axis (see Figure 12.13).

21. Extrude the face in the doorway to fit the doorway, as shown in Figure 12.14.

22. Repeat Steps 18 and 19 for the other three doors on the bottom floor and the four doors on the balcony level (see Figure 12.15).

23. Create a cylinder, as shown in Figure 12.16.

24. Move and scale the cylinder to fit just outside of one of the columns, as shown in Figure 12.17.

25. Now you will need to move the vertices along the length of the cylinder to the base and crown of the column, as shown in Figure 12.18.

26. Scale the top and bottom of the cylinder to match the size of the crown and base of the column, as shown in Figure 12.19.

27. You don't need the faces on the top and bottom of the cylinder because they will be above the ceiling or below the floor. Therefore, you can select and delete the faces on the top and bottom of the cylinder.

28. Group the cylinder to center the pivot point.

29. Duplicate the cylinder and rotate it to fit over the next column the same way you did when you built the room.

30. Repeat Step 29 until all the columns are covered, as shown in Figure 12.20.

31. Create a new cylinder, as shown in Figure 12.21.

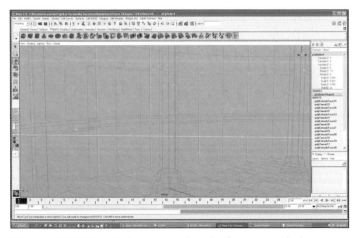

Figure 12.13 Rotate the room to line the faces up with the doorways.

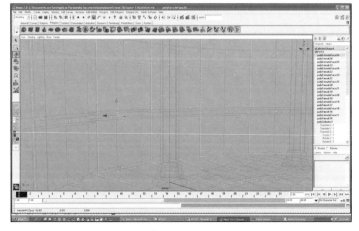

Figure 12.14 Extrude the face to the door.

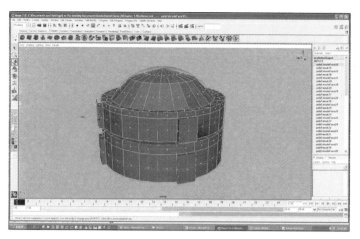

Figure 12.15 Extrude each doorway.

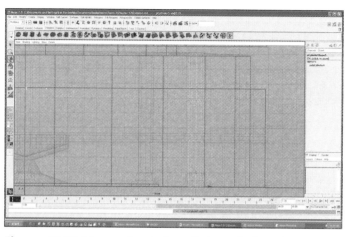

Figure 12.17 Move and scale the cylinder to fit the column.

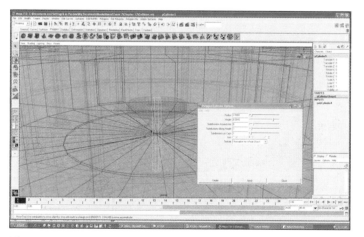

Figure 12.16 Create a cylinder.

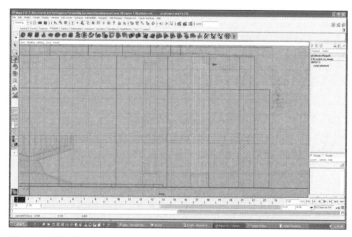

Figure 12.18 Fit the vertices to the crown and base.

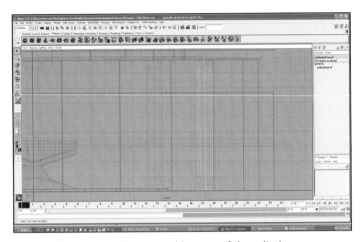

Figure 12.19 Scale the top and bottom of the cylinder.

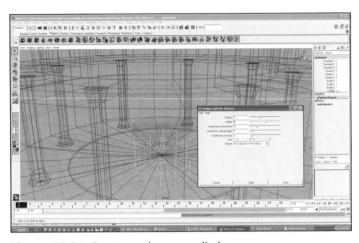

Figure 12.21 Create another new cylinder.

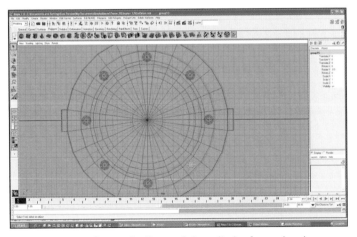

Figure 12.20 Place a duplicate of the cylinder for each column.

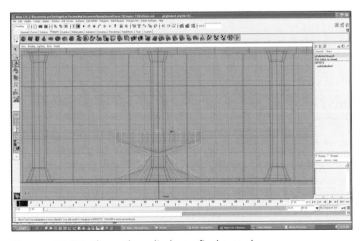

Figure 12.22 Shape the cylinder to fit the pool.

32. Adjust the new cylinder to fit around the challis pool, as shown in Figure 12.22.

33. Select the top faces of the pool collisions and extrude them inward, then extrude them downward to form the inside of the pool, as shown in Figure 12.23. Pull the center vertex down to the bottom of the pool.

34. Delete the faces on the bottom of the pool cylinder.

35. Everything is finished except one important aspect of the room. Remember when you built the room you had to reverse the normals because they were facing outward? The same thing is true for the collision map because you created it in the same way you did the room. Select the room collision geometry and reverse the normals.

36. The collision mask is now finished and ready to export. Select all the objects in the collision map and combine them.

The collision map is now finished. Notice that it has far fewer polygons than the original model. The collision map does not contain any textures, so it should run very fast in the engine.

Exporting Data

So far in this book we have covered many aspects of developing game art, but the book would not be complete if we didn't talk a little about exporting data to a game engine. Seldom will a game engine accept native Maya files. Most of the time the art has to be converted into a specific format for the game. Game engine formats are generally streamlined and only contain essential data that the engine actually uses. Native Maya files, on the other hand, contain extensive data, some of which is not needed in the engine.

Because game engine formats contain limited data, some features in Maya do not export to the game. It is vital that game artist study the features that do export and those that don't. It does the artist little good to spend a lot of time building advanced models with complex materials and mapping, if the engine doesn't support those features. That is one reason that this

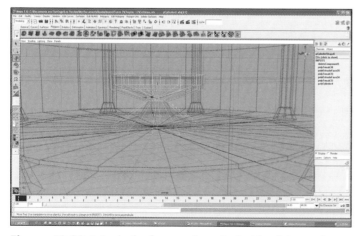

Figure 12.23 Extrude the faces to form the inside of the pool.

book has not dealt with things like layered shaders or bump maps or complex modeling systems. While some of the high-end game engines might support these features, most do not.

Maya is a very popular 3D software program and is supported by almost all game engines for exporting data. Because there are so many types of game engines, I can't cover every one in this book. However, I can show you how most exporters work. If you still have the collision map from the previous exercise up, select Export Selection from the File menu, as shown in Figure 12.24, to bring up the Export dialog box.

Under the General Options area of the dialog box there is a pull-down menu. This is where the exporters are usually located (see Figure 12.25). Right now, the only exporters loaded into Maya are the default ones that come with the program.

If you were working on a game project with a specific engine, your exporter would be on this list, provided you installed the plug-in from the engine. Close the dialog box and go to Window > Settings/Preferences > Plug-in Manager to bring up the Plug-in Manager, as shown in Figure 12.26.

The Plug-in Manager has a list of several plug-ins that are available with the basic install of Maya. Most of the plug-ins on the list are not exporters but rather tools to help with specific aspects of 3D development. Take a brief look at the list. You will notice that there are several that include the word "export" in the plug-in name.

Once you install an exporter plug-in, it will appear on this list. To make it active, all you need to do is check the check boxes next to the plug-in. Let's give it a try. Scroll down the list until

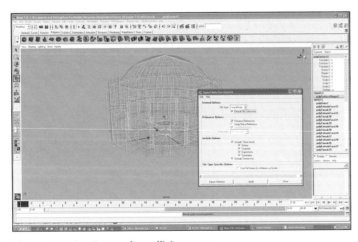

Figure 12.24 Export the collision map.

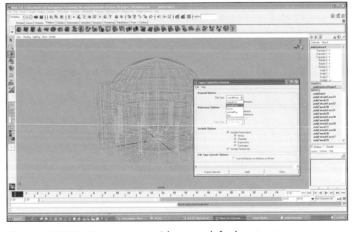

Figure 12.25 Maya comes with some default exporters.

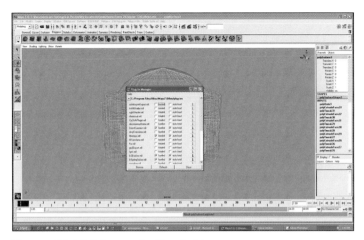

Figure 12.26 Bring up the Plug-in Manager.

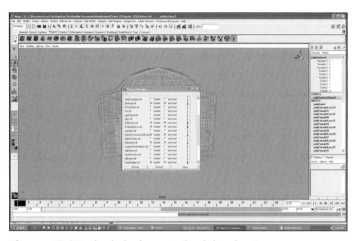

Figure 12.27 Check the boxes to load the plug-in.

you come to the one titled ObjExport.mll. Check the loaded and auto load boxes as shown in Figure 12.27; then click on the Close button.

Now when you go to Export Selection like you did before, the new plug-in will be on the list of exporters in the pull-down menu. Select it and notice how the dialog box changes. It gives you options for the specific exporter (see Figure 12.28). Each exporter will have options for what you want to export. Click Export Selection to export the collision map created earlier.

That is about it for exporting data from Maya. Some exporters will be different, but most of them work with plug-ins. Specific instruction for exporting from specific engines usually comes with the engine documentation.

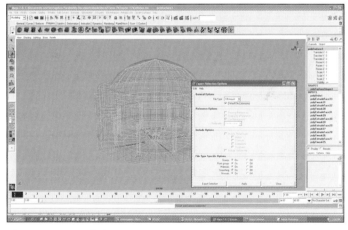

Figure 12.28 Click Export Selection to export your model.

Triggers and Other Invisible Objects

Many engines use polygonal objects to store game information. These objects are set up so they can be used to trigger events in the game. They also are used to place objects in the game, such as characters, vehicles, traps, pick-ups, breakable items, doors, spawning points, and so on. The list is endless, limited only by the engine and the imagination of the development team.

In some game engines, these invisible objects are placed in the game world using a World editor, which is a program that is part of the engine. In other game engines, the artist uses the 3D modeling software to place the objects in the world. In either case the process is similar; I will show you how to do it in Maya.

1. If you don't have it open already, load the dome room and set the model to a template.

2. Create a single-polygon plane, as shown in Figure 12.29.

3. Select Polygon Components > Normals from the Display menu to show the direction of the face of the polygon.

4. Move the polygon over to one of the doorways and scale it to cover the doorway area.

5. In the Visor, rename the polygon trig01, as shown in Figure 12.30.

That's about it; it's not too hard. You just created a trigger object. When your character enters the room and walks through that doorway, he will pass through the trigger object. When that occurs, it will cause something in the game to happen. The face is pointing toward the door, so the trigger only goes off if the character is entering the room.

The name of the trigger could be anything; in this case, you called it trig01. In the game engine, all objects with the trigXX name will cause the same

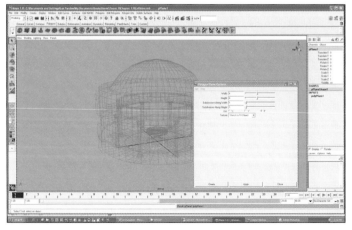

Figure 12.29 Create a single-polygon plane.

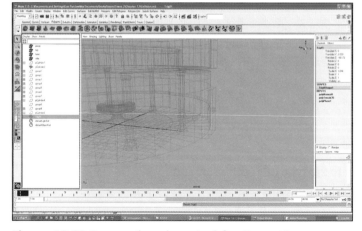

Figure 12.30 Rename the polygon to define it as a trigger.

action to happen. The name is used to tell the programmers what action to tie to the geometry.

Game levels are filled with places where actions or events must occur. A typical level might have anywhere from a few to a few hundred invisible objects in it. Placing these objects is a time-consuming task, but getting them just right can make all the difference in how the game plays. It is an important job for the game artist. Some game companies hire artists to do nothing else but set up great levels. These artists are called *level editors*, and they perform a very important function in game development.

Creating Special Effects

Games today are filled with special effects. The term *special effect* comes from the movie industry. In motion pictures, special effects are elements added during or after filming to enhance the movie. In games, special effects include lighting effects, particle effects, or other elements that simulate the type of effects seen in movies. Over the years, special effects in movies and games have grown to

include almost any fantastic or unique visual elements. Next, you will learn about some of the basic special effects used in games.

Particle Effects

Particle effects are the most common type of special effect used in games. Particles are small, single polygons. Many of these polygons grouped and moving together can simulate effects such as smoke, fire, or rain. Particle effects have some common elements, which include:

- Emitters
- Paths
- Turbulence
- Dissipation

An *emitter* is the origin point or area of a particle effect. In a game the artist will designate a place for an emitter. For example, your game might have a torch in a sconce by the door to a castle. You can place a directional emitter near the top of a torch pointing up. Then you specify the type of particle the emitter will release—in this case, a flame particle.

The *path* is the line of movement of the particle. In the case of the torch, the line of movement is upward and away from the top of the torch.

Turbulence is the variation in the path of each individual particle. If all the particles of the torch moved in exactly the same direction, the flame effect would not be very believable. By adding variability to the paths of each particle, you can achieve a more believable flame effect.

Dissipation is the gradual transition of each particle from solid to transparent. The *dissipation rate* is the time it takes for a particle to go from solid to transparent; the *dissipation range* is the range in which a set of particles will go from solid to transparent.

To understand how particle systems work in games, you can create one in Maya.

1. Create a cylinder, as shown in Figure 12.31.
2. Create two materials and load the bark.bmp and end.bmp textures from the CD in the directory for Chapter 12, as shown in Figure 12.32.

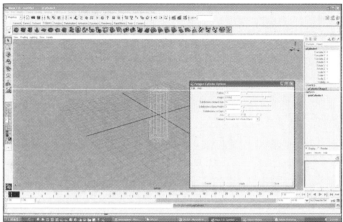

Figure 12.31 Create a polygon cylinder for a log.

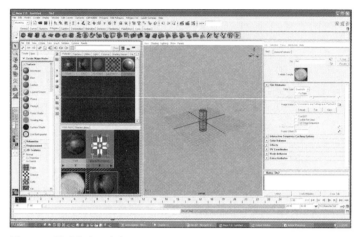

Figure 12.32 Load the textures.

3. Use the Cylindrical Mapping tool to apply the bark to the cylinder, as shown in Figure 12.33.

4. Use the Planar Mapping tool to apply the end material to the cylinder, as shown in Figure 12.34. You now have a nice-looking log. Rotate it 90 degrees in the Z axis.

5. Now you need to go to the Dynamics menu set. Select it from the drop-down menu on the top-right portion of the screen, as shown in Figure 12.35.

6. In the visor, change the cylinder's name to Log, as shown in Figure 12.36.

7. Now you need to bring up an Effects dialog box. Select Fire from the Effects menu to bring up the Create Fire Effect Options dialog box.

8. Adjust the options to match those shown in Figure 12.37 and apply them to the log object.

9. The small ball that appears inside the log is the particle emitter. The other settings in the dialog box are for adjusting the fire. Change the frame to 24, as shown in Figure 12.38. The magenta circles represent the particles.

10. To see the particles, you will need to add a light. Create a light, as shown in Figure 12.39.

11. Position the light, as shown in Figure 12.40.

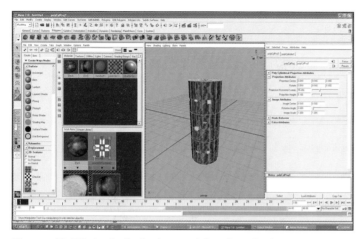

Figure 12.33 Apply the bark material to the cylinder.

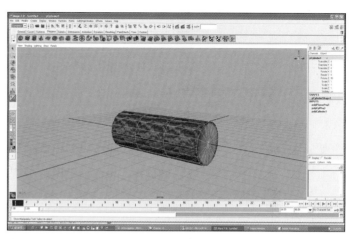

Figure 12.35 Change the menu set to Dynamics.

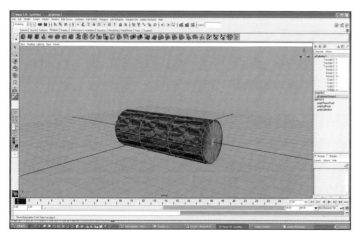

Figure 12.34 Apply the end material to the cylinder.

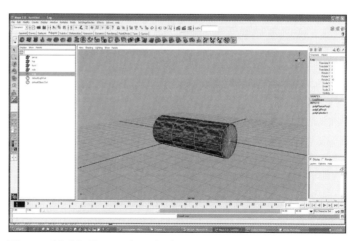

Figure 12.36 Change the cylinder name to Log.

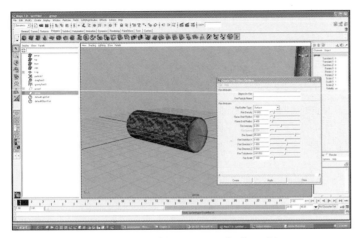

Figure 12.37 Apply a particle emitter to the log object.

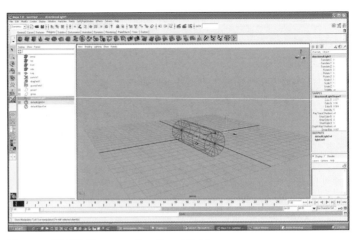

Figure 12.39 Create a directional light.

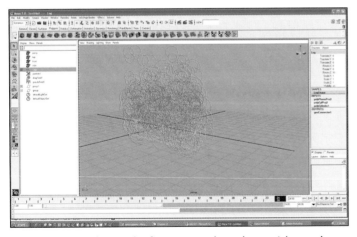

Figure 12.38 Change the frame to see how the particles work.

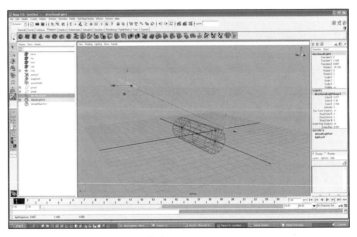

Figure 12.40 Position the light.

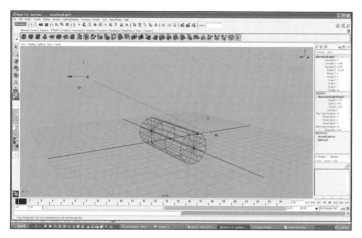

Figure 12.41 Change to the Rendering menu set.

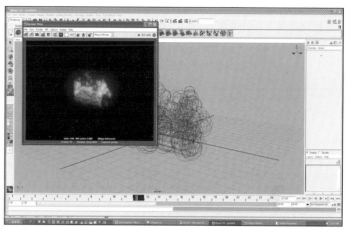

Figure 12.42 Render frame 12 of the animation.

12. Change the menu set to Rendering, as shown in Figure 12.41.

13. Move to frame 12 of the animation. Select Render Current Frame from the Render menu. A small Render View window will appear, as shown in Figure 12.42.

14. You can render a couple more frames of the animation by setting the current frame to another number and then selecting Render Current Frame again.

15. Now you can set some rendering attributes and render the whole animation so you can take a good look at how the particles work. In the Render view, select Render Settings from the Options menu, as shown in Figure 12.43.

16. Set your options to match the options shown on the Common tab in Figure 12.44.

17. Now switch to the Maya Software tab and set those, as shown in Figure 12.45.

18. Now you can batch render the animation. Select Batch Render from the Render menu, as shown in Figure 12.46.

19. When the Batch Render Animation dialog box appears, you will notice that the options are in gray. This is because the Personal Learning Edition of Maya does not support rendering on multiple machines. You should be fine rendering this project on one machine. Click on the Batch Render button to start the render.

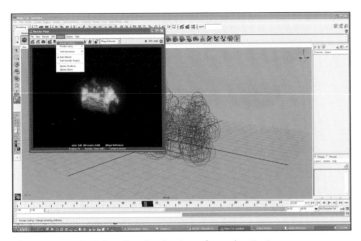

Figure 12.43 Select Render Settings from the Options menu.

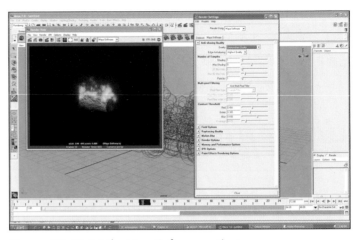

Figure 12.45 Set the Maya Software options.

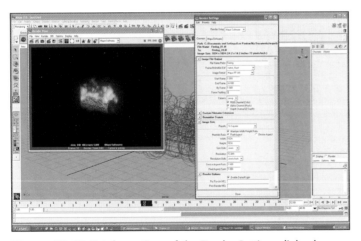

Figure 12.44 Set the options of the Render Settings dialog box on the Common tab.

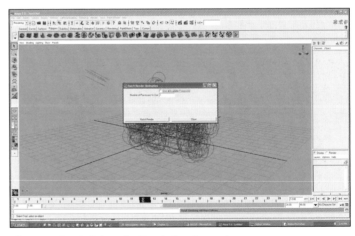

Figure 12.46 Select the Batch Render option.

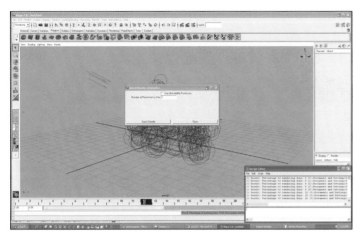

Figure 12.47 The Script editor shows the progress of each frame.

20. If you want to see the progress of the rendering, click on the Script editor in the lower-right corner of your display to expand that window, as shown in Figure 12.47. The Script editor will show you the progress of each frame and the location to which the frame is saved.

Once the rendering is finished, you can look at the results of your flame particles. Figures 12.48 and 12.49 are examples of how the particles should look.

Take some time and experiment with the settings of the flame effect. Change the turbulence and see how it affects the flame. Try adjusting some of the other attributes to see what happens. You will quickly see that even small adjustments can sometimes have dramatic effects. Try creating some other effects from the Effects menu options.

Creating Particles

In Maya you can have as many particles as you want because you are not rendering them in real time. In games, on the other hand, you are rendering

Figure 12.48 A rendered frame from the firelog animation.

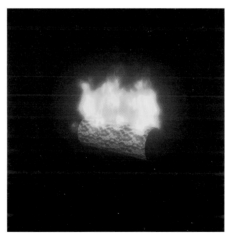

Figure 12.49 Another rendered frame from the firelog animation

in real time so the number of particles is limited. Most particles in games are small polygons with textures applied. The way you create the textures for your game will depend on how your game engine treats transparency. Most game engines support an alpha channel; however, some use a mask. Particles almost always have some element of transparency.

Figure 12.50 shows two particles; one is a flaming rock and the other is a shard of ice. These two particles were created for a fantasy game in which the main character could call fire or ice from the sky. By combining these textures with some semi-transparent, cloudlike particles, I was able to get a nice-looking effect.

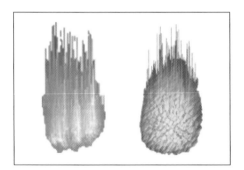

Figure 12.50 Particle textures used in a game.

Animated Billboards

A *billboard* is a single polygon that is programmed to always face the camera. Billboards are often used to simulate effects that might require more particles than the game machine can run successfully. Basically, a billboard is a single polygon with an animated texture. Figure 12.51 shows an example of a billboard animation. Here I used a color map and a mask for the transparent area to create an explosion. The explosion was created in Maya using more than a thousand polygons. The billboard animation only required one polygon.

You can use billboard animation for other things than simply special effects. I have seen them used successfully for animated crowds, individual characters, signs, and lights.

Figure 12.51 A billboard animation sequence.

Summary

In this chapter I covered some elements of game art that aren't seen by the player, as well as some that are.

- Collision maps
- 3D collision maps
- Triggers
- Particle effects
- Particles
- Billboards

The specialized geometry for games might not be seen, but it is a critical part of game development. The special effects are definitely seen by the player. Both are extremely important for making a good game.

If you have gone through everything in this book, you have only just begun your journey to becoming a real game artist. There is still a lot to learn. I suggest you practice the skills you have learned thus far and see what you can create. If you are interested in a career in game art development, learn as much as you can about art. The better artist you are, the better game artist you will become. Good luck! This is a fascinating and exciting field.

INDEX

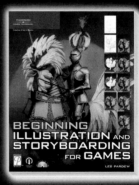
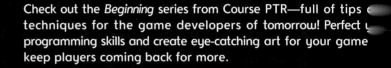

License Agreement/Notice of Limited Warranty